For Suzann
Thanks,
Support at T...

Also by Wilmont R. Kreis

The Allards Historical Series:
The New World
The Hunter
Peace and War
The Voyageur
The City in the Wilderness
The Medallion
The Witch
The Chief

Fearful Passage North

Contemporary Medical Thrillers
The Labyrinth
The Pain Doc
The Corridor

Available in print and e-books from
Amazon.com

Visit the Author at
www.wilmontkreis.co
And on Facebook

1634
RETURN TO THE
NEW WORLD

Wilmont R. Kreis

Port Huron, Michigan
2016

Prologue

History is the record of *known* things past, a collection of facts generally taken from written records. Historical fiction allows the author leeway to fill in missing details—those delicious bits of life that may have escaped the historian's quill, or may have occurred only within the imaginative re-creation of the author's mind.

When I began The Allards series many years ago, I began writing history, but soon fell prey to the historical fiction sirens, whispering to me to add details to bring these stories and these people to life. Since this liberty was well received, I continued it throughout my writing of the family's history. The Allards stretched from the mid-seventeenth century to the mid-twentieth. Since that completion, readers have asked me to tell them about *Québec* and its people *before* that time.

For a starting point, I chose 1628 which seemed to represent the beginning of French-Canada as a viable entity. Primarily an outpost for trade in raw goods, the French king and ruling class did not seem to believe in or support the establishment of it as a colony. Samuel Champlain, however, envisioned more. The 1634 arrival of the first French families, most from the region of Perche aboard the so-called Percheron Express, anchored that beginning in reality as they built their new homes and determined its continuity and permanent place in history.

I was especially enthralled by a particularly enigmatic young woman, Françoise Grenier. I noticed her when I began my historic and genealogic research in the pre-internet era. Unlike other pioneers from Perche, she had no *known* origin. A few years ago some further interest in her began among the circle of French-Canadian genealogists. Was she French? Was she a native? Pros and cons were advanced for both theories, but in the end, she remained a mystery for me. In fact, her first historical record is her marriage to Noël Langlois one month after the ship arrived in Canada. That marriage was said to be only the third recorded marriage in *Québec*.

To see my theory on her and how I present this bit of historical mystery, you must read on. I sincerely hope you will enjoy it.

Although most characters are based upon historical research records, some of the minor characters are fictitious as are Guy, the Mortagne nuns, Étienne Forton, and the natives (except for *Ouébadinoukoué)*. Among the many historical and genealogic references used are two excellent books, Champlain's Dream by David Hackett Fischer and Hélène's World by Susan McNelley.

As with all my works I will discuss and answer any questions on my blogs, both at www.wilmontkreis.com, and on Facebook. Enjoy.

For everyone at Orthopedic Associates of Port Huron

for making my career such a delight

while reading my books at the same time

Acknowledgements

It takes more than an author to create a book, and since beginning several years ago, I have relied heavily on the support and encouragement of others, who bring their own individual skills and knowledge to the project. Susanna Defever has been my teacher, editor, critic and cheerleader, always urging me to do it again but this time better. Carrie Mclean's technical talent with her computer skills, website creation and networking are valued along with her map and cover design.

Finally, I am forever indebted to my wonderful and patient wife, Susan, nurse turned healthcare attorney and voracious reader of books, for her encouragement and honest advice without which I would never have written a book, and for all the evenings she has quietly returned to her reading, understanding when I disappear up the stairs to answer the call of the muse.

www.wilmontkreis.com

The secret of getting ahead is getting started.

—Mark Twain

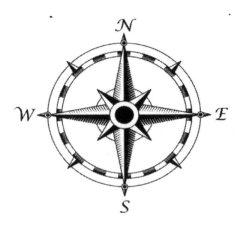

Cover Photo:

Fleuve Saint-Laurent

Saint Lawrence River

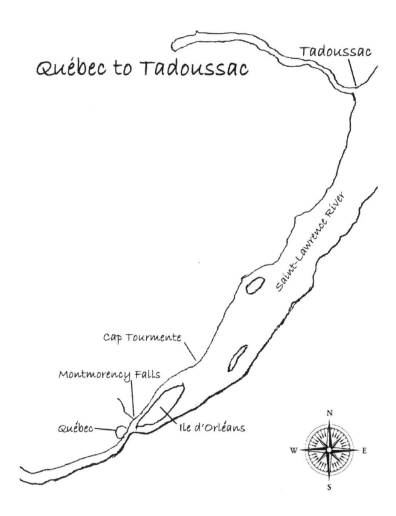

Québec to Tadoussac

Tadoussac

Saint-Lawrence River

Cap Tourmente

Montmorency Falls

Québec

Ile d'Orléans

N
W   E
S

1634

RETURN TO THE NEW WORLD

Québec City, July 9, 1628

Perched two meters from Samuel, the squirrel had not moved for at least five minutes. Finally Samuel broke the silence. "Don't think I'm about to feed you, *mon vieux*. I can scarcely feed my people—or myself. Had I a nut, I would devour it myself." The rodent merely cocked his head in apparent interest, remaining on his rock seat while Samuel arose from his. Stretching his aging frame, he surveyed the glorious summer day from his favorite spot, halfway up the steep hill known as *Cap Diamant* rising from *Fleuve Saint-Laurent* below to the plateau above—where today there was a rudimentary palisade and decrepit cannon with no powder and where Samuel had hoped someday to build a truly solid fortress.

Having begun gloomy and overcast, the day had become clear and fine as any July day could be. A mild northeast breeze brought clear skies and a wonderful freshness to the air. Due to the arrival of high pressure, he could see clearly to the town below with its few ragged shops where the *habitants* went about their business. Beyond sat the small cabins and farms of the few resident families. To the north was the home of the *Récollet* missionaries near the mouth of *Riviére Saint-Charles* flowing from the mountains to the deep blue of *Fleuve Saint-Laurent* as the French called their greatest river. Unfortunately, the flow this year was lower than normal due to the lack of precipitation, which now threatened the few small farms. Downstream was the long, densely forested *Île d'Orléans* dividing the wide *Fleuve Saint-Laurent* into two channels. He could see mist rising over the northernmost channel from the thunderous Montmorency Falls, even though the flow was less impressive than most years. This year had been as bleak as today was bright. Poor weather brought poorer crops, and a winter brutal, even by *Québec* standards, had thinned the forest animals upon which the settlers of the small colony relied for meat. Even the usually excellent fishing was poor.

Lacking a better audience, he turned again to his four-legged listener. "If the people and supplies promised by France don't arrive, we may well all perish. They were scheduled to depart at the very beginning of the season. If they have not arrived by now, I must assume they have floundered and France will not be aware before it is too late to send more—that is, if they could afford more."

The squirrel shook his tail, also made shabby by the poor season, in apparent sympathy with the plight of his uninvited guests. "It's that damned Richelieu!" Samuel claimed, crossing himself quickly to avoid irritating the Almighty before staring at the squirrel, who seemed to be a sympathetic ear, and continuing, "Why in God's name..." crossing himself again, "would you put a cleric in charge of important matters of state? Particularly one who is more interested in a holy war than aiding his people and handling other more important issues at hand? Why..."

The one-sided conversation was cut short by a young man who suddenly appeared without a sound along the trail to the top. The four-legged audience quickly departed when the newcomer called, "*Général!*"

Samuel turned to see the familiar figure. "What is it, Étienne?"

Sweating, but not out of breath—he was never out of breath, Étienne Brûlé, who had come to *Québec* as a young boy on one of Champlain's first voyages, stayed in Canada where Champlain had him travel with *voyageurs* and live with the natives. Now in his thirties, it was said he knew the wilderness better than any European, and, in spite of many scars, the few French women living in the *Québec* found him handsome.

"*Général*," he replied, "A man has just arrived in a small shallop. He says he was near *Tadoussac* and saw ocean boats anchored. He thought they might be the ships from France."

"Praise God!" Champlain exclaimed, "Let us go speak with him. You're faster, Étienne—*allez vite!* Find one of

3

the shipping people to meet me. See if Captain Martin is about."

Brûlé was off like a jackrabbit and soon out of sight while Samuel Champlain worked his 54-year-old frame down the hill in a more prudent fashion. Approaching the harbor, he saw Brûlé with Captain Abraham Martin speaking to a third man he recognized as Nicolas Pivert who worked a farm downstream of the city near *Cap Tourmente*.

Champlain greeted Pivert who began his story again. "I was telling Captain Martin, I was delivering some goods to a farm south of *Tadoussac* with my shallop," referring to the small sailboat used by some of the colonists. "Upon leaving I could see the harbor to the north and could not fail to see these ocean boats at anchor."

"How many were there?" Champlain inquired eagerly.

"At least four, maybe more—I knew the colony was awaiting boats from France, and thought rather than sail up to the harbor I would come here quickly to report. I know people are anxious for the boats."

"Thank you, *Monsieur,* I pray you are correct. Perhaps I should send *un bateau* to see."

"I believe that will not be necessary, *Général*. It appeared they were ready to set sail. I suspect they will be here shortly. But if you will excuse me, *Général*, I must away to my family at *Cap Tourmente*."

Nodding, Champlain dismissed Pivert so he could consult with Martin alone. The two men standing in the square facing the harbor provided a stark contrast. Born to a family of mariners in the French harbor town of *Brouage* just south of the large maritime city and Huguenot stronghold of *La Rochelle*, Samuel Champlain was slightly taller and more slender than the average *habitant*,

4

but he continued to dress in the European fashion of either a black suit or a military uniform. His hair and goatee were always neatly trimmed and though once black now showed a salt and pepper record of time. A thoughtful man, he was generally soft spoken. His words were carefully chosen and thought out. He was 54 years old and looked and felt every year.

Abraham Martin, on the other hand, was huge both in height and girth. Also born in France, but to a family of Scottish heritage, he was called *l'Écossais* by the locals. His coiffure, the opposite of Champlain, was a wild mop of curly hair on both his head and face. Once dark brown it was now nearly white. He either wore the leather suit the *habitants* had modified from the native dress or the coat of a mariner. Compared to Champlain, he was casual to the point of disheveled. His words were impulsive and loud. As a boy he was said to have taken up with an uncle who was a navigator so Abraham developed a skill in ship piloting and navigating that proved immensely valuable to the new colony.

Once the two were alone, Champlain inquired, "So, Abraham, how do you take this? It sounds encouraging— more help than I had hoped."

"Bullshit! *Général*, pure bullshit."

"Well, it does seem a bit too good—should I say— to be true?"

"*Général*, that fop, Richelieu, begrudges every *sou* he sends us. No sir, if this is true, and there are that many boats, this is not the French and not someone we would like to see."

Champlain pensively scratched his goatee. "You may be correct, sir. I see young Brûlé at the dock with two

Montagnais braves. I'll have them take a canoe downstream to investigate."

They waited less than two hours before they saw the canoe returning at a speed only achievable by Brûlé and two young Indians. An additional passenger was soon apparent, and as the canoe approached shore, Champlain recognized Father Joseph Le Caron, the *Récollet* missionary. When the boat reached the dock, Champlain saw a fifth man, lying injured on the floor of the canoe.

Father Joseph hopped quickly onto the dock to address Champlain. "I was attending to a farmer when two native men met me, informing me the English have come to *Tadoussac* with many ships, I know not how many. Apparently they had ravaged *Tadoussac* and were on their way to torch *Cap Tourmente. Monsieur* Foucher," motioning to the man groaning on the floor of the canoe, "was unfortunately in their path." The priest continued, "We can only suspect their next stop will be here—and soon. We must pray for guidance," ordered Father Joseph.

Martin scratched his formidable beard in thought, "Perhaps we should plan. The very place to do it is just here. Come along, Father, we'll need prayers as well."

One of the few small and possibly most disreputable tavern-type facilities was the *Terre Sauvage.* Martin opened the decrepit door for his two companions who were not nearly so acquainted with the pub as he. Dark and reeking of rotten wood and spoiled food, it was blessedly empty. Of the two tables, Martin suggested the one closest to the door. While his conspirators were seated, he approached a man smoking behind a small counter and returned with three cups and a pitcher. "In light of our current shortages, this is all *Monsieur* Forton has," he explained. "He calls it *calvados*, but it tastes like it first passed through a horse." After being the sole drinker to laugh at his joke, he added, "I don't know why a village of Normans can't find one soul who knows how to make it properly." Filling each glass, he raised his. "To good counsel!" He downed his glass while his colleagues sipped theirs. "The first sip is the most difficult," he explained.

Champlain sat back with a professorial pose, "I only see two options. Either we fight them or surrender."

Father Joseph nodded and downed his drink, finishing with a gasp and nodded again. Abraham Martin looked uncharacteristically pensive. "Yes, well, if we fight, we die, and you two may go to paradise, but I fear I may have—should I say, a warmer reward waiting. Or we can surrender and live out our lives in English prison. I guess I prefer the former, but perhaps we have another option—a long shot." Pulling his chair closer, he declared, "There can be no doubt this is infamous Kirke brothers."

Father Joseph's mouth dropped, and he suddenly ordered another drink while asking, "Aren't they pirates?"

"They call them privateers, Father—freebooters. They work the same way but they are in the, should I say, employ, of a nation or empire? They attack vessels—or whole colonies of countries hostile to their patron nation. They take and do what they please with the blessing and protection of their patron state so long as they share the proceeds with that state. These five men are extremely well trained and equipped. A couple of them are ferocious warriors, although like most pirates, they are mainly interested in booty." His companions hung on his words while he explained on into the evening.

7

＊

The morning was dreary with a slow, cold drizzle. The three men met at the dock to wait. By now the community of less than 100 souls had some inkling as to what was up. The answer came in the form of the return of Nicolas Pivert's shallop. In the boat was Pivert, his wife, niece and six Basques captives seized by the English from a Basque fishing boat in *Tadoussac*. Pivert handed a letter to Champlain, who, after reading it, explained to his colleagues, "It is from David Kirke who claims to have a commission from the English King with 18 warships at his disposal—possibly an exaggeration. He offers easy terms if we capitulate and difficult terms if we do not." Continuing to read, he added, "No surprises other than this one…"

"What's that?" Father Joseph asked.

Champlain frowned, "The solitary boat from France *has* arrived. Kirke has commandeered it and taken all the supplies and passengers." His colleagues groaned, feeling the last vestige of hope slipping away.

As he had planned, Champlain then met with the few city leaders and explained a proposition that led to great discussion and consternation, but in the end, they decided, with no small amount of misgiving, to agree with the *Général*. He had already penned a letter to Kirke and immediately sent it back with the Basques prisoners. The following day, he received word that David Kirke had turned and headed his fleet, with the booty he had acquired, back to England.

＊

That evening Champlain and Martin returned to the *Terre Sauvage*. "Well, *Général*, what magic words did you use?"

Champlain gave an uncharacteristic grin. "Simply that we were doing well and were well supplied and armed. I even invited him to visit for an inspection if he wished."

"A bluff!" Martin replied in surprise. "Begging your pardon, sir, but I never thought you had such large balls."

Champlain blushed at the profane phrase, replying, "Actually, Abraham, I considered with all the looting he had done, he probably had little room for any more. In addition, he's a business man—though a thieving one, and understands how to cut losses."

Martin nodded—but clearly did not entirely understand the concept of cutting losses. Chaplain continued, "What upsets me is Richelieu, who is willing to risk untold lives and property over a religious question I find relatively minor. I mean, French or English, we are all Christians, are we not? Do you know that the Kirkes, with their Scottish name, live in the French harbor town of *Dieppe*? Richelieu has forbidden us to harbor or employ any Huguenots in the colony. For the most part, these are talented, educated, prosperous people. They are the bulk of the shipping center of *La Rochelle*. These are the sort of people we desperately need in *Québec*, and he not only throws them away, but he causes them to fight us." The *Général* ordered another drink before asserting, "One more thing."

"And what is that?"

"They will be back. Probably not this season, but they will be back and this time will not be fooled. We will then be forced to make that decision."

Champlain rose and took a long look out the door. "I will make you one promise, Abraham. We may be chased home—but we shall return!"

CHAPTER 1

Québec: June 15, 1629-One year later

W inter of 1628-1629 was not as severe as Champlain had feared, although no *Québec* winter was easy. The ninety or so colonists stretched their rations to the limit, and the generally well-fed Québécois were looking gaunt. The Algonquin and Montagnais tribes had helped by fishing for eel and bringing in what game they could to share. When spring arrived, they helped the *habitants* become hunters and gatherers, as well as farmers, to survive.

Today Samuel had returned to his favorite perch to think. From this position high above the river, the colony looked serene even though he knew it was anything but. Having avoided a *habitant* frying pan over the winter, his squirrel friend had made a habit of joining him when he appeared. The fact that Champlain now collected a few

11

fallen acorns on his way up certainly helped, and Champlain appreciated a non-critical ear.

"Well, my friend, this week I heard more discouraging news. It seems when we were visited by our Anglican adversaries last summer, the entire four-boat French fleet had indeed arrived. Unfortunately they came in behind the Kirkes who were able to defeat them, take all the provisions and return the new settlers to France—without our knowledge!" Standing to provide another acorn, he continued, "Just think, all those supplies and 400 new citizens! Moreover, there has been no official word from France. Damn Richelieu! I am certain it is his fault—I don't know why exactly, but I am certain it is." Tossing down the last acorn, he concluded, "That's it for today, unless you would like to show me how you forage. Perhaps I'll find a bug to eat on the way down."

Hiking back to the harbor, he was unaware that all five Kirke brothers had already arrived, well-armed and well-equipped, at the *Gaspé* Peninsula.

Québec: August 1, 1629

One week earlier—one year after their first visit, all five infamous Kirke brothers had sailed into *Québec* harbor with a fleet of well-manned and heavily-armed ships. This time there was no hesitation, and no question about what was to happen. They carried a license from King Charles I of England giving them a monopoly on fur trade in the colony. Samuel Champlain was forced to surrender his beloved *Québec* without a struggle.

❧

Entering his house, Samuel threw his hat on the table and sank into a chair. He could scarcely muster his words. "So, my dear, I have met today with the city leaders to clear up the details, and we will be ready to leave when ordered."

Hélène Champlain came behind her husband and massaged his shoulders. "We will survive, my dear, you've done all you could. Anyway, I think a stay in Paris will do us both good."

Born Hélène Boulle to a rich Parisian family, with a father who was Secretary to the King of France, she was chosen to marry the famous, dashing Champlain. Unfortunately, she was only twelve years old at the time of the marriage. She had never considered her marriage happy and certainly not passionate. They had no children and lived in virtual celibacy. Much of her married life had been spent in France while her husband explored the world, but she had been with him during his later years in *Québec* where she worked with the missionaries teaching the native children. The blonde Hélène looked as young and beautiful as ever and, in truth, she was secretly ecstatic about the prospect of returning to France.

Hélène came around the table and sat across, asking calmly, "And what did the leaders decide?"

"Most of the single men and some families are going," Samuel began in frustration. "Unfortunately that is most of the colony. The Kirkes have agreed to allow a few of the families to remain and retain their lands and their privileges. Then our five translators will stay with the Indians, but those two turncoats, Marsolet and Étienne Brûlé have agreed to translate for the English. I'm particularly disappointed in Étienne. The rascal's been like a son since he stowed away aboard one of my first voyages."

"I suppose that's reasonable," Hélène suggested. "They have both spent their lives translating for the natives. What would they do in France?" After a short pause she asked casually, "When do you suppose we will leave?"

Attempting in vain to hide his anger, he answered, "They seem to think in a month or two."

"Oh…" Hélène replied, successfully hiding her happiness.

In September 1629, the Kirke brothers loaded a ship to transport the *Québécois* to England. Prior to the departure, those leaving said their sad goodbyes to those left behind. Hélène said goodbye to the native children with whom she had become so attached. Samuel tried to bring three of her favorites, but the Kirke brothers flatly refused. Abraham Martin's wife, Marguerite, was at the dock as the group of passengers gathered. Searching the group, she saw the person she wanted and shouted, "Françoise!" An attractive but somewhat disheveled younger lady standing forlorn in a corner looked up and waved. Marguerite greeted her with an embrace. "I came to wish you *bon voyage*."

"Thank you, Madame, but are you not going?"

"Yes, we are, but Abraham said he and I may have a cabin above decks with *Général* Champlain and I may not be able to see you during the voyage—or even after landing. I do have a favor to ask." Marguerite reached into her pack producing an envelope. "Are you still going to the region of *Perche*?"

Françoise nodded sadly, "I suppose. I don't really have anyone left in France, only a cousin who was in *Mortagne*."

"I have a letter for my brother, and the Lord alone knows when the next post will go to France. My sister and her family are heading toward Paris with us, so she can't deliver it. I wondered if you could…?"

Françoise took the envelope, "Of course I will see that he gets it."

Relieved, Marguerite smiled for the first time, "You're a dear. His name is on it, Noël Langlois. He was in *Saint-Leonard*, but I believe he will now be in *Mortagne*. Anyway, ask around, people will know him." With a grin, she added, "He's devilishly handsome."

The gangplank was extended and the passengers ordered aboard. "I must go," Françoise whispered, "I'll see that your brother gets this." Hugging her friend, Françoise added, "I don't know when we shall see each other again— or if…" Sobbing, she turned and ran up the plank. Once aboard she tried to see her friend going with the group remaining aboveboard, but she could scarcely see for the tears in her eyes.

Françoise Grenier had arrived in *Québec* two years earlier with a man she was to marry. Soon after their arrival, he died and she remained single. Although *Québec* was crawling with single men, none suited her, so when the question of leaving or staying in *Québec* arose, she readily opted to leave.

Due to the seasonal lateness of the departure, seas were rough and several storms caused havoc among the English.

Fifteen of their number succumbed to dysentery, but the hardy French-Canadians rode out the storms with little difficulty during the two month voyage,

They landed in Plymouth, England, on November 3, 1629 where Champlain was greeted with three issues. First, he discovered peace had been declared on April 24, three months *before* the Kirkes landed in *Québec*, suggesting they had taken the colony under false pretenses. Secondly, the King of France had entered a new battle with Italy and so had neither time nor money to help get *Québec* back into the hands of France. Thirdly, Hélène told him she would never return to *Québec*, and was leaving him to return to Paris.

In the face of all the adversity, Champlain planned to stay in England and negotiate with the English himself while the remainder of the captives were taken to Dover, from where they would be returned to France.

CHAPTER 2

Dover: November 16, 1629

One week later, most of the returnees from *Québec* boarded a smaller ship sailing on from Dover to the harbor town of *Dieppe*. The only single woman aboard, Françoise was housed in a small compartment with no light or ventilation. When she felt it safe, she would go aboveboard where she could visit with her immigrant companions—and breathe. Françoise had been the only child of working-class parents, and her father had taught her how to defend and take care of herself. Since her parents died young, these were good skills to have. She had been a waif of the streets from the age of twelve. When she was only fifteen she met Guy. A strong man, twenty years her senior with a few rough edges, he also had a charming smile and curly red hair. He seemed as good as she could do. When he had approached her with the plan to sail to the New World, she agreed, having neither an alternative nor a firm grasp of what she was getting into.

He had promised once settled they would marry, but instead he soon took to the woods with renegade fur traders. Most of the time she was alone—until one day when he failed to return. His associates told her he had run afoul of the hostile Iroquois Indians and she should not plan to see him again. Turning to the Church where she could help with the friendly Algonquin Indians, she was befriended by a few of the women like Madame Martin. She had told them she was twenty, but actually, she was just seventeen.

Standing at the rail, Françoise breathed in the brisk salt air, attempting to forget her worries for a while. The day was clear and the seas fair, a grand improvement over the torrid weather they had endured in the open Atlantic.

The voice shook her from her solitude. "It will be good to get home."

She turned suddenly to see the speaker who had appeared without her notice. She had seen Noël Morin in *Québec*, but scarcely knew him. In fact, she had no real friends apart from the few ladies at the church. She merely nodded and agreed. This worked well for Françoise—she was attractive. Her dark hair was wavy but not unruly and her eyes dark piercing brown. Her physique was strong yet still feminine. She had an engaging smile, which she rarely used and had learned how her appearance could be both an advantage as well as a curse.

Noël Morin was tall and too thin. His light brown hair was wild, and his teeth crooked, but he had a personality and demeanor that served him well. He did the bulk of the talking, mostly about insignificant trivia until he excused himself, explaining. "They say we will land late this afternoon and should be prepared to unload." Françoise returned to her closet to wait. She owned almost nothing and had little to pack. She began to doze just as the ship's bell rang.

When she and Guy had departed from *Dieppe*, she recalled it was a rough and tumble harbor town, but then she had been with Guy while today she was alone and would need lodging for the night. After studying her poor choices, she finally settled on a small inn with an elderly lady rocking on the porch who, when Françoise inquired, invited her in. Realizing she had little money, she asked the price. The old lady grinned a toothless smile, "If you're not too fussy, I can give you a room for three sous and that includes a bowl of soup and cup of wine tonight."

Françoise agreed and, considering her financial state, asked, "Is there any work I could find around here?"

The old lady chuckled, "Honey, I could find you a job around here, and you'd make a lot of money." Looking at her up and down, she added, "But I don't know that it's the type of work you'd favor."

Blushing, Françoise merely answered, "Oh."

"You headed anywhere?"

"Uh, yes, to *Perche—Mortagne* to be exact."

"There's a coach first thing in the morning. Stand is just across the way. I'll get your room ready and you can go get a ticket so you're sure you will get a seat. I'll have a meal ready when you return. By the way, I'm Madame Allard."

Françoise went for the ticket, and when she returned, Madame Allard had the table set for two. "Just you and me tonight, Honey."

The soup was good, the bread fresh and the wine tolerable by *Québécoise* low standards. Madame Allard regaled Françoise with tales of an inn in a harbor town. Françoise had not laughed since she met Guy and had never felt safe before tonight. Finally the Madame asked, "You got a man?"

She considered her answer and its implication, then chose the truth, "No, Madame."

Madame Allard pulled out a pipe and lit it. Sitting back she said, "Let me give you a little advice. You are a pretty girl, and you sure ain't stupid. Hold out for the right one, dear. Believe me, he's out there, sometimes just takes some lookin'—and patience."

Later in her room, Françoise opened her petite sac and retrieved a small box her mother had given her just before her death. Opening it carefully she found its contents intact. They consisted of a rosary, a few pieces of jewelry Françoise believed were precious only to her, and a folded paper on which her mother had written the name of her cousin—*Nicole Lemére, Mortagne, Perche.*

Françoise was up with the sun, and Madame greeted her with coffee and a roll.

"Well, I guess you better get to the coach, Honey." She came over and kissed her cheek, "Good luck—and don't forget what I told you."

Approaching the coach stand, she saw her luck changing. Standing and waiting was Noël Morin. "Good morning," she said with renewed confidence. "I didn't know you were headed this way."

They boarded and sat next to one another. Once seated, he asked, "Where are you going?"

"*Mortagne,*" she answered.

"Family there?"

"I have no family…except a cousin I have never met. I'm delivering a letter for a friend," she explained before asking, "Do you live there?"

"I have in the past—for a short while," he answered, "but today I have some business for the *Général*."

"Oh?"

"There's a friend of his there, a *Monsieur* Giffard. He's a surgeon, but he's doing some work for the company—recruiting settlers."

"I see."

"Who is the letter for?"

She looked inside her bag, "A *Monsieur* Noël Langlois."

He chuckled, "I know him."

"Really?"

"He does carpentry and I was a carriage builder. We worked together. Isn't it a small world?"

She smiled for the second time this year, "I hope so—it has seemed too big just lately."

As the morning went by, Françoise watched the countryside, comparing the soft charm of Normandie to the rough bravado of *Québec*. She was ready to embrace soft charm.

CHAPTER 3

I think we are coming into *Rouen*."

Françoise jumped. It took her a minute to orient. She had fallen asleep, apparently for a long while. Sitting up, she realized she had used *Monsieur* Morin as a pillow. "Oh…forgive me, I must have fallen asleep."

"It's all right, you must have been exhausted."

"I didn't sleep well on the boat," she confessed. "My cabin was more like a coffin."

Morin smiled, "I hadn't thought of that, I was in a space below with some other single men… Why you must have been the only single woman?"

"Yes," she replied softly, feeling her face turn red in embarrassment, realizing he knew the awkward truth.

"Well, you did not miss much. I think we have to change coaches here."

Françoise remembered the man at the stand saying something about this, but she hadn't understood what he meant. So she asked, "Oh, how does one..?"

More smiling, "Don't fear, I know what to do."

When they exited the coach, she staggered, "Good God, I think my legs are dead."

Morin chuckled, "I doubt it. We have two hours before our next coach departs. Come, we shall find a place to eat."

Although she was starving, she realized her funds were near zero. "Oh, I think maybe I'll just wait here."

"You have to eat, it's a long ride."

"Well, I..."

"I'll even pay."

"Oh, you don't..."

"My mother would kill me if she discovered I allowed a woman to pay. At any rate, *Monsieur* Giffard is paying for this. I'll tell him I talked you into signing up for his next voyage back—whenever that may be." When she had left *Québec*, returning was, and continued to be, the furthest thing from her mind; however she simply smiled and agreed.

Selecting a modest café, he ordered chicken stew and Normand beer. He did most of the talking as Françoise felt she had nothing to say that she wanted to share. By the end of dinner she was feeling almost content. "We can take a short stroll," he said while they exited into the late afternoon. Finally it came up, "Didn't you come to *Québec* with a man?"

"Uh, yes, he was a *voyageur* and was killed by the Indians," she blurted out, trying in vain to sound nonchalant.

Now it was out, but to her relief, he asked no prying questions, only, "Iroquois?"

23

She merely nodded, attempting to stifle her sobs.

Trying to escape the subject, he said in a failed attempt to be subtle, "Well, I suppose we are safe from Indians here in *Rouen*."

She had not mentioned it, but she spent a night here with Guy on their way to Canada. *Rouen* seemed large at the time but after two years in *Québec*, it now seemed mammoth. Its giant churches and throngs of people almost seemed incomprehensible. Eventually they found the coach and boarded. They rode in relative silence, as the sun began to set. Françoise was feeling safe, maybe it was *Monsieur* Morin—or maybe the beer.

When she opened her eyes it was daylight. "Oh, my goodness. I slept again."

"I wish I could sleep like that," Morin replied with a grin.

Looking out she saw the rolling countryside of *Perche*. "Where are we?"

"We just passed *Alençon*. We will be in *Mortagne* in about two hours."

Now fully awake for her first time in France, she began to study the countryside. It was not rugged hills and mountains like *Québec*, nor flat plains like her girlhood home on the outskirts of Paris, but a gentle rolling terrain that she found almost hypnotic as the coach rolled along— always quietly up or down. Alternating from dense forest to open, undulating pastures and fields of grain, it was safe or so it seemed, frequently crossing small rivers and smaller streams. In their final autumn splendor, the leaves had turned, but their colors were muted, not like the Canadian maples that shouted their bold reds and gold throughout the forests around *Québec*.

Towns were small, sometimes miniscule, housing ranged from huts to moderate stone structures and the occasional grand chateau of the local *Seigneur*. An hour later they reached *Mortagne*. "This is where you disembark," *Monsieur* Morin announced. Françoise stepped down from the coach into a large square facing what appeared to be an official building next to a lovely stone church topped with a wonderful spire. The street was lined with small shops and enterprises interspersed among the row of small houses. A few citizens gathered by the coach to greet relatives or visitors, but no one for her.

"Do you know where to go?" he inquired.

"No, I have only this name from my late mother."

"What is it? Perhaps I know her."

Retrieving the paper, she read, "Nicole Lemére."

Frowning, he told her, "I don't recognize it. Perhaps you could go into the convent next to the church, I suspect if anyone knows her it will be the nuns."

Looking hesitantly at the convent, she replied. "Yes…thank you."

He smiled, "At any rate, I must continue on to *Tourouvre*—it's just down the road. My contact lives there, but I will be back here. Perhaps I'll see you around town." His smile widened, "Actually I know I will—it's not a big town."

She watched him re-board the coach before turning toward the convent which gave her a sudden flashback. When she was about eight, her parents told her they had to leave her as they went on *dangerous business*. They deposited her at the orphanage of a local convent where the sisters told her she would not see them again. However, they did return two years later to retrieve their conflicted and confused daughter.

The diminutive young nun critically surveyed the stranger at her door before asking, "May I help you?"

Losing her confidence, Françoise stammered, "I am… searching for a lady in the village."

Without changing her expression, the nun asked, "And who might that be?"

Françoise fumbled through her bag to find the paper before blurting, "Nicole Lemére… she is… my mother's cousin."

With a puzzled look the young sister replied, "I do not seem to recall such a person…"

Françoise was losing hope when the nun asked, "Is this her married or maiden name?"

Françoise thought, "It would be maiden."

"Ah! You see I am new to the parish and know only the married names. But it is no problem. Come with me to the school."

She ushered Françoise into a small school room where a lone boy about eight sat diligently reading. The nun went to a large book on a podium in back. "Here is the parish record." Beginning to page through the large tome, she said, "You see, we have here all the records…Ah! *Voila!* I should have known this one." Addressing the lad at the desk, she asked, "Pierre, is your mother home?"

The boy stood and snapped to attention. "Yes, Sister."

"Well then, please escort Madame here to your mother."

Remaining at attention, "Yes, Sister."

Returning to Françoise, she explained, "The woman you seek is his mother." Changing from stern to gracious, the nun added, "If you require lodging later, return here and we will arrange something, Madame…?"

Françoise almost smiled, "Grenier, Sister, Françoise Grenier. And it is *mademoiselle*."

Extending her hand, the sister replied, "And I am Sister Marie-Angelique." The young *religieuse* was *petite*, less than five feet tall and thin to the point of risking being whisked away in a stiff breeze. However, she maintained the nun-like aura of total authority that had held the Catholic faithful in fear for more than a millennium.

Turning to her young pupil, the nun ordered, "Introduce yourself to *Mademoiselle*, Pierre."

Extending his hand, he announced, "Pierre Boucher, *Mademoiselle*." The boy was average height for his age but stocky in a muscular way." His hair was sandy brown and curly and he had piecing blue eyes, possibly belying some Viking ancestry.

Picking up his book, she told him, "This is quite a book for a young man."

Sister Marie-Angelique stated proudly, "Young *Monsieur* Boucher is the finest student in the village."

As Françoise left Sister Marie-Angelique, who had morphed from security guard to girlfriend in a matter of minutes, Pierre assured her, "It's not far. Just follow me." Now that he was free of the scrutiny of the nun, he added, "Someday *I'm* going to write a book."

"Oh? About what?"

"Something I know everything about."

"And what is that?"

"Why, I don't know yet, I'm just learning."

Françoise was appreciating *Mortagne* more and more. "Do you have brothers and sisters, Pierre?"

"Oh yes. Six—I'm oldest—actually I would be third, but my oldest brother died when he was just a baby, and my oldest sister died when she was three." He took her by the hand and led her into a walled cemetery adjacent the church. Pointing to a row of small wooden crosses, "They are buried here." Crossing himself, he led her back to the road to continue the journey.

"How old are you, Pierre?" Françoise asked casually.

"Seven years—almost eight," he announced proudly. Françoise began to wonder if there was something special in the water of *Mortagne*.

Strolling along the main route, passing homes, stores and artisan shops, people would greet young Boucher, and men would tip their hats to the young lady. While they walked, Pierre began to question Françoise. By the time they reached their destination, she thought he knew everything about her—almost everything.

The Boucher home appeared prosperous compared to the average *habitation* in *Québec*. When they entered, Madame Boucher was busy at the fire while two youngsters played at her feet, and a third sat in a highchair.

"Mother," Pierre announced, "This is *Mademoiselle* Grenier. She is your cousin."

Madame Boucher left her task and wiped her hands on her apron. Before she could speak, Françoise took the floor. "Forgive me, Madame, my mother was Agnes Lemére, she..."

Madame Boucher interrupted, "My God, Cousin Agnes! I have not seen her since she left with her parents many years ago. I believe they went towards Paris. We were the best of friends as children. How is she, dear?"

"She died five years ago..."

"Oh, I am so sorry..."

"Perhaps I should explain, Madame." Françoise summarized the untimely death of her parents, her adventure to *Québec* and the recent events, skipping some of the more sordid details, and concluding with, "She said if I needed help, I could call on you." She broke into tears.

Nicole Boucher embraced her cousin saying, "Come, sit and tell me more while I prepare dinner. You may stay with us as long as necessary." Françoise protested but Madame assured her, "It is no trouble, I'll put you in our 'girls' room. We only have Marie now," pointing to the baby in the chair "and she sleeps with us—no trouble at all."

Madame Boucher was short and stocky with the type of physique meant for childbearing. Her hair was dark brown and straight, her eyes also dark brown and her ample breasts were made to feed children. She treated Françoise in such a motherly fashion, it seemed she still had milk to spare.

Madame Boucher explained that her husband was away on business. After Françoise joined the family to dine on a grand porridge with pumpkin pie for dessert, she could scarcely make it to bed, but when the Boucher rooster crowed, she was ready to rise, thoroughly rested. When she appeared, Madame Boucher was dressed with breakfast on the table. She invited Françoise to sit, and as she served the breakfast porridge, announced, "Once we have eaten, my young cousin, we shall go out and decide what to do with your one wild and savage life."

When the house and children were in order, the women retired to chairs on the front stoop with a view of the society of *Mortagne* passing by. There Françoise poured out the details of her story, from the death of her parents to her arrival in *Perche*, in a more calm and organized fashion than the jumbled version given upon her arrival. She did, however, again avoid certain episodes concerning Guy. Finally Madame Boucher gave her advice in her simple cut-to-the-chase fashion Françoise would come to love.

"It's simple, my dear. First, we find something for you to do and then find you a man—a good man!" As if she had planned her timing perfectly, the church bell began to chime, and Madame Boucher arose. "That signals the market. Let us go see it."

CHAPTER 4

Mortagne: November 19, 1629

Held each week in the main square, market day drew every citizen not otherwise occupied with a pressing task. Each farmer's stand held its special wares and crops of the season. Today pumpkin, squash, melons, apples and pears were plentiful along with the last of this season's tomatoes and beans. Corn, which Françoise had obtained from the natives in *Québec*, was still nowhere to be seen in France. Some had milk, cheese and various meats—poultry was most common. Others had wine and liquor along with cider and *calvados*, which would have shamed the *Québécoise* version of the libation.

The two ladies worked their way along the stalls, stopping frequently so Madame Boucher could introduce Françoise, who realized she would have difficulty remembering names in this throng of strangers. Along with the identity of each, Madame Boucher added the occupation of the spouse. Almost every shopper's husband was a tradesman or artisan. The full-time farmers were working their fields or working behind their stands. Passing *Notre-Dame de Mortagne*, they encountered Sister Marie-Angelique who was pleased to see her new friend doing well. Making the turn toward home, Françoise noticed the autumn leaves were still falling, thinking the trees in *Québec* would likely have been bare for some time.

"Gaspard," Madame Boucher began, "will be home this evening. I want to have something special."

"What work does your husband do, Madame?"

"He is a furniture and cabinet builder and has a wonderful contract for one of the *Seigneurs* outside *Tourouvre* to the north and east of here. I'm anxious for you to meet him—he's a fine man."

As they made their way through the autumn splendor, Françoise wondered what it would be like to have a wonderful man. At home they were greeted by young Pierre. "I know you must think I'm negligent to leave the children with someone his age," Madame admitted, "but he is more mature and responsible than most children in their teens."

Françoise smiled, "I've noticed, Madame."

"And you must call me Nicole, my dear. We are cousins after all, and I doubt we are that far apart in age."

"Yes, Madame."

Once home, Madame Nicole Boucher unpacked her purchases and began the assault on dinner while she discussed the nature of this quite rural region of France with her new friend. *"Perche* is a quiet collection of small towns. We do not have these riots they have in places like *La Rochelle.* People move from time to time from one village to another but rarely leave the region.

"We are very near *Tourouvre,* another delightful village which is just a bit smaller. Perhaps we could take a walk there someday before winter."

"One can walk?" Françoise asked in surprise.

"Oh yes, only an hour or two."

Eventually the preparation of the feast was complete, and Nicole declared, "I think we can now sit a spell and wait."

Before she could reach the door, it burst open with the announcement, *"Papa est ici!"*

Gaspard Boucher was tall and thin, with long graying black hair tied in back to be kept out of the way. He had the weathered skin of an outdoor worker, long arms and very long, thin, gnarly fingers. The three ambulatory children came rushing and Gaspard hugged the two youngest before offering his hand to Pierre with, "Did you keep the castle ordered and protected in my absence, *Mon petit?"*

Pierre stood straight and answered, *"Oui, Mon Général."*

With this, Gaspard embraced his wife with a long passionate kiss before turning to Françoise. "And you must be the lovely and *exotique* cousin Françoise Grenier."

Françoise stood in amazement as he laughed, "There are no secrets in a small village, *Mademoiselle."* He extended his hand—it was dry, calloused, and obviously very strong.

Nicole came forward with a bottle, "Dinner will be ready soon, but we have time for a short toast." She poured three glasses of the sweet red local wine and raised her glass, *"Santé."* They each took a sip and Gaspard told them, "I am pleased to say, my project is over, and next week I start on one locally. You will no longer be deprived of my company."

"How did you finish so quickly?" his wife inquired.

"Things went well, and I was able to hire excellent help."

"Oh?"

"Yes, that young Langlois—he is becoming quite talented."

Françoise almost dropped her glass as her eyes opened wide. "Oh, my goodness!" She burst from her chair and went into her small corner to recover her bag. Returning with the letter in hand, she said, "I was so confused upon arrival, I completely forgot…"

"What is it, dear?" Nicole asked.

"When I left *Québec*, a friend gave me this letter for her brother. I completely forgot."

Gaspard looked at the envelope, "Noël Langlois. The very name of my helper. He is young and dashing, does it sound like him?"

"Yes, can I get it to him?"

Gaspard handed the envelope back. "Eventually, but it may be a while. Before I left, he took the coach to *Le Mans*. He has a job there that will take some time."

"How long?"

Gaspard shrugged, "Hard to say, a few months. It is indoors so they will work in the winter."

"How far away is it?"

Shrugging again, "A day or so by coach."

"How can I get the letter to him?"

"He will return, my dear, there are a few Langlois in *Perche*. I would just wait."

34

Once dinner was served, Gaspard brought back the subject. "Now that I think about it, there are a few Langlois right around here. I can never remember which is a sibling or a cousin. There is a young man, Jean, who recently ran off to sea and the wife of the man I was just working for—rich man named Juchereau, I believe she is a Langlois. Then I seem to remember two of the girls went to Canada—Marguerite and Fannie, I believe."

Françoise interjected, "I only knew Madame Martin—Marguerite, from the church. I was only there two years and didn't know everyone."

Nicole added, "Well, I think it sounds like a cold, wild place. I like it here."

Françoise added softly, "Amen to that."

"Like I said, my dear," Gaspard closed, "have no fear, Noël Langlois will return and you can deliver his letter."

CHAPTER 5

Mortagne to *Tourouvre* Road: November 20, 1629

I continue to be amazed that it is so warm this far into autumn," Françoise said while the two ladies made their way down the lane connecting the two villages.

Kicking her way playfully through the fallen leaves, Nicole replied, "This is a particularly mild November."

"In *Québec* there would likely be snow by now."

"Sounds dreadful to me. How did you find it?"

Françoise thought for a while. "At first it seemed wild and exciting, and I guess it was, but the long cold winter with no respite…"

"Why did you go?"

"I think I told you, I met a man. My parents were both dead and I had no prospects. He had heard about Canada and convinced me to go with him."

"But you were not married?" Nicole asked.

"No, he said he would marry me there. I believed him. The ship was ready to go, and he said we had no time."

"Had you slept with him?" Françoise remained silent until Nicole added, "We are family. You can tell me, I won't gossip."

"Yes," she confessed, her voice breaking. "I was young—and stupid. Then, afterwards, I thought, 'no man will want me.' So I went with him." She suddenly felt relieved of her sin.

Nicole took her hand, "Many men would want you, cousin, believe me. I know men."

Françoise blew her nose before continuing, "When we arrived, it was summer, the weather was warm and the country was spectacular. Like nothing you've seen in France. The Indians, that's what they call the natives, were exotic, and sometimes friendly. Soon Guy—that was his name, took a job getting furs."

"Did they trap them, or shoot them?"

"Actually neither, they went into the wilderness and traded European items with the Indians for the pelts—that's what they call the furs. The Indians trapped the animals. Most of it is beaver, but other animals as well."

"And they make a living with that?"

"A very good living I am told. Guy would be gone for months at a time, I was alone. Most of the people are single men there to work and trade. I believe many cannot return to France for *certain reasons*. They are a very rough group indeed. There were a few families, mostly artisans—like Gaspard, but almost no single ladies. I was constantly bothered by stray men." Beginning to whimper, she continued, "When Guy would return, he would drink and have violent sex with me until he left again. I don't know if I was more relieved to see him return or leave."

37

"Sounds perfectly awful."

Françoise finished sobbing. Drying her tears, she continued, "It was. Then one day they said he had trouble with the Iroquois—they are the bad Indians—and that Guy would not come back."

"Was he dead?"

"I assumed so. What is terrible is that I was secretly pleased. It was then I went to help the women of the church teach the friendly Algonquin Indians. That saved me. It was there I met Madame Martin."

They became silent and continued the stroll, watching the fields, pastures and forests as they went. Suddenly Françoise stopped. "Is that a horse?" she shouted in amazement.

Nicole laughed, "Yes, it's a *Percheron*, the local breed."

"It's a monster—and white."

"Yes," Nicole answered, "They are used as draft horses to pull heavy loads. But they are very smart and surprisingly gentle. You can ride one—if you can manage to climb onto it."

Eventually they came to *Tourouvre*. A slightly smaller town than *Mortagne*, it had all the same characteristics, rolling country, shops, homes and a large stone church, *Saint-Aubin de Tourouvre*.

Strolling through the street, they were greeted by several people, all who seemed to know Nicole. Approaching the end of town, Françoise heard a familiar voice, "I knew I'd see you eventually."

Turning to see Noël Morin, she almost hugged him but decided better and only took his hand, introducing him to Nicole.

"Did you find *Monsieur* Langlois?" he asked.

When she told her tale of woe, he replied, "I told him you had the letter, so at least he knows about it, but I heard he had to hurry off to *Le Mans* for another job. He will return."

"And how is your job?" Françoise inquired.

"Very interesting, and if you two ladies would like, we could go sit at this café and I'll tell you about it."

Once they were seated, Nicole said, "We will have tea."

Morin nodded, adding, "You could have beer if you like. It's very good here."

Françoise frowned, "Do you think we are in *Québec*?"

He laughed and to his surprise, Nicole said, "I'll have beer. I've never been to *Québec*."

Morin ordered three beers and began, "I am working for a Robert Giffard. He is a businessman and surgeon who went to *Québec* but comes back periodically. He was returning when the Kirkes came the first time but was intercepted and taken prisoner. With the treaty, he was eventually released and he and Champlain are determined to make *Québec* a *real* colony."

"What do you mean?" the ladies asked almost in unison.

He took a deep breath, "Going back to the beginning, France felt it only needed to send single men because its interest was in fish and furs—not families and colonies like the English. Champlain and Cartier had seen the Indians and thought the men could breed with them and make little Frenchmen." Both women frowned while he continued. "What they did do was disappear into the woods and made little Indians. Now that the English have interest in the area, France does not have the manpower to hold the country. The Kirkes taught them that—if they didn't know it already."

39

"So what will you do now?" Françoise asked, becoming interested.

Morin drained his beer and ordered another. "Would you ladies..?" They both shook their heads, no. He continued. "We plan to send many more people and many families—enough to farm and support the enterprise. "

"And how do you propose luring people to that God-forsaken place?" Françoise questioned.

"By making it a good place to live," he boasted, "and I'll tell you how."

Nicole said, "I would like another beer." Françoise agreed.

After ordering, he continued. "First, we plan to send a large group of men to build an infrastructure."

"Whatever is that?" the ladies questioned.

"Build roads, and a solid fort, a good church, and many houses in a defensible city. We plan to send enough soldiers to defend it and priests and nuns to run a proper church. And..." he said with a dramatic flair, "the Company of 100 Associates will pay their way."

"Where will you find these people?" Nicole asked.

With a smile, he concluded, "We plan to get the first settlers right here in *Perche*."

"In *Perche*?" the women asked in unison, with a skeptical air.

"Yes, *Monsieur* Juchereau is a large investor and lives nearby."

"My husband was just working for him," Nicole explained, before asking, "Isn't his wife a Langlois?"

"Yes, she is," he agreed, then looking at Françoise, "In fact, I believe she may be the cousin of *your Monsieur* Langlois."

Eventually they parted company and the ladies began the trek back to *Mortagne*. They were silent most of the way, both personally considering the possibilities of Morin's plan.

CHAPTER 6

The tower bells of *Notre-Dame* were already pealing, before the Boucher family finished breakfast. Nicole stood and gave orders, "Pierre, help Nicolas dress while we clear the table. We must not be late for mass."

While Françoise and Nicole cleared the dishes, Gaspard actually helped. Françoise smiled as she realized this man was threatening to change her attitude toward men in general. Once in order, they marched off to church. Pierre and Nicolas led the way with the adults behind. Gaspard held one-year-old Charles, and Nicole carried Marie in a pack. Nicole had given Françoise a dress she had outgrown to provide a Sunday dress in place of her singular garment brought with her back from the New World. Françoise protested, but it no longer fit Nicole and fit Françoise quite well.

The square was filled with parishioners as most of the community attended regularly. There was only time for the briefest of greetings before the bells rang, signaling entry. Like most French churches, *Notre-Dame de Mortagne* was the most substantial structure in the village, boasting fine stonework and a prominent tower with not one, but two bells. The interior was as ornate as the community could provide with statues of the crucifix, Saint-Joseph, and of course, *Notre-Dame* herself, holding the infant Jesus.

Françoise had scarcely ever attended mass with her parents, and it was not until her two-year stay in the convent that she went regularly and was properly instructed in the faith. Again with Guy, she fell away only to return when she sought refuge with the ladies of *Québec* at their small and simple church.

Today's Latin Mass was tolerable in length, and the sermon in French dealt with the approach of Advent and the evils of Protestantism. The high point of the mass for Françoise was a short period of music played on a flute with singing in Latin by a rather large lady.

Following mass, the parish stayed in the square to socialize. Sister Marie-Angelique came to visit with her favorite pupil and his family. Nicole asked, "How is the school coming, Sister?"

"If the students were all like your son, it would be wonderful, but since Sister Marie-Monique left us for Heaven, leaving only me, it is a challenge."

Françoise remained silent but on the way home asked "Is Sister Marie-Angelique the only teacher at the school?"

Nicole responded, "Sadly, yes."

"But I saw other nuns at mass."

Nicole nodded, "Yes, but unfortunately, none of the others have the vocation to teach. They aid the sick, work the garden or have other duties."

That evening when the young children were in bed, the adults visited while Pierre laid reading by the fire. Approaching his mother, he asked, "What is this word?"

Nicole looked, squinting at the fire, "I don't know, dear, it's quite long."

Turning, he showed it to Françoise, who replied, "*Hirondelle*, it's a small bird, the sort that nests in your father's barn."

Monday, while Nicole and Françoise were preparing dinner, Nicole asked, "How did you know that word last night? I thought you hadn't been to school."

Françoise stopped, placing the stack of plates on the table. "That's not entirely true. When I was Pierre's age, my parents left me at a convent. I did not know when, or even if, they would retrieve me." Thinking to herself, *how I wish they had not,* but continuing, "There was a small school, and I did learn some letters and numbers. Actually I was not bad. I can read some things, write some and add and subtract."

Françoise picked up her stack of plates, and Nicole set down her work. "I believe I have the answer to your first task."

In the morning the two women went to visit Sister Marie-Angelique, and by noon, Françoise had something to do—assistant instructor. That evening she returned for dinner and announced, "There is a room for me at the convent. I'm going to take it, I have burdened you long enough."

Nicole knew she would miss the companionship and assistance, but realizing it was for the best, she merely nodded. In the morning, amid a few tears, hugs and reassurance she would still be nearby, Françoise left for a new chapter in her life.

What Françoise did not know was that same week Samuel Champlain, who had remained in England, convinced King Charles I to return *Québec* to the French. He, too, finally left for the country of his birth to face the long and arduous task of convincing his nemesis, Cardinal Richelieu, and the King to allow him to return to *Québec*.

CHAPTER 7

During the previous six months, Françoise and Sister Marie-Angelique would meet regularly after class to discuss school matters. Younger than the other nuns, they found this provided a chance to visit as friends, causing them to form a close relationship. Françoise had shared her story of *Québec* with her new friend even including the details of her relationship with Guy.

Today, however, they were discussing the school. "I think we have finally won over almost all the village." Sister Marie-Angelique declared. "At first they were concerned about *my* age. Once they were beginning to accept me, you joined and their skepticism returned. When they discovered you had been to *Québec*, they became even more suspicious. A few mothers came to ask me if you were a *savage*. But now I think they have all come to accept you."

Françoise laughed, "That's more amusing than you know. I have told you that after Guy died, I worked with the few French wives helping with the Indian children. At first I was very withdrawn and hesitant around the natives. Eventually Madame Martin took me with two of the *Récollet* missionaries to one of the nearby Algonquin villages. She left me there with the two priests and the tribe for two months."

Sister Marie-Angelique was aghast, "You were there—the only white woman with all those savages?"

Françoise laughed out loud. "After living with Guy and knowing some of the men he traveled with, I would question who the savages were." The nun was speechless while Françoise explained, "They were the kindest and most gentle people I have known. Women and children are especially charming, and the woman is in charge of the family."

Sister Marie-Angelique regarded her in horror, "*Impossible!*"

"It's true." Françoise declared, "I'm told that in the Iroquois culture, tribes are even more *matriarchal.*"

"Is that like Satanic?" her friend whispered.

Françoise continued to grin, "No, it's a word the missionaries used. It means in that society, women are head of the household."

"It can't be."

"Really." Françoise continued, "In French families, the father is in charge. That is called *patriarchal*—but now I'm wondering if that is *actually* true." Sister Marie-Angelique was giggling as Françoise added, "What I wanted to tell you is while I was at the village, they gave me native dress

47

to wear—made of deerskin, it is very comfortable. They braided my hair in back, which was helpful keeping it out of my way. Since it was summer, my skin darkened in the bright sunlight of the village. When we returned to *Québec*, one of the women there asked if I was an Indian. When I lived with Guy, I was a recluse and even after his death, I did not know anyone other than the few ladies who worked with the Indians in the church. Some people in *Québec* may still think I'm native."

Sister Marie-Angelique went to the cupboard and withdrew a bottle. "We keep this for the priests, but I think we should have a taste."

Mortagne: May 1, 1630:

Two weeks later, Françoise was organizing some books for Sister Marie-Angelique when one of the older nuns came in, announcing, "*Mademoiselle*." The older nuns were much more formal than the young Sister Marie-Angelique. "There is a gentleman to see you." Sister Marie-Claude was possibly old enough to be Françoise's mother and what Sister Marie-Angelique lacked in size, the older nun possessed. She towered over Françoise and outweighed her by at least 100 pounds.

Putting down her work, Françoise asked, "Where is he, Sister Marie-Claude?"

"Out front on a bench, he said he would wait there."

Françoise nodded and left for the street while the nun watched her carefully. The older nuns did not know what to think of this unusual girl and this unusual relationship with their convent.

The young man stood as she walked out the door. He was average size, in excellent physical shape and probably

48

in his twenties. Wearing the working clothes of a typical artisan, he had a short growth of beard, which matched his black hair and accentuated his deep blue eyes. He was *disarmingly* handsome.

"I was told you were looking for me." He smiled, his teeth were healthy.

She hesitated a moment before asking cautiously, "*Monsieur* Langlois?"

Bowing slightly while retaining his smile, he replied, "At your service."

Suddenly Françoise ended her trance. "Oh, I have something for you—*excusez-moi.*" She ran quickly to the convent returning with the envelope. Offering it shyly at arm's length, she said, "This is…for you."

Looking at it, he responded, "From my sister Marguerite. Her writing is unmistakable."

He casually shoved it into his pocket. Surprised at his lack of curiosity compared to hers she asked, "Are you *not* going to read it?"

He smiled again, it was a wonderful smile, and replied with indifference, "I know what she will say. I will read it later, but I am starving and was going to *Le Cheval Blanc* for something to eat. Perhaps you would join me?"

Normally it would seem inappropriately forward if an unmarried girl went on such a date, but the community had come to believe that Françoise had been widowed in *Québec,* so that would make such a meeting acceptable. She knew her answer but replied demurely, "I don't know…"

"But I've been eating alone all winter, and you brought this halfway around the world," he pleaded while smiling.

It was the smile that worked. Gaining some confidence, she answered "Well… if you insist."

49

Named for the giant white horse of the region, the establishment's full title was *L'Hôtel du Cheval Blanc*, a typical *Percheron* tavern and inn. Françoise passed it almost daily but never set foot inside where today people Françoise recognized from town occupied three of the six tables. They all watched her and the young man with interest, perhaps wondering what this unusual girl from the wilds of Canada was up to.

Langlois was oblivious as he ordered and began to speak. "So you knew my sisters?"

"Just Marguerite," she responded, "I've only heard about your other sister."

"My other sister is Françoise, like you, but we call her Fannie. She's married to a man named Desportes. Do you know what has become of them?"

"I was not able to see them after we left Canada, but I believe they both returned to France with their families," she reported. "I believe they were going north—toward Paris."

"I also have a cousin, Marie, who is married to *Monsieur* Jean Juchereau," he stated, "They live outside of *Tourouvre*." Françoise nodded, as he added with a twinkle in his blue eye, "He is rich."

"So I have heard," she responded politely.

Looking around the room as well as for something to say, he told her, "I've never been in here, but there is also an inn at *Tourouvre* named, *Le Cheval Blanc.*"

Also searching for conversation, she replied, "I believe I've seen it. Is that odd?"

Again, the wonderful smile, "I suppose if a region has one exceptional feature—like the world's largest horse, it's worth noting."

Françoise only nodded.

Once the food was served, he asked, "How did a beautiful lady like you get to *Québec*?"

Ready for the question but not the compliment, she used her standard response. "I went with a man I was to marry, but he was killed by Indians."

"How sad. How did you find Canada?"

Pleased he had avoided prying into the subject of her man, she used another standard response, "It is a cold and wild place, at first it was exciting, but after…Let me just say, I am happy to be back in France."

Nodding, he switched to non-threatening small-talk while she watched his magical blue eyes, thinking, *"Where were you, before I went to Québec?"*

At the end of the evening, he walked her home and politely bid *bonne nuit* at the door. She watched through the window as he walked away.

Back at his room in *Le Cheval Blanc*, he opened the letter.

Dearest Brother,

As you may or may not have learned, English freebooters have taken Québec, and we are being shipped back to France. Our sister, Fannie, her husband and daughter are going with us, and I believe we will stay somewhere near Paris for the present. Général Champlain assures us this will not last long and France shall ultimately prevail. He and Monsieur Giffard are planning to return when possible to build a new and defensible colony. He plans to begin with settlers from Perche. I believe our Cousin Marie's husband, Monsieur Juchereau, and his brother will help finance it.

My primary motive in this letter is to convince you to come with us when it happens. This is in its own way a wonderful place, and with the proper planning and citizens it can become much better still. The Mademoiselle who carries this letter is a lovely girl. She has had a hard life, but I have come to know her. Along those lines, there are few women here and fewer eligible women. You would do well to find one in France before leaving.

As always, your sister,
Marguerite

Noël's sisters were perpetually trying to run his life. He tossed the letter on his bureau and crawled into his bed.

Mortagne: July 15, 1630

To Françoise's surprise and delight, *Monsieur* Langlois began to call regularly, sometimes for a walk or a visit to a local fair or market, and at least once a week to escort her to dinner. He had taken a job with Gaspard Boucher and was living nearby. Noël was from the small town of *Saint-Léonard des Parcs*, thirty kilometers west of *Mortagne*, and as the couple was becoming a fixture in the community, the locals were pleased to see someone from their area becoming *Mademoiselle Grenier's young man.*

The older nuns at the convent would wait for his arrival, all three heads peering out the window and giggling throughout the evening, all living vicariously through their young assistant. Françoise was beginning to realize her life was not at its end, but actually that it was only beginning. This evening he had taken her back to *Le Cheval Blanc* where he was more enthusiastic than ever.

"I finally heard back from my sister, Marguerite," he reported. "She and Abraham have settled the family in

Paris. The best part is Abraham has taken a job as navigator on a ship and has asked me to come to be his apprentice."

Françoise tried to hide her surprise and disappointment. "How does that work?"

Noël was oblivious to the downside of the plan from her perspective. "I will go to Paris from where we will leave for and depart from *Dieppe*."

"When will you leave?"

"As soon as possible," he replied, "maybe tomorrow. I'm very excited. This has been my dream."

She tried to remain calm and supportive in face of this disastrous turn, at least in her view. "When will you...return?"

His excitement remained high, "No one knows. Maybe a month or a year...or never."

Never shook her very soul, but she merely nodded.

He continued to discuss the plan while she sat silently, stirring the remains of her meal with her spoon, trying to hide her emotions. Finally he suggested they leave as he had to rise early. At the door of the convent, he told her, "I will write you once things are settled. Thank you for these wonderful weeks." He kissed her gently on the cheek and turned into the street.

Watching him disappear into shadows, she whispered under her breath, *"Au revoir, Mon Cher."*

Françoise cried herself to sleep. She awoke having decided she must get on with life. So she rose and went to do her job.

⚜

Six weeks later she received a letter—the first letter she had ever received in her life. She opened it with care.

Dear Françoise

It has been a busy six weeks. Once I arrived in Paris, I stayed with my sister for a week while arrangements were made. Eventually, Abraham and I made our way to Dieppe. There was a great deal to do and learn, but tomorrow we will depart on our first voyage. Our ship is called l'Aigle d'Or. We will be sailing up and down the coast of France. No crossing the Atlantic at this point, but I am very excited. I will try to stay in touch when I can.

Noël

I miss you.

Françoise read it several times, before folding it carefully, and placing it in her mother's box. She would live on those last three words for some time.

CHAPTER 8

Mortagne: November 2, 1630

T he end of the harvest meant the beginning of school, filling the small convent schoolroom with activity. Although Françoise was called *assistant instructor,* Sister Marie-Angelique did all the real teaching and Françoise was mainly in charge of fetch and carry and maintaining order from the rear. While the nun described the basic history of France, Françoise sat realizing she had now been one year in _Mortagne_. Recalling the days of her return, she gravitated, as always, to Noël Langlois—where was he? Would he ever return?

She was scarcely listening to the lecture, but the students were, and something in it would change her life in _Mortagne_. The catalyst would come in the form of none other than eight-year-old Pierre Boucher.

While the class was dismissed and the students filed out, Pierre hung back waiting to speak with Sister Marie-Angelique. This was hardly unusual, Pierre always had questions and the young nun only hoped they were questions she could answer.

"Yes, Pierre," she said while the last students were escaping to the square, "do you have a question?"

Pierre stood at military attention as any good Catholic boy does when facing a nun. "Yes, Sister."

"And it is..?

"Well, Sister, your lecture was very instructive." Pierre had already honed the skill that someday would be called *brown-nosing the teacher,* and Sister Marie-Angelique was not oblivious to the fact. "I was wondering," he continued, "since *Mademoiselle* Grenier has been to *New France,* perhaps she could teach us about it."

The nun smiled, "That is a very good idea, Pierre. We will think about it and I'll also ask Father. Now, why don't you go join the others?"

Pierre marched proudly to the door but turned before he reached it, "I could help her if you like."

Smiling again, she replied, "We shall see."

Once they were alone, the nun said, "Out of the mouths of children...what do you think, Françoise?"

Françoise was already frightened by the idea, "I don't know, Sister, I mean..."

"I think it is a marvelous idea," the nun declared. "I must discuss it with the Father, but I'm certain, he'll have no objection." Françoise was obviously not on board, but the nun added, "I'll help you, it will be fun."

⚜

Dinner at the convent generally involved only the four nuns and Françoise. By tradition there was no conversation during the meal, but following they took the opportunity to visit. The elder three looked forward each evening to hearing about the school.

"I have spoken to Father and he has met with some of the parish leaders. They have no objection to Françoise speaking—so long as it is within parish guidelines." The older nuns were particularly enthused as they had been since they first heard the idea. Françoise remained nervous while Sister Marie-Angelique continued. "Françoise, you and I will work on an outline. We shall keep it simple and non-threatening." Françoise realized she must co-operate. She owed it to the convent and to Sister Marie-Angelique, but she thought simple and non-threatening would be a difficult way to portray *Québec*.

Three weeks later they were ready, or the nuns and children were ready. Françoise was astounded that she could be so frightened by children between six and twelve years of age. However, she took a deep breath when Sister Marie-Angelique introduced her and the topic, knowing full well the students already knew all about it from young Pierre.

Taking another deep breath, Françoise began, "Three years ago, I left home to take a large ship across the ocean to another land."

"How long did it take?" a voice rang out.

Sister Marie-Angelique stood and frowned. The students knew they were not to interrupt.

Oblivious to this rule, Françoise answered, "Two months."

"Why did you go?" asked another voice drawing another frown from the nun.

Françoise had anticipated this one. "I went with my husband," she declared, wondering if one need confess lies told in lectures.

"What happened to him?" was next.

Suddenly Barbe Guyon, the oldest girl in school, stood. "Quiet! All of you! This is important and we all want to hear it. No more questions!" She sat and the questions ended, sometimes peer pressure is more forceful than nun pressure.

Françoise continued and soon became comfortable. She was amused when she noticed the three older nuns listening outside the doorway. They had decided to do this twice a week for one half-hour. In this half-hour, she brought the ship safely across the sea approaching the long *Fleuve Saint-Laurent* into the wilds of *Québec*. At the end the students rose clapping and drew another admonishment from Sister Marie-Angelique.

After dinner that night, the women discussed the program and the older nuns had more questions than the children. Sister Marie-Claude said, "I now wish I had been a teacher."

Françoise used this to ask a question that had bothered her from the beginning. "Why are you not all teachers?"

"We were trained at the Ursuline Convent in Tours. Our order is mainly teaching young children, but they trained some of us for other things. The three of us did not become teachers like Sister Marie-Angelique—I regret that now."

By Christmas, Françoise was feeling comfortable in her new role and believed she had accomplished the first of Nicole Boucher's two goals—but now she must find a man.

More than a year from her first lesson on New France, Françoise was amazed the children continued to have questions, bringing up new topics on which she would try to speak. This caused her to call occasionally on *Monsieur* Morin in *Tourouvre* for tutoring on the facts. Her lessons had gained notoriety in the town. Although there was much skepticism at first, the adults had come to embrace the concept with the occasional stray adult attending the sessions. However, she had been less successful in finding a permanent man. She had won the interest of a few local bachelors, but she was hampered by her awful memory of Guy and her hopeful belief that *Monsieur* Langlois would someday return.

Recently, she had begun speaking about the native people and her experience in the Algonquin camp.

"So the Algonquin are good and the Iroquois are bad?" her most ardent listener asked.

No matter how much she studied and thought about her subjects, she could never keep up with the quick mind of young Pierre Boucher. "Not exactly, Pierre," she responded, not totally certain of her answer. "The French get along better with the Algonquin. I am certain there are many reasons."

To her dismay, Pierre's hand was again in the air. "Yes, Pierre."

"You said the Iroquois live in villages—where they farm and don't move about."

"Yes?"

"And the Algonquin hunt and don't have regular villages that stay the same."

Not certain where her young genius was going, she simply agreed while he concluded, "Maybe the Algonquin are more like the French who, you said, do not have a stable village, and the Iroquois have villages like the English."

Françoise realized her pupil had a better insight than she did. "That's all for today," she said in surrender.

At dinner she told Sister Marie-Angelique, "I believe I should get away from the Indian topic."

Her friend laughed, "Don't feel bad, Pierre knows his numbers better than I do." Then smiling, "In addition, there are only two school days remaining."

The following evening, Sister Marie-Angelique came to dinner and greeted Françoise in excitement. "The Father just received word from Paris. It seems on March 20th, England surrendered *Québec* to France. Father says, your friend, *Monsieur* Champlain, is making plans to return even as we speak."

Françoise replied, "And I have only one day to explain this to young Boucher?"

That night she lay awake in her bed, contemplating that two years ago, she had no interest in *Québec*, especially in returning, but now she was not so certain.

CHAPTER 9

Mortagne: October 1632

S
ummer in _Perche_ had been delightful. Françoise helped the older nuns in the convent garden and was beginning to feel at home. She attended the summer fairs and markets sometimes with Sister Marie-Angelique, sometimes alone, and sometimes with the occasional suitor. However, she always watched the coach stop, hoping someday to see the long absent _Monsieur_ Langlois return.

At the end of harvest, school commenced as usual and along with it, her twice-weekly discussion of New France. In the beginning, she and Sister Marie-Angelique had expected this to take several weeks, but the increased interest of the students, and some adults, was turning it into a permanent fixture.

One afternoon when Françoise was straightening out the classroom, Sister Marie-Claude entered. "_Mademoiselle,_ two men are calling for you. I put them in the Father's office."

Françoise had rarely been in the priest's office and certainly never to receive her own caller. Uncertain if this was a good or a bad omen, she knew Marie-Claude would not voice an opinion, so straightening her dress and hair, she headed to the office.

She recognized Noël Morin immediately, but did not know the older gentlemen. In his forties, he was clean and well dressed with an air of authority. She had only *heard* of Robert Giffard in *Québec*, but felt certain he was the other visitor.

Morin extended his hand, "*Mademoiselle* Grenier, how good to see you again." She took his hand with a subtle curtsey as he continued, "Permit me to introduce Doctor Robert Giffard."

Françoise curtsied again, simply saying, "*Enchanté*." She still had a premonition this was not going to be anything good.

Giffard began, "*Mademoiselle*, I understand you were in *Québec* the last two years before the English invasion." She only nodded as he added, "I'm surprised I never met you. But I was gone much of the last year conferring with the Minister. I was returning when those devil Kirkes apprehended me." He rose and looked out the solitary window onto the street, "I would like to visit with you for a while. I spoke with Sister Marie-Claude and she tells me you are a widow so it would be permissible for us to go have something to eat." Françoise merely nodded again in agreement, but she still had a bad feeling.

Françoise had never seen the private room at the back of *Le Cheval Blanc* where the threesome were seated, and Doctor Giffard ordered the meal. "Let me get straight to the

62

point," Giffard said, once the server had left. "I understand you are teaching a class about *Québec* to the village children."

Françoise felt the walls were closing in, "Well, *Monsieur* Doctor, it is not really a class. Why some of the children asked about it and I...I did get permission from the Father. And Sister Marie-Angelique, she's the teacher...I promise I won't..."

Giffard began to laugh, "*Mademoiselle*, I am not asking you to stop. Quite the contrary, I want you to continue. In fact, I am wondering how we can expose more citizens to your class."

Nearly speechless, the only word she could squeak out was, "Oh."

The waiter brought the food and once they had been served, Giffard said, "Let me explain this to you from the beginning." She didn't know what to do with the food until he said, "Please, go ahead and eat, I'll do the talking."

She took a cautious bite while he began. "I was born here in *Mortagne*. After school, I went to Paris where I studied to become an apothecary and surgeon. I had an interest in travel. Vessels that cross the Atlantic are required to carry a surgeon, so I began to sail with various ships. It was there I met *Général* Champlain. We have developed a close business and personal relationship."

Françoise could not believe this was happening but tried to eat as she was ordered while Giffard continued, "Originally the colony was established as a source of valuable fish and furs with the hope of finding a northwest passage to the Orient. Just before the English came to *Québec*, we had planned to recruit *real* settlers to the colony. Not just workers, traders or missionaries, but families—people who would come and start a new life in the New World. Unfortunately the Kirkes slowed us down, but since the colony has been returned to France we are back to our plan. The *Général* is going to send workers and soldiers this year to begin building, and I hope to bring families the next year—families from *Perche*."

He took a few bites before proceeding, "I was disappointed at the lack of interest I was encountering here, until some months ago when enthusiasm began to build, but it was almost entirely from the region around *Mortagne*. Recently we heard about your program at school and realized you, not I, are the reason for our new success. No, *Mademoiselle,* I do not want you to stop. I want you to *expand*."

For the remainder of the afternoon, Giffard explained his plans and vision for the new *Québec*. "*Général* Champlain will begin this spring to build the foundation of the colony. He will cross the sea with soldiers, priests and perhaps 200 workers and artisans. This time they will build a proper city. A well-equipped fortress on the top of *Cap Diamant* fortified with cannon, no enemy force will take the city again. A proper church will be maintained by Jesuits with plans to add a convent and school as well as a hospital. Then there will be generous plots of land where families can build their homes, their farms—their lives. You have seen *Québec, Mademoiselle.* There is more land than could ever be needed." Sweeping his hand through the air he continued, "More land than the eye can behold or the mind comprehend!"

"Will settlers *own* their land?" she inquired.

Giffard did not blink an eye, "The *Seigneurs* will own the land and let it to the farmer, just as in France, but consider, *Mademoiselle*, there is more land than can ever be tilled so the farmer will be the virtual master of his fields."

"Will you build roads?"

Giffard smiled. "In towns where needed, but remember, the colony has God's own roads, a river system that moves traffic faster than any land road. Just think, *Mademoiselle*, before we had but workers and trappers, now we will have homes, families, and the beginning of the greatest colony in the Americas!" By the end of the meeting, Françoise was almost ready to return. She certainly had more information for her course, which she was already organizing in her head when the men deposited her back at the convent. When she found the nuns, she shared her enthusiasm.

On the way back to *Tourouvre*, Noël Morin asked Giffard. "You give such a wonderful presentation, why do you need her?"

Giffard laughed, "I'm going to get rich on this, son. Most of the men will realize this. But there is little gain for this girl—they will trust her."

Françoise awoke refreshed well before sunrise, ready to face the world. Last night she retired with the knowledge she had been treated with respect by men, and not any men, but important men. Not because she was an attractive young woman, rather because they were interested in an accomplishment, something she herself had done. Dressing quickly, she was in the kitchen well before the nuns, humming and beginning to prepare breakfast.

Having spent her life under the shadow of inferiority that haunts women in her position, always afraid of what was around the corner and how it may harm her, this morning she was ready, and for the first time in her life, she was not afraid. When the nuns arrived, breakfast was prepared and Françoise greeted them cheerfully.

"My goodness," exclaimed Sister Marie-Claude inspecting the kitchen. "Did you get into Father's communion wine last night?"

Françoise laughed casually, "No, Sister, it is just that I awoke ready this morning."

"Ready for what?" the portly *religieuse* queried.

"Ready for whatever life brings, Sister, *whatever* it brings."

Sister Marie-Claude looked to her colleagues, whispering, "Communion wine—for certain."

Classroom activity proceeded as usual until it became time for Françoise's half-hour. She took her notes that had been carefully prepared with Sister Marie-Angelique and abandoned them face down on the desk before she began.

"When *Monsieur* Cartier first saw Canada in 1535, *almost one-hundred years ago,* he saw it as a possible passage through to the Orient and nothing else. Later he saw value in the codfish that could be caught along the coast, and later men discovered a profitable business in the animal furs of the region." Pausing for a moment it was apparent she had her audience's attention. "In 1608, *Général* Champlain founded a town 800 miles down a great river at a place he called *Québec*, meaning *narrow strait* in the Indian language. For more than twenty years, it remained a small town with few people and again only a source of fish and furs. Only now has France deemed it time to make this a new city in the new world of New France…"

Françoise's course continued to delight the students, and its renewed vigor had caused them to discuss it at home, sharing some enthusiasm with their families. School was soon out for the Christmas season, allowing Françoise to run some errands for the convent. Entering the *boulangerie* to buy special bread for the holiday, she encountered Nicole Boucher. The two women had remained friends but never seemed to have time to visit. Once her purchases were made, Nicole suggested they share tea at the café across the way.

Once they had traded pleasantries about the Boucher family and the convent, Nicole said, "Pierre has always talked about your class, but it seems lately he talks of nothing else."

Françoise smiled but said, "I'm sure he talks about other things, but you're kind to…"

Nicole went on, "Actually all the children are talking, and there has been some discussion among the mothers." Françoise frowned, wondering where this was going, as Nicole added, "And *Monsieur* Giffard has been around the tavern talking to the men about going to *Québec*."

Françoise replied, "Oh, I didn't mean to…"

Nicole interrupted again, "No, Françoise, we aren't upset. What I was going to ask is that you might come talk to some of the mothers. We would like to learn more."

Françoise responded, "How would we…?"

"We have it all arranged, I spoke with the Father and he would let us use the church to hear you. The children say you are the most interesting part of school."

Beginning to feel a return of her old insecurity, Françoise said, "Well, I…"

"Don't worry, *Mademoiselle*," Nicole told her, "Just tell them what you have been telling the children. Now, let me see, I think we have five ladies." Beginning to count on her fingers she reeled off the names, "Madame Guyon, Cloutier, Pinguet, and two Bouchers, myself and my sister-in-law, Périnne. Father said we can use the church room Tuesday after Christmas."

Françoise left the café a bit unsettled, but school was now out and over the next few days, she regained her confidence. She knew all the people other than Madame Pinguet, Sister Marie-Angelique helped her prepare her presentation, and along with the joy of the Christmas celebration, she began to feel ready.

On the appointed evening, she arrived in the small anteroom the Father had deemed appropriate for such a gathering with Sister Marie-Angelique in tow to provide moral support. Nicole appeared soon after followed by the others. As Nicole was introducing Madame Pinguet, a sixth lady appeared. Nicole exclaimed, "How nice you could come! I had heard you were not able to attend."

The stranger replied, "With the interest my husband had, I could not restrain my curiosity."

Nicole brought Françoise over, saying, "*Mademoiselle* Grenier, may I present Madame Juchereau."

Françoise's heart almost stopped at the name. Having never met the woman, she knew she was the wife of the man planning to finance the voyage as well as the cousin of the long absent Noël Langlois. "*Enchanté, Mademoiselle*," Madame Juchereau said, "My husband has spoken of this project, and I am quite interested in what you have to say. In addition, I believe you know my cousin, Marguerite Abraham, and have met my cousin, Noël."

Trying to be as brief as possible, Françoise replied only, "*Oui*, Madame."

Françoise managed to give her presentation buoyed by the presence of Nicole and Sister Marie-Angelique. At the end, all the ladies were complimentary and politely thanked her. Madame Juchereau said, "Thank you, *Mademoiselle*. I suspect you are anxious to make this voyage."

Speechless, Françoise had not actually made a decision about going. In fact, she had been inclined to stay in Perche, but now faced with the question she felt she could only reply, "*Oui*."

CHAPTER 10

Québec, May 23, 1633:

With three ships carrying more than 150 souls: artisans, laborers and soldiers, Samuel Champlain sailed triumphantly into *Québec* harbor where his mood quickly changed as he saw the two armed English ships at anchor. He had encountered two similar craft near Tadoussac the day before but discovered they were fishing boats just ordered back to England that were getting ready to set sail.

Ordering his mate to ready a skiff to visit these crafts in the harbor, he noticed a rotund English officer on the dock. Wearing a formal uniform that fit him poorly, he greeted Champlain cordially, explaining his orders were to remain until Champlain landed. "And with that *Général*, I am off to my vessel," he announced, "and bid you *au revoir*."

Turning back to Champlain, the Englishman added, "I must say it is with no regrets I leave this hell-hole."

Champlain tried to hide his joy, asking, "I pray you did not find the winter hard."

"I fear I did, sir," the Captain confessed, "but it is the savages. I don't know how you tolerate the vermin." With that, he stepped awkwardly into his skiff and did not look back.

Enormously relieved, Samuel watched the English weigh anchor before turning to the few on the dock—a small but enthusiastic gathering of those left behind.

First in line was Marie Rolet, widow of Louis Hébert, Champlain's old friend who had been the first settler in *Québec*. With Marie was her new husband, Guillaume Hubou. Next in line were Marie's daughter Guillemette and her husband Guillaume Couillard with their four young children. Needless to say, nicknames were a necessity in this family. Last was his friend and interpreter, Olivier Tardif. As he shook Tardif's hand, Champlain realized this represented all the families remaining in the city.

Before he could speak, he was interrupted by a tall slender figure running down the dock as fast as he could manage in his long black robe. "Governor," he gasped out of breath, "sorry to be late, I lost track of time. I have a long list of things to consider. Perhaps we can take *Monsieur* Couillard and go discuss them."

Champlain had met the Jesuit, Paul LeJeune, in Paris before the priest sailed to *Québec* in 1632. Champlain much preferred the Franciscan *Récollects* like Father Joseph Caron, but Richelieu had withdrawn them from *Québec*, leaving him with the Jesuits who, in Champlain's opinion, spent too much time in distant Indian villages and not enough with the French citizens. Clearly, Champlain felt it was he that should make the decisions, not the priest. He replied, "Thank you for recognizing I am now governor, Father. However, I still prefer to be called, *Général.*" When LeJeune went to turn, Champlain held up his hand, "One more person, Father,—Abraham!"

Abraham Martin appeared on the deck with more white hair and girth than ever. "*Je viens!*" the mariner shouted, as he sauntered down the plank. After greeting his old friends, he nodded to LeJeune indifferently.

Champlain explained, "Captain Martin agreed to accompany me as navigator—and advisor. He will leave in time to bring his wife and family from France next year."

While the men walked into the lower town, LeJeune suggested, "First we shall see the church, it is in desperate condition."

Before he could make the turn, Martin replied, "Hell, Father, you can pray outside—Jesus did. Let us go see the fort." The other men agreed, turning to the left.

The City of *Québec* was a fat peninsula, the tip of which pointed east. On the northern side ran the river *Riviére Saint-Charles.* The land mass continued on the western side and the great *Fleuve Saint-Laurent* ran on the south side and in front of the tip. The peninsula consisted of three distinct levels, the eastern tip was lowest. At river level and cleverly named the lower town, Champlain planned to put markets here. The medium level looked to the north, sporting a wonderful view of the waterway and countryside. Called the upper town, it would eventually contain the church and other important buildings along with fine homes. The upper level was the majestic *Cap Diamant* which had drawn Champlain to this place twenty-five years before. From here, one could see forever, and here Champlain had built his original fort now lying in tatters.

Viewing the 360-degree panorama from *Cap Diamant*, Champlain explained, "We will build strong, well-fortified palisades and ramparts with periodic towers along the entire western land mass, from *Riviére Saint-Charles* to *Fleuve Saint-Laurent*. Then we will ring the cliffs on the other three sides with similar structures which need not be so strong due to the excellent height of the cliffs." Surveying the group, he said, "Couillard, you are the builder. I have brought excellent artisans and workers and have detailed plans on the ship. This is our first priority, and I plan to begin tomorrow." Looking over the countryside, he added, "Thank God we have enough trees."

As they walked to the northern cliff, he looked down at the lower town. "We will then build my *Habitation* down there to include living quarters, offices, a small temporary hospital and blacksmith shop. We will set it at the *Place Royal*," referring to a flat area of the lower town, "and fortify it with cannon for protection from a water assault. Then in the upper town, Father, we shall get to work on your church."

Turning to Abraham Martin, he instructed, "Let us go look at the plans for the fort."

The following morning Champlain rose early from his makeshift quarters in the already crowded temporary Jesuit Seminary. Walking down to the port, he planned to meet Couillard and Martin to begin construction of the fort. When the dock came into view, he realized he would have other issues. There were nearly twenty Indian canoes and their owners at the dock. Coming to the lower town, he met his three companions. "Abraham, you and Couillard go, see to the fort. Father, you can come with me."

Not knowing what to expect, he was pleased to see his friend and interpreter, Olivier Tardif, at the dock, speaking with the native leaders. "Montagnais," Champlain identified the tribe to LeJeune, as they came closer.

Most French-Canadians considered Indians either Algonquin or Iroquois. This distinction was based mainly on language similarities. The difficulty came with the many variations. In general, Algonquin were friendly with the French. As young Pierre Boucher had realized half a world away, they shared cultural similarities. The Montagnais would be classed with Algonquin.

When they arrived at the dock, Tardif explained, "They came to welcome you back."

"*Kedaramihiken,*" Champlain thanked the chief. He knew some Algonquin words but relied on Tardif for conversation and important matters.

After more conversation, Tardif said, "He wants to know why the great country of France would abandon their friends to such evil people as the English," adding, "The term he used was less gracious than *evil.*"

Champlain frowned, "Tell him I wondered the same thing," abruptly adding, "Don't say that!" Pondering for a moment, he said, "Tell him the great King of France allowed us to return to save our Montagnais brothers from the evils of the English."

This brought smiles to the native group, but they also had concerns regarding the activities of the many renegade fur trappers and traders who had enjoyed a free hand in the area during the English occupation much to the detriment of the Indians. Champlain assured them he was back now, to bring these unregulated thugs to justice—although privately he had no idea how he would do it.

The two men exchanged compliments and pleasantries through the talented Tardif until they parted friends, and the Montagnais returned to their tribe.

The following morning a similar group of other Algonquin tribes with similar concerns greeted him. Champlain dealt with them again through the abilities of *Monsieur* Tardif, thankfully with similar results. As he then expected, the Huron came with a like agenda. The Huron were a bit more complicated. They spoke an Iroquois dialect but did not associate with those tribes. Again, Champlain reassured them.

Québec: June 1633

Four weeks after their arrival, Champlain and Abraham Martin walked up *Cap Diamant* to view the progress and ongoing bevy of activity. "Damn, Samuel," Martin remarked, "This is proceeding well above my expectations."

"Mine, too, Abraham. It will likely be three years or so before it is entirely finished, but we should have some defensible structure by autumn."

Walking to the proposed location of the western wall and the great land mass beyond, Martin said, "Samuel, I believe I would like this land for my place."

Looking at the thicket of trees, Champlain suggested, "Wouldn't you rather have a place in Beauport where you wouldn't have to mount the hill to farm and have ready access to the waterway?"

"Don't know how much farming I'll do," Martin replied. "I'll be doing my boating from the harbor. As the only river pilot in the area, I'm certain that will occupy most of my time—and I enjoy the view up here."

"Of course, it's ultimately up to the company, Abraham, but I see no problem. Let us get back to the lower town, I have a different issue, and perhaps you can help."

"Not the fur trade?" Martin asked painfully.

"I'm afraid so. At the moment, it's in total shambles, and I don't see the solution. Before the Kirkes, many of the legitimate traders—the true *voyageurs*—worked with the blessing of the state. They would go to the wilderness and trade goods with the Indians for the pelts the Indians had trapped and prepared as they have forever. The traders would then come back and sell them at the market, and the fur merchants would send them to France."

"We've always had outsiders," Martin said. "You know, the *coureurs de bois*. Some would trade independently with the natives or run traps themselves, then sell them on the various black markets."

"Yes," Champlain replied, "but now that is virtually everyone. I don't even know ninety percent of these men, and I have no idea where they are selling the pelts." When they made the turn toward the lower town, Champlain added, "I have found two men who may be able to help. Their names are Benoît and Bernier. I don't know when or from where they came. They have no families, but they have been trading honestly for years."

At the lower town they easily identified their contacts. Sporting *voyageur* clothes and *voyageur* hats, they appeared to have never bathed or shaved. Champlain made introductions and pointing to the squalid remains of the

Terre Sauvage suggested, "Let me buy you a drink." For a *voyageur*, this was as close to an angel choir as there was.

When seated Benoît said, "Shots and beers." When the drinks arrived, Champlain simply asked, "How has the fur trade been?"

Benoît, who appeared the more articulate opposed to his comrade who may have been a mute, replied, "Ain't worth a shit, yer honor. Most lads out there don't know nothin'. They botch their traps, ruin their pelts, piss off the Indians and don't have no one to sell to."

Champlain nodded in interest, asking, "What will they do?"

"The ones that don't know what to do will starve, kill each other, or become hair donors."

Realizing *Monsieur* Benoît was likely more intelligent than he let on, Champlain asked, "What about the competent *voyageurs*?"

"Well, yer honor, if things don't change here, they'll move down to the Hudson River and trade with the Dutch in that town, *Beverwijck* or somethin', but over there, you got them dammed Iroquois of the five nations. Sooner or later they kill ya over somethin, yer honor."

Champlain told him, "France and the Company of 100 Associates are going to start regulating. The good traders get licenses and can trade with the Algonquin and sell in the Québec market. The company will take care of shipping the furs to France."

Benoît signaled for more drinks and said, "That sounds good to us, yer honor, but there's one other thing to worry about."

"What's that?"

"Well, yer honor, there's this bunch of guys—been out there a long time. They understand pelts—not rules. Their leader is this guy they call, *Half-face*, at least that's what the Indians call him. Mean as a snake—steals, cheats and treats the Algonquin real bad. Trouble is, even they's afraid of him."

"Is he an Indian?"

"No—Frenchman. Let me tell ya a story. Once he and his boys is in a Mohawk camp where he's been stealin' pelts and cheatin' the natives. Can you imagine someone with the balls to cheat the Mohawk?" Champlain nodded and Benoît continued. "Well, he gets into it with this big old Mohawk and they really go at it. Finally Half-face, he's got the Mohawk around the neck and's stranglin' him. They're rollin' on the ground by the campfire and it looks like Half-face is gonna win. Anyhow, the Indian can't breathe, but he gets ahold of a stick, like a club, from the fire and hits old Half-face with it, he holds the fire on his face, but Half-face won't let go. This goes on like forever until the Iroquois finally goes down. This is where old Half-face gets his name. He gets up lookin worse than shit—like half his face is burnt right off. We thought he'd be dead, but I saw him maybe a year later, still alive and meaner than ever. Ain't got no ear, eye's all gone, and he got scars on that face look like a turtle's ass. I don't know how you're gonna control, him, yer honor. And if you see him comin', head for the hills."

Champlain ordered another round for the *voyageurs* before telling them, "What I would appreciate from you gentlemen is to tell all the *legitimate voyageurs* you see what we discussed. The Company will be here by the beginning of next season to negotiate on licenses."

"Whadda we do till then, yer honor?"

"Tell them I am not in a position to buy pelts, but I will store them for you until the Company does come. Also have them come in and give me their names, so we'll be ready for licenses when the Company comes."

"Mighty kind of you, yer honor."

Champlain stood and announced, "Well, gentlemen, thank you for your help and good luck. We must go, but you may stay. I will tell *Monsieur* Forton at the bar that I will pay your bill."

"*Merci,* your honor, we'll spread the news as we can." When the men reached the door, Benoît called out, "Don't forget, yer honor. Stay away from Half-face, you'll never find a viper that mean."

Entering into the bright summer sunlight, the two men made their way toward the site of the *Habitation* construction. While they walked, Abraham pulled out his pipe. "Got this Iroquois tobacco from Tardif. Ain't nothin' else like it." Once it was lit, he added, "Don't you think you're taking on too much responsibility storing pelts? Hell, we got enough to do."

"Abraham, the fur trade is the only enterprise we turn a profit on at this time. We need to foster it any way we can." Staring off at the big river, Champlain added, "That Benoît seems to be an intelligent man."

Martin blew a smoke ring, "I just realized who he is."

"Oh?"

"He came over in the old days, before 1620 anyhow, but you wouldn't have recognized him then."

"Why not?"

Martin blew another ring. "He was a dandy. Word was his old man was a Lord of some kind. Benoît, I don't think that was his real name, said he wanted no part of it. The gossip was that he killed someone."

"Oh, well, he did seem bright."

"He went to the Sorbonne in Paris."

Samuel smiled, "That explains a lot. I wonder what he studied."

Martin pondered, "I think the theater."

Champlain stopped to survey the waterfront. Gazing up to the high country and the beauty of the wild, he whispered, "God! It is good to be back!"

CHAPTER 11

Mortagne: Christmas Day 1633

Françoise would mark this as her fifth Christmas. Her parents never celebrated and, in fact, rarely entered a church. During her two-year stay in the French convent, mass was longer on Christmas, and each orphan was given a small hard candy. With Guy, the Holy Day was never mentioned, and though after his death, she was aware of the celebration, *Québec* was too cold in December to celebrate anything.

Only in *Mortagne* did she begin to understand the festivity. Her first Christmas was two weeks after her move to the convent, and that was a blur. However, each successive year she began to appreciate and enjoy it more as she became accepted into the community. Today was particularly special due to her close friendship with the women who had come to her to learn about *Québec*.

Mass was a grand affair, and *Notre-Dame de Mortagne* was dressed in its finest. Following mass, the parishioners gathered to visit and wish well to one another, in spite of the chill in the air. Each lady wore her finest, many with a colored ribbon on her coat. Françoise wore one given to her by Nicole Boucher who had invited her to Christmas dinner. While the socializers began to leave for home, Pierre Boucher was sent to escort Françoise. Nearly twelve years old, he was nearly as tall as Françoise and beginning to look as mature as he had always behaved.

Removing his cap, he announced, "*Tante Françoise*, I am to escort you to dinner."

Françoise struggled to stifle her giggle and replied, "*Oui, Monsieur* Boucher," taking the arm he offered.

The Boucher home was warm and welcoming, a huge fire roared with the traditional Yule log, and a crèche of finely carved figures, created by Gaspard in his wood shop, sat close by. Each of Pierre's younger siblings, Nicolas age 9, Marie age 6, and Marguerite age 2, showed *Tante Françoise* their treats, which had been left in their shoe by *Père Noël*. Pierre, too mature for such things, showed her his new book.

Gaspard produced a bottle of local red wine, pouring a glass for each including a small glass for each child before proposing a toast, "Joyeux Noël!"

Soon more company arrived. Gaspard's older brother, Marin, with his young wife, Perrine, whom Françoise knew from the *Québec* talks, along with their children: 3-year-old Louis and one-year-old Jean. Dinner was a feast, and Françoise began to experience family for the very first time in her life.

The celebration lasted into the evening, and eventually only the adults and Pierre remained. The topic turned to *Québec*, a common subject nowadays in *Perche*.

Gaspard reported, "Noël Morin tells me *Monsieur* Giffard has nearly forty people from the region with interest. He says it is only a matter of formality before the King and Company of 100 Associates makes the contract. He believes he shall sail in early spring."

By the time Françoise began her trek back to the convent, the streets were empty and she was alone with her thoughts and concerns, still pulled between compelling reasons to remain in France and an almost irrational pull to return to the wild. Arriving at the convent, she was surprised to see the candle in the window, and more surprised to see Sister Marie-Claude sitting by the fire.

"I thought I would wait up, my dear, to learn about your visit." Françoise sat by the fire, surprised when the portly nun brought out a bottle of wine. "I thought we could toast the birth of our Lord," she explained, while she poured two very generous servings. Françoise realized more wine was the last thing she needed but did not want to appear rude. She related the evening to the nun including the discussion and her concerns about *Québec*. She had not discussed this much with the sister, but tonight Marie-Claude was filled with questions. Eventually she looked at the now empty bottle and told Françoise, "I suppose we should be to bed, my dear," and when they arose she added, "But I am compelled to say, that were I young and in your position, I would go in a second."

Surprised, Françoise responded, "Really, Sister?"

The old nun smiled, "In a heartbeat, child—and *never* look back."

<u>*Mortagne*</u>: January 9, 1634

Returning from her errands, Françoise found winter arriving in force. Pulling her coat tight with her head down, she pushed through the pelting snow. *This is nearly like Québec,* she thought, approaching the convent. Lost in her thoughts and the blizzard, she nearly tripped over the seated figure on the bench. "Oh," she exclaimed in surprise, followed by, "It's you!"

Noël Langlois rose, brushing the snow from his coat. "Sister Marie-Angelique said you'd be back any time."

"Why did you not wait inside?" she asked.

"I told her I would stay out here," he replied. "If I'm going to *Québec*, I must get used to it." She stared speechless while he added with his wonderful smile, "Come with me to *Le Cheval Blanc*. I think I've had enough cold for today."

"But the sisters are expecting me."

He smiled again, "Not anymore. I told them you'd go with me—they didn't seem to mind."

Not one of the more solid structures in *Mortagne*, *Le Cheval Blanc* was warm nonetheless thanks to a roaring fire. Once they had ordered, Langlois asked about her life in *Mortagne*. She briefly described her time at the convent and work at the school.

"I was told you have taught the children about *Québec*," he claimed.

"Yes, they asked me to."

"I'm going to *Québec*," he announced.

"Oh?"

"Yes, now that I'm a river pilot, it looks like a wonderful opportunity."

Trying not to sound too uninformed, she asked, "What exactly does a river pilot do?"

"He pilots ships in the rivers."

"How does that differ from a captain of a ship on the ocean?"

He disarmed her again with the smile, "The open sea is vast. The trick is keeping the boat safe in rough seas while maintaining the direction to your destination. On a river, direction is obvious but the rivers are narrow and oftentimes deep in places and shallow in others— frequently treacherous. Generally once a ship reaches the river, the captain turns the helm over to the river pilot."

"I never knew that," she confessed. "It sounds dreadfully complicated."

"It is what my brother-in-law, Abraham Martin, has done for some time. He took me as an apprentice and now I am licensed. So I will ship out with him and my sister." Taking a bite of his meal, he added, "I assume you are coming."

"In truth, I am still not certain."

"But you must," he declared, signaling for more wine.

"It's different for a single lady."

"But you won't be single forever. I hear *Québec* has many single men."

I know, I have seen them, she thought to herself as she merely shrugged, then to alter the subject, asked, "What of your other sister?"

"She died," he said softly. "She and her husband, Pierre Desportes."

"How awful," she said. "What happened?"

"He was infirm and died soon after their crossing, she died this year. Their daughter, Hélène, is returning to *Québec* with Marguerite and Abraham. Abraham is in

85

Québec now. He left with Champlain but will return to France in time to sail back with us."

They moved on to more pleasant subjects and only departed when it was apparent the proprietor was ready to close. She took his arm while they braved the winter back to the convent.

"May I call on you?" he asked at the convent door.

"If you wish."

"Good I'll call before dinner tomorrow." He kissed his finger and touched it to her cheek, then turned and disappeared into the snowfall.

The candle was burning and Sister Marie-Claude was sitting in the window. "How is your *young man*?" she asked, causing Françoise to give her a summary of the evening. The nun hung on every word and at the end said, "Then you are going to *Québec* for certain."

Françoise shrugged, "I don't know, Sister."

"What?" the nun clutched her more than ample breast in protest. "Dear God, what more do you want, child?"

"I guess I don't know, Sister." Françoise reported as she rose and headed to bed.

At the end of January, Doctor Robert Giffard received his commission from the King and began to actively sign recruits to the colony.

Mortagne: February 1, 1634

Entering the general store to buy for the convent, Françoise encountered Nicole Boucher. Due to the frigid weather, they had not visited for a while. "Are you signed up for *Québec*?" Françoise asked.

86

Her friend frowned, "No, we may not go." Françoise stood speechless while her friend continued, "When Gaspard went to sign, he found they were not willing to take the whole family for the first season."

"What?"

"Apparently, the Company will take the man, sometimes with his wife but with no more than one child. Well, as you can imagine..."

They discussed this for a while and Françoise left the store perplexed. That evening she had dinner with Noël. "I had the most alarming conversation with Madame Boucher today," she began.

Once she had aired the problem, Noël scratched his well-trimmed beard and said, "I can see the Company's position. The wives and especially the children cost as much to transport and support as the men who do most of the work that is needed at first. Of course, this makes the families less likely to agree to come. It will be difficult to split the family and at the end of the engagement, it is as likely the man will return to France rather than bring the family to *Québec*."

"But what can be done?" she wondered.

He smiled as usual. "You need to explain it to Doctor Giffard."

"Me?" Her mouth hung open.

"Who else?"

"But how?"

He smiled again, "Just wait, he will come to you."

"What? Are you deranged, *Monsieur*?"

He looked over his shoulders, then leaned in. *Le Cheval Blanc* was virtually empty. "He came to you before when things were not going well. He'll come to you again."

"But how do I..."

Moving closer still, he confided, "Doctor Giffard is charming, articulate, and persuasive. However, I fear he is, like my dear father used to say, *not the sharpest tool in the shed.*"

Laughing, she almost choked on her wine, and he continued. "He will come to you, and you need to do what all women do well."

Aghast, she questioned, "You don't mean?"

Smiling once more, he whispered, "You tell him what to do and make him think it is his idea."

Mortagne: February 12, 1634

"Gentleman to see you, Françoise," Sister Marie-Claude announced. "He's in the Father's office."

Putting down the broom she was using to sweep the classroom, she entered the office to find *Monsieur* Giffard, just as Noël had predicted. She did not know whether to laugh or scream, and had no idea how to handle this. Giffard stood, "Good day, *Mademoiselle*, I came for your advice."

"My advice, *Monsieur*?" she asked demurely.

"Well, your opinion. You see, I am in the process of signing families for the voyage to *Québec*." She nodded and he continued. "There seems to be some reluctance about which family members to bring on the first voyage. Now all the children would raise the cost, and of course, there is the question of safety at sea, not to mention in Canada…" Giffard went on rambling for a while, giving Françoise a chance to think.

When he stopped, she jumped in, "I believe you are *exactly* correct, *Monsieur*. It will be more costly, and not without risk, but as you say, once the families are in

88

Québec, they will be more stable and the men will be inclined to work harder. The women will keep them in order, and of course, they will produce more children—more citizens for the new colony. I think it is genius! I am always in awe of men as intelligent as you."

Giffard thought for a while. This was not exactly what he had said—or even close, but she seemed to think it was, and it did make a good deal of sense. He thanked her and was on his way.

One month to the day, Giffard had signed agreements from all the families—with one additional passenger, Françoise Grenier.

Mortagne: March 12, 1634

With all contracts signed, *Monsieur* Giffard posted a notice—all passengers were expected to be in *Dieppe* in one month, ready to sail. In most corners of the world, this would seem impossible, but in the close communities of *Perche,* there was always enough extended family to deal with possessions, property and even family members left behind. The narrow deadline merely served to heighten the excitement of this life-changing endeavor.

To Françoise's delight, *Monsieur* Langlois began to call regularly and invite her to dine twice each week. The nuns were on pins and needles, wondering when and where this was headed, asking Françoise after each date if the *Monsieur* had made his intentions known. The answer came on the evening of March 20.

The couple was seated at their usual table at *Le Cheval Blanc*. It was only because Noël had spent very little of his pay for his time at sea that he was able to afford such opulence. Françoise was discussing the activities of each of the other women preparing their families for the voyage when Noël interrupted her in midsentence, "I think we should be married."

Françoise went silent. She had been hoping for this but had not yet decided how to deal with her *history*. She had never mentioned it to Noël, and, to her knowledge, he knew nothing of her personal affairs in *Québec*. Françoise's life, with the exception of the time spent in convents, had not stressed honesty and virtue. She could probably ignore the past, and Noël would be none the wiser. However, her life had changed, and this man was like no other she had known. He deserved the truth.

Biting her lower lip, she began, "I have a past."

He merely smiled, "Everyone has a past."

The tears began to well up in her eyes. "Not like this past." He merely looked at her with only a hint of worry. He asked no questions, but she chose to continue. "When I was young, my parents died. I was alone on the streets outside Paris. I met a man, an older man. It seemed he would protect me. I gave myself to him—he didn't even force me." Now that it was out, she could finish. "He wanted to go to Canada and take me with him. I felt I had no alternative. He said the boat would sail soon and he would marry me in Québec. I was stupid enough to believe him."

Drying her eyes, she continued, "When we arrived, he took up with outlaw trappers. He would leave me for weeks, even months, for the wild. I was all alone in a small cabin outside of town. I had no friends. He would come home and do terrible things to me. Eventually he failed to return. I heard Indians had killed him. The few people I knew thought we were married. I did not tell them

90

otherwise. It was then I went to help the ladies with the Indians."

Finishing her wine in one mighty swallow, she declared, "And now you may take me home."

Noël remained immobile, "But you haven't answered my question."

"What?"

"Will you marry me?"

"But I just told you…"

He interrupted, "I knew all that."

Her jaw dropped, "What? How did you...?" suddenly she realized the answer, "Your sister!"

"Of course, Marguerite told me everything. His name was Guy. He was a monster. I wish you had not known him, but I still want to marry you—I love you."

Her mind was spinning in confusion, "But…" Suddenly she took another drink, and tried to smile, "When?"

He reached across the table taking her hand, "We don't have time to read banns before we leave. We shall do it as soon as we get to Québec. It will be more romantic. Marguerite said it might be just the third marriage there. We could never say that in France."

Noël ordered more wine, and they sat holding hands, discussing their future until the proprietor began to close the shutters. At the convent door, he gave her the most passionate and sincere kiss, promising to return tomorrow.

The nuns were stacked at the door. "You were gone a long while," said Sister Marie-Claude, stating the obvious. "Did he?"

She calmly replied, "Yes."

The nuns began jumping up and down, and Sister Marie-Claude pulled her into the kitchen to open a bottle of wine.

Françoise knew she certainly did not need it but could not refuse.

Once she was in her small room, there was a gentle knock. Sister Marie-Angelique peeked in, "May I enter?"

The young nun sat on the bed. "Did you tell him?"

"Yes, everything."

"Everything?" the *religieuse* asked in astonishment. Françoise nodded and Sister Marie-Angelique continued, "And he still agreed?"

"He already knew."

"What? How?"

Françoise smiled. "His sister."

The diminutive nun rose, "I guess we can call this the Lord's compensation for your past trials." As she opened the door, she turned with a smile. "Don't ever let go of this one."

Françoise collapsed on the bed watching the ceiling spin in the moonlight as she realized for the second time in her young life, she had agreed to go halfway around the world with a man—and only the *promise* of marriage. But this one felt right.

CHAPTER 12

Mortagne: April 8, 1634

As the travelers arranged to leave for *Dieppe,* the entire town was filled with emotion. Departure for the port was to be in three days, and the citizens were saying their final farewells to their many friends and neighbors whom they might never see again. Françoise had already said her tearful goodbyes to the nuns and other friends in the village to allow her to travel with Noël, who was to report three days early to meet with Abraham Martin and the shipping company. Although Françoise had not lived a happy life, her time in *Perche* had certainly been the best. The four nuns stood at the coach stop, clutching their handkerchiefs for that last farewell to the friend who would not likely see *Mortagne*, France, or them again. As the coach pulled into the countryside, she was again struck by the softness of *Perche*, the forest floor carpeted with wildflowers while the tree leaves were just emerging from buds.

Passing through the miniscule town of *Saint-Léonard-des-Parcs*, Noël told her, "I was born here. It was not very exciting." He launched into tales of his youth while Françoise remained quiet, feeling there was little good to tell about in her childhood. Eventually they drifted off until the coach reached the metropolis of *Rouen* where they were instructed to switch coaches. "We have some time," he announced and led her to a great square with the enormous ornate cathedral. She was understandably awestruck as they entered, and Noël began to point out the architecture and art. She had never been in a large church before. Her experience with cathedrals was loitering outside, begging or picking pockets.

As they approached the altar, she knelt, giving thanks for the events of the past few years and how they had dramatically changed her life. The remainder of the trip was uneventful, through the green rolling countryside of *Normandie,* ending at the sea. *Dieppe* had changed little in the past four years. "I know where we can stay," she announced. She led him down the street to where Madame Allard sat on her rocker as if she had never moved.

"I'll take care of this," Noël volunteered, and he disappeared inside with Madame. When he returned, he said, "We are all settled, let's go down and see the harbor." Although it was her third time in the harbor town, Françoise felt she was seeing it for the first time. Previously frightened and conflicted, she now felt secure for the first time in her life. They walked along the piers where Noël explained each boat, what it was and what it did. Eventually they stopped at a prosperous looking tavern, *L'Albatros*.

As they were seated, she whispered, "This must be the best restaurant in the world."

He smiled, "It's nice, but not the best."

"Isn't it frightfully expensive?"

He looked about, "Possibly, but we leave in two days and may never have another chance to dine like this."

There were two waiters, white tablecloths and fine glass and dishes. The food was delicious. Making their way back to the hotel, she asked, "What did the name mean?"

"The albatross is a large seagoing bird that flies great distances from the shore. It is said to bring good luck to sailors, but one must never kill it."

Back at Madame Allard's, he showed her to the room. It had one bed on which her pack was placed. "I'm across the hall," he told her.

"But, why couldn't we…"

"I want to do this properly," he explained. "You deserve it." He gave her a passionate kiss and continued, "I must go to the harbor early to meet Captain Martin, and I shall see you in the afternoon."

In the morning, she breakfasted with Madame Allard. "I remember you from a few years ago, Honey. Recognized you the minute you came in, but I didn't say anything to your young man, in case there was somethin' you didn't want him to know."

Françoise smiled, "Thank you, Madame, but you can speak freely."

"That's what I thought, but I reasoned I'd ask first. He is a beauty, Honey. We had a fine chat this morning. I told you to wait for a good one and it seems you did. Don't go spittin' him out."

Noël returned in the afternoon and they had another delightful, although not so expensive, evening. The next day their fellow travelers began to arrive along with the news the ships would be *delayed a few days.*

The passengers for Canada crowded the port town settling in to wait impatiently. The two Boucher families had found Madame Allard and joined Françoise and Noël. Noël was gone during the day to work with Abraham Martin, leaving Françoise to visit with the ladies. On the fifth day of the wait, Françoise and Nicole sat on Madame's porch guarding the young children playing in the street when they saw young Pierre returning from town.

Enthusiastic as ever, he reported, "I went to the church where they have a room with books. A nice monk helped me. I found a book of letters written by priests in Canada and sent back to France. It is called *The Jesuit Relations.* Brother Thomas helped me with it. He said there are several other books—all about Canada."

Sitting on the steps, he continued. "I read a story by a priest who was there at the same time as *Tante Françoise.* He was taken prisoner by the English, too. He was on a different ship. They were in a great storm and had to go south to a place called Virginia." He continued his tale ending with, "I'm going back tomorrow to read more."

Two days later, the ships were at the docks preparing to leave. Noël had taken time to walk the dock with Françoise and show her their vessels. Three similar three-mast ships, they sat at anchor a short way off. "*Saint-Pierre*, and *Notre-Dame*," he explained, "will hold soldiers and day-laborers. Ours is the third. It will carry the people from *Perche* along with a few other workers and soldiers."

She smiled when she saw the name. "*L'Hirondelle*," she remarked. "Pierre will like that." Noël was puzzled so she related the story of helping him with his reading. "In a way it was that word that brought me to the convent and teaching the children about *Québec*," taking his hand, she continued, "which seems to have brought me here with you."

Noël returned to work while Françoise continued to watch the boats being readied for the voyage. Sitting majestically in the harbor, each with eight mighty cannon peering out the sides, she marveled at how enormous the vessels seemed. Remembering this from her first two trips, she also remembered how small they became once at sea. She had been conflicted, and frightened on both her previous voyages, but today she was confident and alert, studying the circumstances with new interest and some courage.

Viewed from the sides, the deck was lowest in the center, the front was higher as it rose to the majestic bowsprit, and the aft deck was highest. It was from here the ship was steered and where Noël and Abraham Martin would work to navigate the craft. Below were cabins for the Captain and officers along with the Martin, Giffard, and Juchereau families. Space below decks held cargo but would also accommodate other passengers. Overflow soldiers and a few laborers from the other two ships were housed in the narrow front and the five remaining families from *Perche* in the rear where there was considerably more space.

"Tante Françoise!" She was jolted from her musing by the enthusiastic voice of Pierre Boucher. Looking up she saw him approaching with a tall thin man in a long black robe. *"Tante Françoise,"* Pierre repeated, out of breath with excitement, "This is Father Lalemant—he wrote the book!"

Still getting her bearings, she responded, "The book?"

"Yes—the book about Canada—from the church."

"Oh, yes..."

In his forties, his hair graying, his skin withered and scarred from exposure, the priest bowed slightly, extending his equally weathered hand. "Father Charles Lalemant, *enchanté Mademoiselle.*"

She took the priest's hand, and Pierre told them, "Excuse me, I must go help my father."

Watching Pierre run off, Lalemant chuckled, "That is one remarkable boy." Françoise agreed, and the priest continued, "Walk with me, we still have time to see some of the harbor." They began down the dock when he said, "Pierre told me you have been to *Québec.*"

Amazed as well as frightened that she could be walking and visiting with a real priest, she answered, "Yes."

"I was there as well," he told her, "But I was with the Huron mission and not in the city. I was taken captive by the English on another boat. We had rough seas and went to the English colonies for refuge. It took longer to get home. I had been in Canada since 1625, but always in the missions. Only the Récollects were in the city then, but now we Jesuits will be there. Father LeJeune from our order is there now and I will join him along with the priests on the other two ships."

Men had begun loading one of the ships. Pointing to it, the priest said, "I see *Saint-Pierre* is ready to board." Then he explained, "You and I are on *L'Hirondelle*, we board last." They stopped to watch as the throng of workers and soldiers began to gather to board *Saint-Pierre*, while he told her, "Pierre told me you taught about *Québec* in his school."

"Yes," she answered, still nervous. "But I wasn't a teacher, I only helped the nuns. They asked me to speak with the children."

"Listening to Pierre," the priest added, "it sounds as if you were an excellent teacher."

Not knowing how to answer, she remained silent as he questioned, "How did you come to be in Canada?"

Now faced with the question she had been dreading, she replied simply. "I came with a man. He was a fur trader and was killed by the Iroquois."

"How awful," he consoled, and went to other topics much to Françoise's relief.

They continued to visit until they saw activity at *L'Hirondelle*. "I believe we must go," he told her as they headed back. Françoise did not know, nor would she ever fully appreciate, that she had been visiting with the man who was writing and would continue to write some of the most widely read popular work of French literature of the century.

Noël was waiting by the gangplank. "Your bag is with Nicole Boucher. She said you would be bunking with them. I am going to be with three other single men from *Perche* toward the center of the deck, so we won't be far away."

Walking up to the deck, she asked, "Who are the men?"

Counting on his fingers, he replied, "Noël Morin, whom you know, and two I have only met, François Bélanger is a mason and Robert Drouin, a bricklayer."

Although the walls were lined with cannon, the family area in the rear had the most space. The ladies had already divided the area hanging some tarps to provide some modicum of privacy. Françoise was aware of toilet, sanitation and water issues from her previous voyages. Noël had told her sailors referred to this wide area as the *Sainte-Barbe*, the patron saint of cannon gunners.

"Everybody!" Nicole shouted. "The Captain has invited us all to go above to watch our departure."

When they were assembled on the deck, they saw the other two ships sailing ahead. Two skiffs with oarsmen guided *L'Hirondelle* to the harbor exit where the crew raised the sails, snapping smartly as they filled with the fresh breeze.

The families leaned together along the port railing as the city of *Dieppe* began to fade into the distance. The northern coast of *Normandie* remained visible thanks to the wonderful clear day, while the starboard side of the ship looked over nothing but blue. Some hours later, a crewmember came and pointed to the south, "Those are the famous Cliffs of *Etretat*." The granite cliffs had been carved into high upright slices of granite protruding into the sea, many with holes in the center worn by eons of waves. "My father," he told them, "said they looked like an elephant drinking from the sea." He then explained what an elephant was to the children—and some of the parents. Soon the land began to disappear, and he announced, "If we continue to make such excellent time, we may see the land point at Cherbourg before dark. That will be our last glimpse of land until Canada. After that, it will be nothing but sea."

That evening dinner was tolerable and the ride continued smooth with only the gentle roll of the ocean. Françoise crawled into her makeshift sleeping bag and closed her eyes, realizing she was once again the only single woman in a crowd of humanity.

CHAPTER 13

Enjoying the idyllic weather of the first week at sea, Françoise was becoming familiar with the routine. Even though it was her third voyage, it was the first time she was able to comprehend all the ship's activities. When she came with Guy, he rarely allowed her to come above decks. He would go to do as he pleased making certain she remained in their place in the hold. On her return trip with the English, the French had no freedom whatsoever.

This voyage was entirely different. Each morning Father Lalemant said a brief mass for the families followed by breakfast of a hard roll and weak herbal tea. Afterwards they would deal with the sanitary and toilette issues, emptying used buckets into the sea and filling them with fresh seawater. They were then free to visit above deck in a small corner reserved for families and out of the way of the sailors.

Today, however, Father Lalemant was hearing confession from a makeshift confessional near the family residence. Françoise took the last place in line. During her time in convents, she had confessed regularly but always an abbreviated version and always avoiding the most dreadful issues. When all other sinners were absolved and had departed for above deck, she took a deep breath and cautiously entered the small chamber—today, she had decided, was *the day.*

"Bless me, Father, for I have sinned—I have sinned terribly." She began with her youth and proceeded through her days on the streets around Paris to her life with Guy and beyond, leaving no sin, large or small, unrevealed. Finishing half an hour later, she became silent.

"Is that all?" asked Lalemant. It would be a while before she realized, in spite of the mantle of the clergy, the man possessed a sense of humor.

"Isn't that enough?" she replied, before recognizing this was not the correct thing to say.

Lalemant simply replied. "Say the rosary once and you will be clean. Go and sin no more."

Leaving the cubicle, she did feel lighter and appreciated her penance. She had thought lashes or dunking might be called for. Returning to her small space, she took her mother's box from her bag. Removing her mother's rosary, she wondered for the first time why a woman who had never been known to go to church would have such a treasure, and why she would give it to her equally wayward daughter. Completing her penance, she went above to meet the day a free woman.

Joining Périnne Boucher at the rail, she felt the fresh wind in her hair and breathed in the clean salt air. "What a wonderful day!" she exclaimed.

Périnne pointed to the dark black clouds gathering in the southeastern sky. "Probably not for long."

As the first bolt of lightning sent a shiver of thunder over *L'Hirondelle*, Françoise announced, "Nothing can bother me today." The next bolt was close and the thunder rocked the boat as the pelting rain began.

"Better get below, ladies," the sailor told them. "We are about to batten the hatches."

Below decks was a bevy of activity as the crew secured everything they could, taking particular care to check and reinforce lines that secured the cannons lining the wide *Sainte-Barbe*. "Nothin' worse than loose cannon on a ship in a storm," a sailor told her. Soon Françoise began to regret her statement of contentment as the ship began to roll, then tilt, before lunging violently over a wave crashing into another just ahead. Soon many family members succumbed to the dreaded *mal de mer*. Fortunately, this had not affected Françoise who had not been ill even in storms she had considered fierce while leaving *Québec* with the English.

The following day brought no respite as winds continued to build. She had not seen Noël since the beginning and prayed it was only because he was too busy with the ship. During the course of the day, more and more of her shipmates fell ill, and she tried as she could to keep them comfortable and hydrated. Madame Xainte Cloutier and Madame Mathurine Guyon were the only other women unaffected. All the men and most of the children were infirm with the exception of young Pierre Boucher who was circulating with pails of fresh water as well as pails to clean the ever-present vomit and other excrement.

During a brief period of quiet, the three ladies sat down to rest. Xainte Cloutier brought three cups of cold tea brewed from wild herbs around *Perche.* "No one else can keep this down," she said, "I suppose we should drink it." Mathurine Guyon asked Françoise, "How is Nicole?"

"She finally stopped vomiting," Françoise answered, "I think she has nothing left in her."

"How far along is the pregnancy?" Xainte asked.

"Not too long, three or four months I believe."

Xainte stood to stretch her back. "She should be all right then. I am going to lie down. I seem a bit queasy."

By morning, only Françoise and Pierre were standing as the storm continued unabated.

"It would appear you two need some assistance."

Françoise looked up from her nursing duties. She recognized Madame Juchereau from her class with the ladies. "Oh, well…" she said as she stood. Looking at the moaning bodies on the deck, she smiled, "I guess we do."

"The crew is caring for those above deck. I seem to be the only one unfazed and thought I would lend a hand down here."

Pleasantly surprised by the assistance Madame Juchereau provided, Françoise had always regarded rich women as haughty and lazy, although she never knew one well. Eventually it seemed all their charges were under control, and Françoise suggested, "Would you care for some tea?"

"I'd love it," the Madame answered, "But I'll get it, you have done enough."

Madame Juchereau was nearly as tall as Sister Marie-Claude, but thin. Her sandy hair seemed to stay obediently in place where, after the last three days, Françoise's was wild. In spite of the appearance of one who rarely worked, Madame had proven she was quite strong and not a shirker. She soon returned with two cups and was seated. "So you are the young lady who has stolen my cousin's heart."

"Well, Madame…"

"Please, my name is Marie-Geneviève. I shall call you Françoise. We shall soon be related, after all."

"Very well," Françoise started, "It is just…"

"That I'm rich?"

"Well…"

"I'm not rich, Françoise, my husband is. Well, I am not *very* rich. You see, my father and Noël's were brothers. The family had property that could not be divided and it went to the oldest, my father. It provided me with enough dowry to marry well." The women continued to visit into the evening. Marie-Geneviève seemed to know something of Françoise's background but did not pry or indicate she knew the *awkward* portions. Soon they were laughing, and Françoise began feeling as if she were talking to Nicole.

"Do you have siblings, Françoise?"

"No, Madame—Marie-Geneviève."

"Nor do I. My husband Jean's brother, Noël Juchereau, is single. He is above decks on the ship. He is also in *the business*," whispering, "He's odd. He philanders with

106

women but shows no genuine interest," adding in a lower whisper, "I think he likes men better."

Before Françoise could respond, Marie-Geneviève put her finger to her lips, "Listen…"

"I don't hear anything," Françoise replied.

"The wind is dying!" Marie-Geneviève stood and listened. Pointing to the stairs, she said, "Let us go see."

Stepping carefully around the resting and recovering passengers, they made their way up the steps where a sailor had just opened the hatch allowing in a gust of blessed fresh air. The women suddenly realized how putrid the air in the hold had become. "Look! It is nearly daylight," Françoise exclaimed, seeing the small orange crescent on the eastern horizon.

The two women went to the port railing where a startled Marie-Geneviève exclaimed. "I see land!" And before thinking asked, "Could it be Canada?"

"Unfortunately not."

The two women turned to the speaker. Noël Langlois smiled his dependable smile, "I see at least you two have survived." Marie-Geneviève gave him a small peck on the cheek and Françoise a more romantic kiss.

"Yes, cousin," Marie-Geneviève replied, "It seems you have found the woman with the strongest stomach in France."

"Sadly that is not Canada," he explained, "rather the coast of Spain."

Françoise had studied the map of Europe in the convent classroom and was certain Spain was nowhere near their course. "How can that be, are we lost?" she asked with a hint of desperation.

"You recall I told you a ship captain must handle rough seas and stay on course."

"Yes"

"Sometimes handling seas takes precedent. For the past three days, high seas required us to sail south and east to meet the waves head on. If we took them from the rear or on the side, we risk capsizing."

"Oh dear!"

"Now that the seas are improved, we shall change course—in fact we already have." He motioned to the rear of the ship. The land mass was now directly behind them and becoming smaller. "There is one other issue," he reported.

"What is that?"

"We have lost sight of the other two ships." The ladies' smiles faded before he added, "Don't worry, we will likely find them—in *Québec* if not before." Tipping his hat, he returned to business and the ladies went to watch the sun freeing itself from the sea.

"I hear Nicole Boucher is with child," announced Marie-Geneviève.

"Yes, but not due for some months."

"That's good, Madame Giffard is also expecting, but soon." Marie-Geneviève reported, "I fear we may still be at sea."

"Oh, my!"

"Her husband begged her not to come, but she would not hear of it. He is a surgeon but not skilled in childbirth, and I have always heard the husband is the last person you want *when the time comes*. Do you know if any of the women below decks are experienced?"

"I'm not certain," Françoise admitted, "I will ask."

⚜

The sun continued to rise and along with it, the passengers, beginning to realize they may actually recover. Crewmembers not actively sailing the boat were assisted by the recovered passengers to take on the task of making the lower decks again *ship-shape*. At noon, the cook announced *déjeuner*. Most of the passengers declined, but Françoise and Marie-Geneviève found they were actually hungry. By time for *dîner*, many more were ready for nourishment.

The evening was as pleasant as the last had been awful. If Noël was free on a pleasant evening, it had become routine for him and Françoise to meet at the railing. "That had to be one of the worst storms ever," she declared.

He paused for a moment before, "This is my first voyage *across* the ocean, and you have been twice. But the experienced crew tells me this was not so bad."

Her jaw dropped. "Not so bad! What could be worse?"

"Did you get wet?"

"From the vomit, and…"

"No," he responded, "from sea water."

She was becoming exasperated, "We were *inside*!"

"You see, the crew tells me," he replied, "in a *big* storm, waves break on the deck—sometimes break over the entire ship." Her mouth dropped as she found this information too awful to comprehend when he continued, "Sea water begins to leak through the deck and floods the lower deck where we sleep."

"Oh dear," she whined. "Now we have something more to look forward to."

As she stared into the blue eyes, he answered, "We have a great deal to look forward to. Most of it will be wonderful."

"Hold me," she whispered, and he did. With her head on his shoulder and moonbeams beginning to bounce off the waves, she realized she now had a man in whose arms she felt secure—not threatened.

CHAPTER 14

F air weather had prevailed since the storm, and *L'Hirondelle* had rejoined *Saint-Pierre,* but not *Notre-Dame.* Typical of people in close quarters, the inhabitants of *L'Hirondelle* were becoming friends. Following dinner it had become common to gather above decks in fair weather and below if cold or raining. Gaspard Boucher played a fiddle and a few of the other men including two of the soldiers played recorders and drumsticks. It had started small but grew with time and now even the privileged of the upper deck frequently attended. Generally, there was no occasion but fellowship. However tonight, the young sleuth, Pierre Boucher, had discovered, was Father Lalemant's birthday.

The evening was perfect, the seas calm and the night clear. A nearly three-quarter moon lit the deck like daylight. Once the passengers were gathered, young Pierre was sent to lure the unsuspecting Jesuit to the deck. Lalemant frequently made a showing at these events but never stayed long. Upon arrival, he was greeted with shouts of *bon anniversaire!*

He was clearly surprised as each of the nine women asked him to dance, including Madame Giffard, great with child. At the end of the dance, they each gave him a priest-like kiss on the cheek. Encouraged by the spectacle, some of the soldiers became bold enough to dance with the ladies. As the ship's sole *Mademoiselle*, Françoise began to draw a bevy of soldiers and even some crewmembers. Some were more forward than others, but she was accustomed to this from her past life.

Eventually, a timid young soldier asked for a dance. He looked no older than Pierre Boucher. Becoming weary of fondling attempts, she agreed. He was a terrible dancer but thanked her profusely at the end. "I have a girl back home," he explained. "We will be married when I return from my three-year tour. I would not have joined, but we needed the money—her name is Françoise, like you."

She smiled and asked, "And what is your name?"

"LaPorte, *Mademoiselle*. André LaPorte."

She gave him an inappropriately passionate kiss. "That is from *your* Françoise, André, *bon chance.*"

The night was like no other. Enjoying the wonderful weather, the total population of *L'Hirondelle* began to bond. Even the elusive Noël Juchereau danced with Françoise and later with a few of the soldiers, and even Father Lalemant.

Françoise helped Marie-Geneviève pull the large chest back to its normal station. Looking around, she groaned, "We'll never get things back in place from this mess."

Suddenly it began to move easily, "Have no fear, *Mesdames*. We shall have her in order soon. I've seen worse, I can tell you that." The weary women looked up at their savior. "*Merci, Monsieur* Bergeron," gasped Marie-Geneviève.

The old mariner stood and smiled a nearly toothless grin, "Ah, it is nothing. I have seen worse, much worse." Clearly, the oldest crewmember, it was said Bergeron had been with Champlain on his initial voyage. Some of the younger men joked that he had been with Cartier in 1535. Taller than most, he had a wiry frame and remained reputed as the strongest man on the ship. Certainly, no one had ever seen that claim successfully challenged.

The storm had come quickly but was blessedly short, a good thing as it made the first storm look like a light breeze. Beginning as its predecessor with black clouds, lightning strikes and a violent shift in wind, this time the wind built rapidly to an unbelievable level. As Noël Langlois had warned, the waves became behemoths crashing violently onto the deck. The seamen reported some rogue waves exceeded the height of the main mast— but seamen were prone to exaggeration.

Wave size aside, seawater had begun to enter the interior of the boat. First in drips, then as flow and finally as if the sea itself were entering the holds. The water reached knee deep in the *Sainte-Barbe* compartment of the ship, but as the storm abated, it began to seep into the hold below

113

where the exhausted crew was now busy pumping it back to its home.

Now kneeling on the floor, Bergeron raised the hatch. Sticking his head below, he called, "That's it, *mes garçons*. You will have it dry soon." Returning to standing, he chuckled, "In a day or two." Returning to the two ladies, he began to help with other heavy lifting, while the remainder of the passengers sat or lay around the periphery in some state of recuperation.

The two upright women began to help their fallen comrades to their feet, and soon several were helping. Eventually things began to look hopeful. Bergeron made a quick survey of the interior, noting broken boards that needed the attention of the ship's carpenter. Returning to the ladies, he said, "I believe we have succeeded. Let us go up. I find the most glorious time at sea is just before and just after the storm."

Mounting the center deck, Françoise was thrilled to see the sun, breaking through storm clouds that were dispersing and moving east to France. The water was smooth, but continued to roll causing the ship to rise and fall, but now at a pleasant and controlled rate. The ship's structure, on the other hand, was not as serene as the sea. Broken boards, parted lines, and torn sails were the norm, but the crew was hard at work beginning repairs. Bergeron led the women to the foredeck from where they could watch the sea from the very front of the ship. "Look there." he said, pointing.

Françoise looked, speechless, as a school of enormous fish was swimming alongside the boat, as though guiding it to its destination. Instead of diving deep, they leapt along the surface often becoming free of the water. "Dolphins," he reported, "always a sign of good things to come." Gazing farther into the distance, he added to no one in

114

particular, "I have made this voyage to the New World more times than I can count. Perhaps I should stay a while this time and experience it."

By dinnertime, the passengers were recovering nicely and everyone was again feeling optimistic, though with a new respect for the sea.

The Atlantic: June 1, 1634—Day 47 at sea

Nicole and Françoise were taking advantage of the beautiful day along the port railing of the foredeck. Normally this was not the usual spot for the families but there was little activity and *Monsieur* Bergeron had given them permission. "I have been keeping a diary," said Nicole. "Today is our forty-seventh day at sea."

"Noël told me the captain believes we shall see land in about two to three weeks," Françoise told her. "But then he said things about tides and currents and winds. I guess, no one really knows."

"They say a ship six years ago took 117 days." Nicole explained pessimistically. Turning around they saw Noël with his customary smile.

"So I suspect we should be pleased with anything less," he suggested.

Pointing to the south, Nicole asked, "What in heaven is that?"

Noël looked and called out, "Whale, ho! To port!" Most the crew stopped their chores to look. "We saw them occasionally when I sailed with Captain Martin off the coast of France," he explained.

"My God, it is huge!" Nicole cried out, as the creature rose in the water, then dove in, eventually slapping the water with its magnificent tail.

"His tail is on wrong," Françoise noted.

Her love laughed, "That's the way they are made. Look! There are two more." Soon most of the ship was absorbed in the antics of these gigantic beasts. Noël added, "They say they come north in summer to feed, but go south many miles to have their young."

"Seems like a lot of work," Françoise said with a giggle. Seeing *Monsieur* Bergeron with a long telescope, she shouted, "*Monsieur*, are you watching the whales?"

The old mariner walked over, "No, I'm watching something much more important," as he pointed to the southwest.

Françoise strained her eyes, "I only see a speck."

He handed her the glass and pointed it in the right direction. She squinted, "A ship?"

"I'm afraid so," he answered. "The question is what sort of ship—and to whom does it belong."

Françoise understood the implication, "Oh dear?" she said, her glee slipping to concern. "What will you do?"

"For now, I must report to the captain, he will decide. If it is going away from us, it may not matter. If it is coming towards, it shall matter. It, of course, does not know who we are as well."

"When will you know?" Nicole asked, realizing this was not a routine concern.

"Maybe in several hours, maybe a day, maybe never, but we must fear the worst. Forewarned is forearmed. I fear we will have to go to battle stations." Tipping his cap, he ended, "Now I must see the captain."

Ordered back to their quarters, the worried passengers waited with unending anxiety. The sailors, aided by some of the soldiers, began to prepare the cannon. Having slept next to the weapons for nearly two months, Françoise had come to view them as part of the décor. Now she had a very different perspective. Previously, accommodations had been public enough, but now rather than a nearby fixture, the cannon was a weapon—armed by a man ready to use it.

Françoise crawled into her bag and covered her head, realizing there was a soldier a few feet away. She was only reassured by the thought that using the weapon was unlikely to happen—at least in the dark. Once covered in her bag, she said a short prayer and closed her eyes hoping for sleep which she knew was unlikely to come.

"*Mademoiselle* Françoise." The voice would have shaken her awake had she been asleep, but she was not. Peering out of her bag, she saw a familiar young face.

"André LaPorte," she whispered, "What are you doing here?"

The young soldier crawled over to her becoming much closer to her than to his cannon. "They did not have enough experienced cannoneers. I had been trained, but only for one day. *Mademoiselle*, I don't think I can do this. Can you help me?"

Françoise climbed out of her bag and crawled to the cannon. "What do you know, André?"

The frightened young soldier replied, "You put powder here. The ball in here. Then trim the fuse and light it. But first it has to be aimed at the target."

She realized she could not do this, nor could this frightened young man. However, it was unlikely they would need to do anything before daylight when other soldiers would be around to help. Putting her hand on André's arm, she reassured him. "I can do this, André," she lied, "just wake me if you need me." She crawled back into her bag and went to sleep—as did André.

In the morning, she was awakened by the sound of a spoon beating on a pan with the call, "Time to rise." While the rolls and tea were distributed, *Monsieur* Bergeron appeared. "The unknown craft is traveling in our direction and drawing closer. We have closed in with *Saint-Pierre* and will continue on our present course—and must remain vigilant."

As Françoise arose, LaPorte was sitting cross-legged watching her. "Thank you for your assistance, *Mademoiselle*."

The captain agreed to allow some freedom for the passengers with the insistence they must be ready to go below at a moment's notice. The day was clear, the winds fair, and with each hour, the mystery ship came closer.

Noël appeared to tell her, "We are no longer at war with England. The only real fear is a pirate ship."

"And what does that mean?" she asked, not certain she wanted the answer.

"A privateer," he began, "like the Kirkes, may take things of value but is not likely harm us." He continued with a serious frown, "However, a renegade pirate may do or take anything."

"Anything, like what?" she queried.

"Like *anything.*"

She chose not to question him further.

Cautioned reigned for the next three days, the mystery ship continued to parallel their course but edging closer as time went on. Françoise retired for the night as usual,

118

reassuring the frightened André LaPorte before she dozed off.

The noise was deafening as she heard calls above deck and the sound of running overhead. Jumping out of her bag, she saw André frozen to his cannon. "André, what is it?"

"I don't know, *Mademoiselle*. It just awakened me as well."

They heard running down the stairs as *Monsieur* Bergeron appeared. "We have identified the ship!" he reported, and then smiling, "It is *Notre-Dame!*"

Passengers congratulated each other in joy and relief before they rushed onto the deck to see their long-lost friend. As they danced around in jubilation in various stages of undress, Françoise looked up. "Look! Look!" she shouted. "A bird!"

<u>Atlantic Ocean: June 12, 1634—Day 58 at sea</u>

Birds had now become commonplace to the point of nuisance, but the crew assured the passengers this meant land was but a few days off. The sky was becoming threatening. However, Françoise reasoned a storm would not be so severe this close to land. Unfortunately, Noël corrected her, reporting storms near land were often the *very* worst. Françoise was helping clean the quarters when Marie-Geneviève appeared down the stairs.

"Françoise, I wonder if you and Madame Guyon could help me."

"What is it?"

"Madame Giffard," Marie-Geneviève reported, "she went into labor last evening but seems to have made no progress. I know Madame Guyon has the most experience." Françoise had explained Mathurine had given birth to eight children, the most recent two months before the departure. "And you said you attended some births at the Indian village."

Françoise put down her broom, "I'll come, but at the village I only watched."

Finding Mathurine Guyon, the three women ascended the stairs while Marie-Geneviève told them, "She says she feels like she should push, but nothing happens. She is becoming hysterical and Madame Abraham and I are at our wits end."

"Isn't her husband a surgeon?" asked Mathurine.

"Yes," Marguerite Abraham said in disgust, "but he's hiding in a room reading a book—he's the most helpless of the lot."

The upper cabins were by comparison plush, with windows and beds. Madame Giffard lay moaning as Mathurine removed the covers. Looking between her legs, she observed, "Some blood, has she had her *show?*"

Marie-Geneviève produced a chamber pot with bloody mucous. "Yes, hours ago, but nothing else. She has delivered two children, both without incidence."

Mathurine ran her hands around the abdomen, "She seems to have *dropped* but…Oh dear!"

"What is it?" Françoise questioned nervously.

Mathurine put Françoise's hand in the upper left side of the protuberant abdomen, "Do you feel that?"

"It's hard."

"The head," she exclaimed. "She needs to *turn* so the head comes first."

"Like a cow?" Marie-Geneviève asked.

"Yes, but with a cow, you reach in and turn it. With women it must be turned from outside." She took her hands and tried to rotate the infant in various ways. "It just won't move."

A sudden crash was deafening. "What was that?" asked Françoise.

Marie-Geneviève looked out the window as a brisk wind entered. "Thunder."

Returning to the bed, Mathurine said, "Marie-Geneviève, put your hand here, and, Françoise, put yours here." Straddling the patient on the bed, Mathurine put both hands in place, "Now everyone push!" Madame Giffard screamed and thunder roared in response while the pelting rain came through the open window. Dismounting, Mathurine was thrown to the floor by a violent roll of the ship. The women continued to try multiple maneuvers as the rain, thunder, lightning, contortions of the ship and Madame Giffard's screams increased rapidly.

As the women recovered their bearings, Françoise suggested, "Let's try something new. I'll get up here," and she straddled the patient's chest again, putting her arm on Madame's left pelvis at the same time as the boat broached, catapulting both women to the floor with Françoise landing with both knees on the patient's pregnant middle. The other two were thrown against the wall and once they came to standing, they carried Madame back to bed. Françoise put her hand on the upper abdomen and shouted, "It has moved!"

Blood and fluid flowed from between her legs and Mathurine took position while her helpers tried to hold the mother and prevent another thrusting exit from bed. Within minutes, the errant head began to crown and a short while later they had a whimpering mother and a screaming infant. Once things were cleaned and the mother was comfortably feeding the infant, the four assistants sat on the floor

121

leaning against the bulkhead. Marguerite Abraham was first to speak, "If *becoming* pregnant was as difficult as that, we would certainly have many fewer children." Her friends broke into laughter and all was right with the world.

By morning, the storm had abated and Françoise paid a visit to the upper deck cabins. Finding Madame Gifford sitting up, holding the infant with a smile, she said, "How are you this morning, Madame?"

Smiling, she replied, "Quite well, other than my bruised *derrière*." Françoise had never seen her smile before.

"Oh, I'm sorry."

Madame laughed, "Don't be, it worked. And don't call me Madame, we must now be friends. My name is Renouard—I hate it. My friends call me Remie."

"Yes, Madame—Remie. What will you name the child?"

Remie smiled, "Françoise, what else?"

Atlantic Ocean to Québec

St. Lawrence River

Nova
Scotia

Gulf St. Lawrence

Tadoussac

Gaspé Peninsula

Atlantic
Ocean

Quebec

Îles de la Madeline

Acadia

CHAPTER 15

From the moment near daybreak when the call, *La Terre Voici*! went up, passengers filled the deck, basking in the sight of land growing ever larger by the hour. Abraham Martin and Noël Langlois came out to boast, "Once we see land we usually spend another two or three days searching for the inland waterway, but today, *nous sommes parfait."* Martin pointed to the strip of land far to the north, "That is *La Nouvelle Terre*. To our south and much closer is *Acadie,* where there are fishing camps. Between them is *Le Golfe Saint-Laurent*. We sail up *Le Golfe* to *Fleuve Saint-Laurent,* but before, we will stop for a night or two at *Les Îles de la Madeleine* where there is dry land, fresh water, and game."

124

"I remember that," Françoise told Noël. "It was one of the few days I actually enjoyed when I first came."

Toward late afternoon, the three ships weighed anchor at an island chain of long golden cliffs interspersed with periodic areas of low sandy beach. Here skiffs began to ferry passengers to the first dry land they had experienced in two months. Even those not prone to seasickness experienced waves of nausea during their first moments on solid land.

As the sun was setting, crews built fires for warmth and to cook food brought from the ship. In the morning, hunting parties were dispatched returning at midday with impressive collections of game. The pioneers would not lack for meat any time soon. After lunch, the men were sent to a large lake to bathe while the women and children taken to a smaller version for their needs. The water was frigid, but clean and fresh—there were no complaints.

By the end of the second day, the ships, now resupplied with fresh water and game, were ready to sail on to *Québec*. Since Françoise was rarely allowed above deck during her previous two crossings, the sights of *Fleuve Saint-Laurent* were new, fresh, and filled with excitement. Leaving the islands, they passed before their enormous golden cliffs. Upon entry to the *Golfe,* the landscape was bleak, jagged granite, bare or at best covered with scrub. As they sailed on, trees began to appear, at first sparse and always conifer. The day after leaving *Les Iles de la Madeleine,* evergreen forests began to prosper and soon hills were covered. Two days later, they encountered deciduous trees in the full green splendor of final days of spring.

Moving on south and west, the river became narrower, and one could occasionally see both sides. At the same

125

time, the hills became ever higher, eventually becoming what the *Percheron* considered mountains. At *Tadoussac,* they began to see civilization, usually a small hut, sometimes deserted, and the occasional man in a canoe or small sailboat called a *shallop*. The few humans they encountered shouted and waved with enthusiasm, realizing the great day had arrived and *Québec* again had a French population.

Natives began to appear and were no less enthusiastic. "These people are Algonquin," Françoise told Noël. "They are the people I worked with"

"How can you tell they aren't the other tribe?" Noël asked.

"Iroquois look different," she replied. "They dress differently, and they act differently."

"But how will I know who is who?"

She smiled, looking into his blue eyes, "Oh, you will know, my darling—believe me, you will know."

They began to see the occasional whale breaking water, not as large as the whales at sea, but larger than one would anticipate in a river. There were even odd appearing white whales. "They are called *Beluga*," *Monsieur* Bergeron told her. On day seven after entering the *Golfe*, the river continued to narrow and the coast became flat. Covered with deciduous and conifer forests, one could imagine when cleared, this flat terrain would be ideal for farming.

On the ninth day, they came to *Île d'Orléans*, a large island that divided *Fleuve Saint-Laurent* into two channels. The northern shore of the mainland had become high again and they encountered the long, spectacular Montmorency Falls.

"We must anchor here for the night," Noël told her, "We will be in *Québec* tomorrow morning, but it is getting too dark to navigate any further."

While the anchor was lowered, there was a commotion on the foredeck as a canoe with three men approached. A ladder was lowered and the men boarded. A tall elderly gentleman, a young priest in a black robe and a man in *voyageur's* leather garb. The captain, Father Lalemant, and Jean Juchereau stood to greet them. Abraham Martin whispered to Françoise and Marguerite, "It is Father LeJeune, Oliver Tardif, the interpreter, and *Général* Champlain himself."

After a while, Champlain invited the families to gather. *"Mesdames et Monsieurs,* for those of you who have been here before, welcome home, and for the new families, welcome to *Québec.* Your eight families shall be the seeds of the new colony, which will now begin to grow. Many more will come, and your numbers shall multiply. Tomorrow when you disembark, we will have a visit of the city and the ongoing construction we have initiated."

Giffard introduced the *Général* individually to the new families. When he came to Noël and Françoise, he explained, "They are to be married as soon as possible. *Monsieur* Langlois is a river pilot and carpenter, and *Mademoiselle* Grenier was here before the English invasion."

As he shook her hand, the *Général* said, "Yes, I believe I remember you." The *Général* had grown frail since she last saw him on the dock before the voyage to France, and she was certain he had no recollection of her.

Eventually the three men returned to their canoe. As Champlain took his seat, he was weary, praying he could last long enough to see his dream come to life.

The next morning the ships reached the docks, and began to unload. In honor of the families, *L'Hirondelle* was first. Walking onto the dock, Françoise thought little had changed from the day she boarded the English boat for Europe. Waves of fear and depression returned as she remembered that awful day. As her new friends began their first taste of *Québec* with enthusiasm, however, her attitude improved. Soon she was pointing out sights to the ladies. Once assembled, Champlain led the families to town while an officer led the soldiers to the fort.

Leaving the dock and heading north through the lower town, they saw a few stalls for a market. Turning toward *Riviére Saint-Charles,* they passed Champlain's *Habitation,* with his home, office, and a small hospital. Looking down toward *Riviére Saint-Charles,* Françoise saw the old church where she had worked with the natives—it was now in ruins.

Turning inland, they climbed to the mid-level called the *upper town.* "Someday we shall have carriages pulled by horses," the *Général* explained with pride, "but first we must use our shipping space for farm animals such as cows that can provide milk as well as pull loads. Currently we have only two cows remaining since the English departed, and they are too valuable to risk as beasts of burden." In the upper town were the small residences of the Hébert and Couillard families with construction starting for the merchants Juchereau, Giffard and Pinguet.

Champlain pointed to a few very small row houses, "These will serve as shelter for the other families until more suitable structures can be built on *your* land." Walking up toward *Cap Diamant*, they saw the construction of the new church. "Until this is finished, we use the Jesuit Chapel across the square." Finally, at the *Cap* they saw the new fort, which was progressing nicely. "We will use some of the cannon from the ships," he told them, "to improve our fortifications."

Returning to the upper town, they had a *déjeuner* better than any meal since France. Then *Monsieur* Tardif assigned temporary quarters in the row houses. Noël was given one but Françoise would be required to bunk with the Boucher family until the marriage. Even so, she was thrilled to be afforded this status. Following lunch was a meeting with Giffard. "I have been given the *concession de la seigneurie de Beauport*," he announced, showing them a simple map of the area. "Beauport is this fine section just across *Riviére Saint-Charles* with the closest proximity to the city. I have outlined each of your plots, and we will travel tomorrow to see them."

Once dismissed, they crowded in to examine the map. The parcels were enormous by French standards, long stretches of riverfront, extending far into the forest. Françoise could scarcely contain herself when she saw Noël's name on one of the closest parcels. The group eventually retired to the row houses where the excitement of land was raging, but soon the reality of the trip descended and all the pioneers were asleep in their new temporary beds.

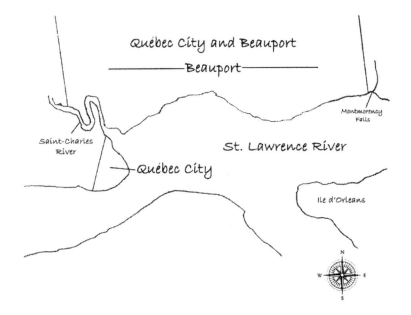

Québec City and Beauport

Beauport

Saint-Charles River

St. Lawrence River

Montmorency Falls

Québec City

Ile d'Orleans

N
W E
S

CHAPTER 16

As the sun broke through the broken puffs of clouds, the light breeze caused small ripples in the deep blue of *Fleuve Saint-Laurent*. Nothing short of spectacular, it was the sort of morning that forces people to love *Québec*. At breakfast, Giffard had posted the list of families, assigning their lots. Closest to *Riviére Saint-Charles* were listed first.

Boucher, Gaspard

Langlois, Noël

Guyon, Jean

Cloutier, Zacharie

Boucher, Marin

Not yet a wife, Françoise would normally not be included in the tour, but her actions during the birth of infant Françoise Giffard gave her favored status with *le seigneur de Beauport.* Taking a short walk down the beach of the lower town to the mouth of *Riviére Saint-Charles,* they saw four canoes at a small dock, each with a native pilot. Arriving at the canoes, Françoise gave an uncharacteristic squeal and rushed to embrace one of the native paddlers. "Jacques-Henri!" she cried, "is it really you?"

The Indian responded, *"Oui, Mademoiselle* Françoise, Madame Martin told me you had returned." Looking at Noël, he asked, "This your new man?"

"Yes. This is *Monsieur* Noël Langlois."

He walked around Noël poking him occasionally like a side of beef. "Good man," Jacques-Henri decreed. Looking at Noël, "You take good care of this woman, or you answer to me. Because of her I have strong son."

Noël was speechless and Françoise explained, "When I went to the village with the Jesuits, Jacques-Henri's wife was having a difficult labor. I sat with her until the baby was born, that's all."

"You good medicine." Jacques-Henri asserted, "That is why."

Gaspard and Nicole Boucher were assigned with Françoise and Noël to Jacques-Henri's canoe. Françoise entered first, staying low and centered. "Stay low," she cautioned Noël. As he stepped in, the canoe rolled and he stood instinctively. Only Françoise grabbing his belt saved him from a plunge. "Stay low," she repeated with a smile. The mouth of the river was about one-half mile, but the crossing took only a few minutes with the expert Indians at the helm. Landing on the beach, the *Percheron* disembarked to examine their new homes.

Françoise was amazed at the size. "What are you going to do with all this land?" she questioned. "You're a carpenter and a pilot, not a farmer."

Noël himself was still getting over the shock of the size of the parcel. "*Monsieur* Giffard said because we are all tradesmen, we should let out some of the land to farmers who come later."

"So you will be a landlord, like Giffard?"

"Not exactly, he owns it. I must give him a share of any rent I collect. It is called *sous-seigneur,* but it may be a good circumstance for us." She loved the word, *us.*

Wandering a short distance from the beach, they came upon a small, dilapidated building. Suddenly filled with dread, she stopped, not knowing where to go. "What's the matter?" Noël asked.

Coming back to the present, she replied nervously, "Oh, nothing. I'm just very tired. Let's go back to the beach."

Once at the beach, she sat by the canoe as Noël and the others explored the land. Back in Québec, she spoke to Jacques-Henri before leaving with Noël. "What was that about?" he asked, as they headed back to the upper town.

"The shack," she began, "That was where I lived with Guy." He remained silent as she continued. "I asked Jacques-Henri to take us back tomorrow. I'll get over it."

"Well, I have some news," he announced.

"What?" she asked, putting her arm around his waist.

"I spoke to Father Lalemant this morning. He said we can come sign a marriage contract and he will read the banns. We can be married a month from today."

Suddenly, Guy was nothing but a distant memory.

⚜

The morning was as bleak as yesterday had been fair. The sky was filled with dark clouds, and a hot humid breeze brought a misty drizzle. "I thought *Québec* was cold," Noël remarked.

"Not always," she replied, "but do not worry, you shall have cold aplenty."

Retracing their steps, they found Jacques-Henri at the canoe dock. Noël boarded first, staying low. "Good," decreed the Indian. "Learn quick."

Before getting in, Françoise asked, "May I paddle?"

Jacques-Henri rubbed his chin, "Okay."

He climbed in front sitting backward, "I watch."

She pushed the craft away and entered, kneeling at the back seat and began. The *Riviére Saint-Charles* current pushed the canoe toward *Fleuve Saint-Laurent,* but she fought back keeping the craft on course. When they reached the shore, Jacques-Henri commented, "Not bad— for white woman."

Noël was speechless. "I learned at the Indian village," she told him.

Returning to the ruined cabin, she pulled the door, which fell to the ground. The interior was overgrown with plant life and the roof had collapsed. Remnants remained of what might have been furniture. She kicked a board and a raccoon appeared, heading to safer ground.

When they exited, Noël said, "Maybe we could fix it."

Ignoring him, she looked to Jacques-Henri. "Burn it!"

The couple headed back to the beach. "Won't it start a big fire?" Noël asked.

Looking about, she said, "The mist will protect the trees, and Indians know how to use fire."

134

Back at the beach she said, "Follow me." Heading inland, they could hear the crackling of the flames devouring the damp wood. When they begin to climb, Noël realized this was the old bank of the great river. Soon they came to the top of the rise, and turning around exposed a grand vista of *Fleuve Saint-Laurent*, *Québec*, and *Île d'Orléans*. "We will build here," she ordained, "follow me." Returning near the beach, they encountered a brush pile.

Beginning to remove branches, she whispered softly, "It is still here." She continued to remove the branches until Noël asked, "A canoe?" Nodding her head, she continued until it was entirely exposed, turned over on two logs. "It looks good," she judged. When she began to turn it over, a mother fox and two cubs ran into the woods. Unfazed, she explained, "It was *his.*"

"Are you going to burn it?" he asked.

"No," she replied with determination, "Canoes are too valuable."

As she continued to inspect it, Jacques-Henri found them, reporting, "House gone." "Good." she responded. "Jacques-Henri, what do you think of this canoe?" He began to inspect it as a jeweler would a rare diamond. "Algonquin built, *voyageur* canoe—the best. This your last man's?"

"Yes," she admitted.

"Jacques-Henri not like him."

"You never knew him."

"No matter, he come back, I kill him. He mean to *Mademoiselle* Françoise."

"I think the Iroquois were ahead of you, Jacques-Henri."

The Indian smiled, "Only thing Iroquois good for," changing the subject, "you want I fix canoe for you?"

She smiled, "Oh, would you? Will it need much?"

He tipped it all the way over and continued to inspect. "Some work, pine tar, few pieces—good as new."

Returning to Jacques-Henri's canoe, they encountered a small space devoid of trees. "I had a kitchen garden here. When we begin to work on the house, I'll replant."

She paddled back with greater efficiency. Jacques-Henri came in Guy's canoe in order to repair it. Back in the city, they hiked to the Jesuit seminary in the upper town where they met Father Lalemant for the marriage contract. French marriage contracts were not simply agreements to marry. They contained financial and ownership records to denote what each party brought to the match. Françoise was pleased with Lalemant's reaction to her canoe.

Two days later, work began in earnest. Each of the men in the five Beauport families was skilled in the building trades. The other three single men, who had shared quarters with Noël Langlois on the ship, were similarly trained. This group of eight was expected to work three days each week on city construction and three days on the Beauport properties. Also assigned to their crew were five single laborers from the *Saint-Pierre* who were strong enough to work as *bûcherons*, cutting trees for lumber.

At their first meeting, they agreed to work as a team on the houses, beginning with the family with the most children. The first days were chaos, but Jean Guyon eventually stepped forward as leader and progress began. The first and most daunting challenge was wood. Although wood was certainly plentiful, these men had been trained in France where mills cut lumber and horses or oxen pulled it.

136

Zacharie Cloutier had the most building experience and devised a plan to minimize unnecessary labor.

Initially the site would be selected, generally on the first rise from the river providing both a magnificent view as well as safety from winter floods. The trees on the site would be cut first and used whole or split for the foundation. Subsequent trees would be cut up the slope to fall parallel to the slope where they could be trimmed before being rolled down to the site. Soon progress in town and in Beauport was impressive. At two weeks, the rustic Guyon home was completed. The families and single men gathered that evening for a celebration with inexpensive libations from the *Terre Sauvage*. The next morning the group moved on to the Cloutier residence.

CHAPTER 17

Surveying the Jesuit Chapel, Father Charles Lalemant had never seen it so full. Along with the few families who remained in 1629, the eight new families were joined by some of the workers and soldiers. Two of _Québec's_ prominent new citizens, Robert Giffard and Noël Juchereau stood as witnesses. The couple, Noël and Françoise, were dressed in their finest, including some items borrowed from friends. Françoise had taken the opportunity to wear her mother's jewelry for the very first time as she was finally to be properly wed. A tear hung in her eye as she wondered how her mother would feel today.

"Having searched the parish records," Father Charles Lalemant began, "it appears this is only the third marriage in _Québec_. It is of further note that Mademoiselle Grenier lived for a while with the people of the Algonquin Village.

During his life's work, *Général* Champlain has strived for a great colony in the New World where the French can live in peace and harmony with the native people. So I am very pleased to see Jacques-Henri," motioning toward the rear of the chapel, "and members of his tribe here today."

Following the ceremony, the congregation spilled into the upper town square called the marketplace. Although most markets were still in the lower town, Étienne Forton, owner of the down-scale *Terre Sauvage*, had seen the future when word of the treaty and return of Champlain was announced. Leaving the lower town establishment and its rough *voyageur* trade in the hands of an assistant, he opened a new facility on the square. *L'Auberge Oie Bleue* was a small Normand style inn with basic tavern and restaurant facilities as well as lodging for the anticipated new civilized trade of *Québec*. While Gaspard Boucher and a few musicians played, Étienne had put out tables and was serving tolerable and sometimes good food and drink.

Nicole told Françoise, "This could be in the square of *Mortagne*." The jubilant Samuel Champlain stood smiling under a tree with a cup in hand, tapping his foot and realizing he was finally seeing his dream come true.

When Françoise and Noël were not dancing, they were visiting with families they knew and a few they had only met today. When she saw the older lady approach with three cups and a bottle of wine in hand, Françoise knew who she was, but had never met her. "*Félicitations! Monsieur et Madame* Langlois," she said, pouring a cup for each. "I am Marie Hébert-Hubou."

Françoise certainly knew who the first lady of Québec was, but merely curtsied, "Merci, Madame."

Although the first lady was likely in her mid-fifties, she appeared much older, yet very spry. She related her story, some of which Françoise knew. "My late husband, Louis, and I came here with *Général* Champlain in 1617. For some time we were the only family." Looking about, she continued, "How we dreamed of a day such as today with a real society to have a genuine celebration. I only wish Louis could have lived to see it."

She touched their glasses and they each took a sip. "We had three children. Our daughter, Anne, was the first marriage in *Québec* when she married *Monsieur* Jonquest. Sadly, she died in childbirth and he—well, he died soon after." She touched glasses again, "*Santé.*" Pointing, she explained, "That is my second daughter, Guillemette. She and Guillaume Couillard were the second marriage. I assure you both marriages could not have such a wonderful *fête* as this.—there were no other families. Now they have four children, three girls and a son. I hope they shall marry like this someday."

She reached to grab the arm of a young man with a younger woman. "And this is my son, Guillaume. I believe you know his *young lady.*"

Noël and Françoise had only recently met Noël's niece, Hélène Desportes. Her parents had returned with her from *Québec* to France, but had both died there. The daughter of Noël's sister, Fannie, Hélène had returned with the Martins and had spent most of her time on ship in her quarters. Madame continued, "They have just completed a contract to be the fourth marriage—in the autumn." The two couples hugged, kissed and exchanged congratulations allowing Madame Hébert-Hubou to wander off to other encounters.

Françoise took her husband's hand and led him to an area where Jacques-Henri and some of his people had gathered. She knew a few and introduced them, "This is Félicity-Angel," she explained, "Jacques-Henri's wife, and this is their son, Jacques-François." The boy was about six years old, and his mother a thin yet muscular beauty with jet-black hair and exquisitely smooth dark skin. Jacques-Henri introduced those natives Françoise did not know. Most of the Algonquin kept to themselves, but Jacques-Henri and a few of the men seemed to know everyone and circulated freely.

As the sun began to set, the weary revelers began to head for home, all convinced today was a landmark day for the colony and a sign of better days ahead. Even the *Général* himself danced triumphantly with the bride.

Françoise would now move into Noël's row house, but tonight, Étienne Forton had offered the solitary room in his new inn. "You will be the first," he told them—"the sheets are still clean."

When they were finally alone, they embraced. Noël said, "You know I have no experience."

She hugged him tighter, "And I have none in *making love,*" she replied. Pulling him toward the clean sheets, she giggled, "We shall learn that together."

By morning, they were both mentally rested and physically exhausted. "Did you learn anything?" he asked.

Embracing him, she replied, "Yes, everything."

The construction team had given Noël the day off, allowing them to stay at Forton's restaurant for breakfast. Leaving, they found Jacques-Henri waiting for them. "Come with me," he ordered, and he led them down to the canoe dock.

She screamed in glee when she saw it. "It is beautiful—like new!"

Jacques-Henri explained what he had done and revealed with great pride the ornate red script of the letter F, for Françoise, in the place for the traditional *marque* of a canoe, identifying its owner. Françoise took it for a short ride after which they spent the rest of the day giving Noël his first of many lessons in how to be a true *Québécois.*

They spent the night in Noël's small row house, and in the morning, took their canoe to rejoin the construction. At this point, the Guyon and Cloutier houses were habitable, and today the builders began on the residence of Gaspard Boucher. Françoise went to their lot where she had cultivated the small cleared area by her old house for her kitchen garden. The following week they arrived to another surprise. Jacques-Henri had erected a temporary Algonquin tent on the rise, "So you can spend nights on your new land," he explained.

Beauport: August 15, 1634

Construction had finally begun on the fifth and final Beauport residence, that of Françoise and Noël. During the cutting of the trees for lumber, wives and children had been collecting the numerous rocks found throughout the woods. Hauling them to each of the houses, the masons and bricklayers could begin to build a proper fireplace for each home. The biggest news, however, was the arrival of a fourth ship from France. It carried no families, but some workers and more importantly, livestock: four cows, two bulls, six sheep and two goats. The community decided to distribute the creatures to maximize their potential. Half went to the upper town families, and the others to be shared by the five families of Beauport.

Nicole and Pierre Boucher were at the Langlois building site just after sunrise. "Is he here yet?" asked the anxious Pierre.

"No, but he will be soon." No sooner had the words left her mouth than Jacques-Henri appeared as if out of nowhere.

"You ready?" the Indian inquired.

"Yes, sir!" Pierre answered with enthusiasm.

Two days before, Françoise had asked her native friend if he would take her for a tour of the back of their property. There had been so much work building, no one had strayed far from the home sites, and she realized that even when she lived with Guy, she rarely went out of sight of the hut. When Nicole heard about it, she asked to go and, of course, Pierre would not miss it for the world. Now in the sixth month of her pregnancy, Nicole felt she was still strong enough for the outing.

"Start upstream," he told them, pointing up the creek that roughly divided their two properties on its way down to *Fleuve Saint-Laurent.* Leading them up the Langlois side of the creek, Jacques-Henri moved rapidly through the thick forest. So long as his followers stuck close by, they had little trouble.

Eventually Pierre asked, "How do you know where to go?"

"Just follow the trail," their guide replied.

"I don't see a trail." Pierre said with a questioning face.

Jacques-Henri simply replied with a patient smile, "Indian trail".

Pierre objected, "But it is just trees."

Jacques-Henri laughed, "White man sees trees, Indian sees spaces." Pierre remained silently perplexed until Jacques-Henri took him by the hand and pointed ahead. "What do you see?"

"Trees?" Pierre answered cautiously.

Jacques-Henri laughed and pointed to the area between two trees, "What do you see?"

"A space?"

Jacques-Henri brought him through the space. "Now what do you see?"

Pierre's eyes sparkled, "Another space!"

Jacques-Henri smiled, "Now you lead."

With greater confidence, Pierre marched ahead easily, much to the ladies' amazement. "But how do I know where it goes?"

Jacques-Henri answered, "This Indian trail. Indians know where it goes,"

"But?"

Jacques-Henri knelt on the ground and motioned for Pierre to join him. Putting his face down, "Look close."

Pierre did without discovering anything. Jacques-Henri then took him over to another opening for the same maneuver. The astonished lad said, "It's different!" His guide smiled while Pierre added, "It's more worn over there. I would have never seen something so subtle."

The women looked but were not so impressed, and Jacques-Henri added, "Also remember, same number of left turns to right to go straight. Otherwise you come back in circle."

"Like geometry!" Pierre exclaimed.

The Indian smiled, "Jesuits teach me geometry when I was your age."

Continuing to follow the creek, they suddenly came to a body of water. "A lake!" Pierre shouted.

Jacques-Henri shook his head. "Big lake up ahead, one day—two or three for white man to get there. This is pond."

"What is the difference?"

"God make lake." Jacques-Henri declared.

"Who made the pond?"

Jacques-Henri motioned him to the lower side of the pond, pointing to a pile of sticks. Pierre looked around it closely until a large furry ball appeared, diving into the pond with a slap of its broad flat tail, drenching Pierre. Jacques-Henri laughed, "Beaver make house, house slows water, makes pond. Pond grows fish for beaver to eat. Beaver very smart. We must always move traps to get beaver. Hard to fool. Not like muskrat. He is easy to fool, like white..." He stopped, thinking better of his statement, but it was not lost on the audience.

They continued just a little way before they entered an enormous clearing, covered in meadow grass with only an occasional small scrub tree. "Five years ago," Jacques-Henri explained, "big fire, all trees gone."

The ladies stared at the spectacle, declaring together, "Pasture!" They spent the rest of the morning exploring the site. Because of the clearing, they could see well to the north. The terrain continued to climb, first rolling, then hills and farther out, almost mountains. "I asked how far back our property goes," Françoise reported, "apparently, no one actually knows. I guess as far as we want."

Nicole said, "Heaven could not be more beautiful." After a pause, she asked, "Jacques-Henri, how far are we from our houses?"

He thought for a minute, "Not far. We came on a curve. If you go straight, one hour. One-half if you go fast." He then led them along the creek, which traversed the clearing to a second pond where they sat to rest. He unpacked his sac and passed out strips of meat, "Pemmican," he told them. "Very good, light to carry—stays good long time."

Watching the few puffs of clouds and the play of the fish and beaver, Nicole said, "This could be better than heaven."

Obviously organizing his thoughts, Pierre asked, "Sir, your French is very good, but sometimes it is... Well, not so good, and other times it is perfect."

Jacques-Henri laughed. "When I was younger than you, the Jesuits taught me French, some Latin and English. They taught me well, but the Indian learns that he must be careful how he speaks to whom." Pierre seemed confused. "If I speak good French around my people, they think I am arrogant. If I do it around many Frenchmen, they think I am... well, they do not seem to like it."

Pierre thought for a while before saying, "I think you should always do your best."

Jacques-Henri smiled, "It depends on what you think is your best."

Eventually, Françoise said, "I could do this forever, but I fear we should return before Madame Boucher has her baby."

Standing, Jacques-Henri said, "If she does, she is with the best woman to help."

Laughing, Nicole added, "I know at least one other woman who thinks that."

Arriving back at the construction area, they reported their hike, with particular emphasis on the clearing. "It is large enough to pasture the new animals," Nicole related, "and there is still enough ground that is ready to plant to satisfy the needs of all of us. Even the stumps are gone."

Since Noël and Françoise could stay in Jacques-Henri's Algonquin tent, all five families remained in Beauport that evening. The wives combined forces for dinner at the Guyon home and discussed plans for the future. Zacharie Cloutier announced, "Once we are finished building, we must continue to cut trees in back, both for access to the land and firewood. Guillaume Couillard told me how much wood we must lay up to get us through the next winter— more than I would have expected. More than we cleared to build the houses!"

After dinner, the Langlois family left to visit the shell of their new house before retiring to the tent. Snuggling up to her husband, she said, "Thank God you convinced me to come to Canada."

CHAPTER 18

Québec: October 1, 1634:

The bell sounded for the very first time—another sign of civilization ringing in the wilderness. Merely a small bell brought on the last ship, the foot-high chime was a bell nonetheless and now rang in the first real church of Canada. *Notre Dame de la Recouvrance,* which Champlain had vowed to name the chapel if God delivered *Québec* back into his hands, would not be completed for a year, but this functional shell would suffice while work went on around it.

"Another landmark of our new land," Father Lalemant announced, "as we celebrate the fourth wedding of our young colony made even more special as it involves the first native-born French-Canadian."

A slightly larger gathering than the Langlois wedding filled the square following the ceremony. Everyone knew the two families. Guillaume Hébert had come from Paris with his parents in 1617, and Hélène Desportes had been born in the New World soon after her parents' arrival from France in 1619. Local musicians played, pioneers danced, and Étienne Forton presented an even larger spread from his expanding *L'Auberge Oie Bleue*. The shower of red and gold maple leaves, delivered with each breeze, made the affair even more Canadian.

The Beauport families composed a sizable contingency. Noël Langlois had let a parcel of his land to his old shipmates, Noël Morin, Robert Drouin and François Bélanger. While today Françoise was proposing another addition. "I have spoken to Jacques-Henri, and he is enthusiastic about joining us. He and his family can live behind our house."

"Will they live all winter in that tent?" Nicole asked with a look of horror.

"No," Françoise laughed, "that is only for temporary quarters in good weather. He would build an Algonquin hut—they're made with the same method as canoes." The whole Indian concept was still a mystery to her neighbors. "We will need their help," Françoise added, "Ask anyone who was here that last awful winter of 1628. We would not have survived without the help of the natives. Who among you knows how to build a canoe?" she asked. "Or shoot a caribou, catch a sturgeon, or harvest a field of corn?"

Xainte laughed, "You've convinced us, Françoise. Now, who among you would like more beer?" All hands went up. It would not be long before the Beauport folks would recognize the wisdom of Françoise's plan.

⚜

Three days later Jacques-Henri, Félicity-Angel and young Jacques-François arrived in Beauport, where they selected a small clearing behind the Langlois house to place the Indian residence. Jacques-Henri announced, "I will work on camp when the men are working in city. Rest of the time, I will help with their work here."

Since the completion of the five cabins, the men had used their time cutting wood. This allowed them to clear a path to the pasture where their new livestock grazed while they collected firewood for the winter. In addition, they had built a barn behind the Guyon cabin to bring the cows for milking as well as housing the livestock in winter. When Jacques-Henri examined the firewood, he suggested the obvious, "May still need more. Is best to have too much rather than too little. However, at this time, cut wood and leave in place. The cattle not strong enough to haul wood this season. I have better method as winter arrives."

He soon began to expertly strip the bark from birch logs, which he used to build his family hut. Using the canoe technique, he took only a few days to build a dome-shaped structure with ample room for his family, a small fire pit inside and a sizable one on the exterior. Once finished with his shelter, he turned his talents to a more a difficult project and in three weeks, had completed a canoe, which he gave to the residents of Beauport. "Now have three canoes," he declared. "Françoise's, mine, and this one. Will make travel to the city more convenient."

A week later, Françoise suggested Noël ask Jacques-Henri to take him hunting. "You have that gun, and we won't be able to go to *Québec* as easily in winter. We need to stock food." Champlain had provided each head of household with a used military musket and had given lessons in its use at the fort. In France, farmers and wealthy landowners hunted. Tradesmen from the villages rarely did. Clearly not excited at the prospect, Noël nodded, knowing he would not win this argument. "I'll go ask him," she suggested.

"I'll do it," he said, heading out to the Indian hut.

To Noël's surprise, Jacques-Henri replied, "Hunting better in late fall or winter. What we should do is fishing."

Noël knew less about fishing than hunting, but agreed and returned to his wife. Early the next morning, Zacharie Cloutier joined Noël and Jacques-Henri heading into the big river with the Indian canoe. Giving each Frenchman a strong line with a rock sinker and metal hook to which he had attached a small fish, Jacques-Henri showed them how to tug periodically on the line as he paddled the boat slowly downstream. It was not long before Cloutier felt a tug that almost tore the line from his hand as the boat began a rapid course in the opposite direction.

"Just hold him," Jacques-Henri counselled, "until he is tired." As the canoe continued to accelerate, Cloutier shouted, "It's cutting my hand!" This was an unusual problem for a man with the calloused hands of a lifelong master carpenter.

Jacques-Henri showed him how to secure the line to a small post giving him the luxury of sitting back to enjoy the ride which took them well upstream of the city. Eventually, the fish tired and the boat came to a stop. Cloutier was now able to haul it toward the boat. When the fish came to the surface in one last act of defiance, the men were stunned by its size. Jacques-Henri stood, instructing, "Stop there." He took his bow and landed two arrows in the creature. Blood spilled into the water, and the giant sturgeon surrendered. Jacques-Henri handed Cloutier a great hook. "Put it behind gills and bring him in the canoe." Then he sat back smiling while the two Frenchmen struggled to bring the monster aboard. Once it was in, he noted, "Not bad for small sturgeon," without losing the smile.

The hook rebaited, the Indian returned to paddling downstream. They were just approaching *Cap Diamant* when Noël had a bite, and the canoe again headed upstream at an even greater rate. This time they were out of sight of the *Cap* by the time the fish folded, and Jacques-Henri repeated the drill before Noël boarded a fish at least two feet longer than the first. As they returned to Beauport, their guide told them, "Best to fish going downstream. Easy to paddle and fish will run upstream and tire sooner. Also easier to return home going downstream."

Arriving at the dock Jacques-Henri had built at the Langlois beach, they unloaded the two behemoths, dragging them to Jacques-Henri's to astound their families. They were, however, surprised to see Françoise, Xainte, and Félicity-Angel cleaning a mountain of sizeable trout on the large flat rock at the Indian camp. With glee, the wives told them, "Félicity-Angel showed us how to catch trout at the beaver pond." All six began to clean the catches, finishing in one hour. The French-Canadians realized had it not been for the Indians, it would have taken all day.

The natives then showed them the local method for preserving the fish. Covered with salt the women had taken from a local salt vein, the fish were then wrapped in leaves and smoked in Jacques-Henri's fire pit. Xainte alerted the neighborhood of the feast—the best meal yet.

With the setting sun, the temperature dropped, and the pioneers gathered around the fire pit to extend the party. Françoise told them, "During that awful winter of 1628-9, we only avoided starving by eating eel. It seemed it was the easiest thing to catch. How is it done, Jacques-Henri?"

Jacques-Henri looked into the fire, "Eel fishing different, I show you tomorrow night."

Noël and Françoise had finished dinner and were sitting by their fire when the knock came. Opening it, she found Jacques-Henri with Félicity-Angel holding a torch. "Good night for eel."

Not quite certain what was to happen, they took their coats and followed their guides down to the dock where Jacques-Henri's canoe was at the ready. Confused by the lack of fishing gear, Noël decided to wait and see. Soon they were away from shore and Félicity-Angel handed the torch to Noël with the instructions, "Hold over water."

As Noël complied, Jacques-Henri took his bow but remained seated. The abrupt commotion caused the Langlois' to jump. The serpentine monster stared menacingly at the torch and Jacques-Henri let his arrow fly. Soon he reached over and retrieved the arrow with the eel attached. The second was just as simple, and Jacques-Henri gave the torch to Françoise who repeated the feat. This time Félicity-Angel shot the beast. Once they had six eel, Jacques-Henri suggested returning. Hauling the snake-like monsters up to the Indian camp, Félicity-Angel skinned and cleaned them with ease. Before she salted the meat, she put four slices on the fire.

Once cooked, she distributed them. Noël was shocked, "Like chicken but—sweeter."

Jacques-Henri explained, "Is better when soaked in Indian sauce. I believe your King Louis XIII says it is his favorite food."

Noël continued to be amazed by his enigmatic native friend.

CHAPTER 19

<u>Beauport: October 25, 1634:</u>

When I was a young girl in Paris," Françoise explained while helping to button his jacket. "I walked one day by *Le Ministère de la Marine.* Two young officers in uniform stood outside. They were the most elegant men I had ever seen, and I thought, *if I knew a man such as this, he would take good care of me."* Finishing the buttons, she stood back. "And now I have one." She gave him a kiss on the cheek, "But each time I see you in your captain's coat, I want to tear it off and take you to our bed."

Smiling broadly, he returned the kiss. "I fear duty calls, but I will only be gone a few days. So keep that thought in mind." Taking his captain's cap, he added, "But duty does call. Let's go."

They walked down to the dock and their canoe where she would do what many future generations would call, *driving your husband to work*. He boarded while she pushed the craft out and hopped in, beginning to paddle to the ship dock. He continued to be astounded, yet a bit chagrinned, that she handled the craft much better than he did. "What are you going to pick up?" she asked.

"A ship from France arrived last week. Apparently, the captain feared being wintered-in and dropped his cargo in *Tadoussac*, returning immediately to *Dieppe*. *Général* Champlain wants us to bring the cargo here as soon as possible. It must be something important."

Noël had done river cruises with Abraham Martin, but this was the first time he was sailing as captain. As the dock came into view, she said, "The barque, I'm impressed."

A smaller, lighter, less costly version of an ocean ship, the barque was for moving large loads in *Fleuve Saint-Laurent*. More common was the shallop, a smaller and less seaworthy sailing vessel used for smaller chores and smaller rivers. Both boats were capable of ocean travel. Indeed that is how they came from France where they were built; however, they were not well suited for severe weather.

Françoise tied to the dock, explaining, "I will go with you. I need to do errands in the village."

As they approached the barque, they noticed an older man standing at attention on the gangplank. Noël chuckled, "Maybe Captain Martin does not *entirely* trust me."

Françoise laughed and followed her husband up the plank to place a daughter-like kiss on the cheek of the venerable *Monsieur* Bergeron from *L'Hirondelle*. "Keep my husband safe, *Monsieur*."

156

Bergeron saluted smartly, "Yes, *Mademoiselle*—I mean *Madame*." Giving her husband a less daughterly smooch, she returned to the dock.

When their ships from *Perche* arrived, the old sailor had told her he had decided to stay in *Québec*. "I have spent my entire career sailing to and from this wild new world. I suspect, before I die I should experience living it."

Once she was ashore, the ship's bell sounded, lines cast, and her husband piloted *Madame Hélène*, a name given the craft by Champlain himself, downstream. Françoise headed to the marketplace and visited a few merchants, obtaining supplies for herself and her neighbors. After arranging for their delivery to her canoe at the dock, she headed to the upper town to meet a friend at *L'Auberge Oie Bleue*.

Harbingers of the coming winter, most of the maple leaves now lay in the square. The quintessential *Canadienne,* Hélène Desportes-Hebert, sat outside, unfettered by the cool temperature while calmly waiting for Françoise. "Hello, my dear," Françoise said, as she gave the young bride a peck on the cheek and was seated. "How is married life?" Looking at the young bride, only 14 years old, Françoise reflected how young Hélène was before recalling she was only one year older when she took up with Guy.

"Not at all bad, thank you," Hélène replied. "We have a fine home in the upper town—very close to the chapel," adding with a giggle, "I even have a servant."

As the two young ladies socialized, Françoise noted three men occupying a nearby table. Any *Québécoise* would recognize *Général* Champlain, but the two backwoodsmen who joined him were unknown to most upper town citizens. The ever-silent *Monsieur* Bernier sat slouched, draining his beer, while *Monsieur* Benoît spoke. Françoise could not help overhearing.

"Overall, it's been good this year, yer honor. Algonquins got the most furs I seen since I come—and that's been some years." Before continuing, he signaled *Monsieur* Forton for more beers. "Best quality I seen, too, gonna bring big money in Paris. Me and Bernier, why, we brought in all we could possibly haul."

"Sounds encouraging, *Monsieur*," Champlain stated, pausing as he suspected there was another shoe to drop.

"There's just this thing, yer honor. It's that Goddamned Half-face. Excuse my English, yer honor. Word is he came to Little-Arrow's camp up in the Huron country. Killed Little-Arrow and some of his men and took his whole stash—just like that. And another thing, when we was on our way back through the high-country, we run into Jacques-Pierre and his boys. They had a whole shitload of furs and was on their way back, too.

"Thing is, yer honor, we been back two weeks and ain't seen hide nor hair of 'em. Ain't like Jacques-Pierre to be late. Either he run off with the Indians or he and his boys is lyin' dead in a ravine back in the high country and old Half-face is got his pelts."

Champlain was getting more concerned, "But how can he sell them? He does not have a license."

"He's a sly one, yer honor, and ain't many that dare to cross him."

"But who..?"

"Maybe one of them Scottish bankers. They can't hardly turn down a good deal."

Champlain tried to protest, but Benoît continued, "Like my old Pa said, 'Scotsman is so nice, he'll *sell* ya the shirt off his back'."

158

Bernier stifled a chuckle—the first sound Champlain had heard him utter.

"I don't know what to tell ya, yer honor," Benoît continued. "Nobody wants to truck with him. Even the soldiers is afeared." Champlain excused himself and left the two *voyageurs* to drink in silence. Françoise returned her attention to Hélène but would not be able to get this conversation out of her head.

Finishing their lunch, Québec's two newest brides said goodbye, and Françoise returned to the canoe dock where she found all her purchases packed and in order. Landing at the Beauport dock, she saw Jacques-Henri waiting to help and together they delivered them to the neighbors. On their way back, she asked him, "Do you know of this man they call Half-face?"

With a shrug, he replied, "I have heard stories but never seen him. It is said he is a *coureurs de bois* who had part of his face burned off in fight with Iroquois. I think he is more *voyageur* legend than fact. Why do you ask?"

"Just something I heard."

Fleuve Saint-Laurent: October 26, 1634

Madame Hélène's bell rang as the first sign of daylight reached the horizon. Noël and his men were already up and fed, and as the bell tolled, they weighed anchor, setting sail to complete their voyage to *Tadoussac*. Over 100 miles downstream of *Québec*, it was the oldest port in Canada. The small trading post had been established by fur traders before the arrival of Champlain in 1603, and in spite of this history, it had changed little in 31 years. Three small wooden structures stood on the northeastern point formed by *Riviére Saguenay* as it entered *Fleuve Saint-Laurent*

159

from the north. The other structures were a scattering of Algonquin huts as most of the year-round population was native.

Noël heard a French inhabitant of *Tadoussac* could count the trading post's Frenchmen on his fingers and toes—and that none of the residents had all their digits. The joke aside, there was a reason for the digit shortage—the singular industry of whaling. In this widening expanse of *Fleuve Saint-Laurent*, small boats using Indian harpoons and native crews harvested the bounty of aquatic mammals. Their success, however, was dependent on the cadre of seasonal Basque whalers who came annually for the whale harvest but returned in winter to their sunny corner in the southwest of France.

Docking offered little difficulty due to low winds and the lack of other ships. Noël went directly to the harbormaster's office in one of the dilapidated cabins. "*Bonjour,* Captain Langlois," greeted the harbormaster, *Monsieur* Perrault. "Has Captain Martin set you free at long last?"

"Yes, sir," Noël replied.

Perrault had the look of someone who had lived most of his life in the wild. What he lacked in teeth he made up for in scars. His hands were as calloused as they were filthy. Taking a paper from his desk, he said, "Here is your list of goods. Your French ship's officer could not escape fast enough. I believe he had heard rumors of *Québec* winter, and those Basque rascals can't get out too quickly. I know they prefer the south of France to Canada—at least in winter." Looking at the paper he added, "You have quite a load here. There are a few soldiers and some workers. They have been holed up in the tavern all week—may take a while to sober them up. Then there is some livestock and several other items. If we can get some work from the men in the tavern, perhaps we can get it all aboard today."

Perrault led him to the tavern where the passengers sat in various stages of consciousness. The harbormaster instructed the proprietor to close the bar, much to the dismay of those still standing. He ushered the crowd out and began barking orders. The more conscious enlisted the others still standing and began to haul the loads of farming tools, guns, wheels, harnesses and other paraphernalia to the ship. As Noël monitored the loading, he noticed a long bulky parcel. On closer inspection, he said, "My God! Can we use this!"

As the men continued loading, Perrault took Noël to a fenced area where he had housed the livestock. "It is impressive how much these creatures have improved with only one week on land," he explained. "They were near death on arrival." When the bulk of cargo was loaded, night was falling and they decided to wait for morning to load the animals.

At first light, all hands were on deck, and with the aid of the locals and passengers, the animals were loaded: cattle, sheep, goats and swine. Noël noted they had double the numbers that had arrived with him in May. In addition was a yard full of frantic chickens with the occasional rooster. "When we unloaded them," Perrault related, "we thought they was all dead, but damn, if they didn't come back to life—every damned one." Once they were caged and loaded, Noël finished the paperwork and headed into the *Saint-Laurent*, sailing towards an ominous sky in the southwest.

No more than ten miles from *Tadoussac*, the first bolt of lightning struck, followed by wind gusts and a pelting rain. Noël proceeded with caution as the wind shifted to northwest and the rain diminished. Over the next ten miles, the temperature continued to drop and the snow began to fall. Wet and scattered at first, as the temperature plummeted, it turned to giant flakes and finally to hard, pelting snow. Noël continued with caution until he lost sight of his bowsprit and took the prudent step of striking the sails and lowering the anchor.

In the next hour, an eight-inch layer developed. As the men cleared the deck and Noël prepared to sail, he asked naively if this was much snow. The grins of the experienced crew answered his question. He weighed anchor and began to fight his way home against the current and headwind. Fortunately, the wind shifted to due north, diminishing the temperature but allowing him to sail more freely with greater speed.

Late morning of their third day, they made *Île d'Orléans* and two hours later moored in *Québec*. Noël went directly to the harbormaster where both Abraham Martin and Champlain awaited him. Following his report, he told them, "There is also something special you should see." As they approached the ship, men were unloading the long contraption.

"What in the world?" Martin asked.

"It's a set of long-saws and a vise," Noël reported. With great enthusiasm, he continued. "You cut a log to length, place it in the box and tighten the vise. The saws each fit in their own slot and two men on either side each work one saw. It requires little skill so you can use your strongest men who can quickly produce *real boards.*"

"Where will we put it?" Martin asked.

Noël had already been thinking, "Where will you put the new animals?"

Champlain answered, "We would like them in Beauport where you have easy access to abundant pasture."

"In that case," Noël said, "we can put it in Beauport and bring the strongest workers. We can quickly make a large barn for the animals before winter hits, and then move the saws to wherever you have the most need of good boards."

"That would be by the fort and the upper town," Champlain smiled inwardly, realizing he had finally surrounded himself with men who possessed the knowledge and drive to make his dream come true.

CHAPTER 20

<u>Beauport: November 20, 1634</u>

S avoring the view, Noël concluded this was his first free time alone since arriving in Canada. He had added a small porch to the front of his house, and although the home and porch were quite basic, the view from the porch was nothing short of spectacular. Bright and sunny, the day was surprisingly cold, but the wonderfully warm deerskin clothes made for him by Félicity-Angel made the coldest day bearable—at least up to the present. In addition, one of the new farm hands had come from Normandie with a talent for making calvados, and Noël had just heated a glass of that wonderful apple brandy.

Sitting in one of the two rocking chairs made by Gaspard Boucher, he gazed across the *Saint-Laurent* to the city where the barque *Madame Hélène* and three shallops sat idle. Abraham Martin told him there would be no more big ships to rescue this year, and they would likely stay idle. With the help of the long saws, the men finished the large barn and Beauport now boasted three cows, a bull, one hog, two sow, four sheep, two goats and a yard full of chickens.

"Now is time for hunting."

Noël looked up from his warm drink to see Jacques-Henri and pleaded, "I need to practice more with the gun."

"Do not need gun," Jacques-Henri claimed, regressing to his primitive French. "Bow," he stated, holding up the weapon. Coaxing Noël from his respite, Jacques-Henri showed him the subtleties of the traditional handmade armament and demonstrated by shooting an arrow into a circle carved on an extremely wide tree. He then handed the weapon to Noël and again tutored him in its use. Noël took the bow, and with some difficulty let the arrow fly to parts unknown. "Try again," his teacher encouraged, and Noël was eventually able to hit the tree. "More practice," the Indian ordered as he returned to his camp. Noël did, and he began to come closer to the mark.

"What in the world?" He turned to see his spouse returning from her visit with Nicole Boucher who had given birth to a daughter, Madeline, three days before.

"I am learning the bow and arrow," he admitted in exasperation.

She came to his side, "Show me."

After he landed a few near misses she said, "Not bad. Is it very difficult?"

"Well, it takes some practice."

"Can I try?" she asked.

Smiling, he retrieved the arrows and showed her how it was done. She took her first shot, which continued well past the tree. "Try again," he said with a grin. "It is harder than you think."

She took another arrow and landed it directly in the center. Then she repeated the feat three more times in rapid succession. "It doesn't seem so difficult," she reported. He looked in amazement as she laughed. "When I lived at the Algonquin village, they taught me. And Félicity-Angel has been working with me while you were away." Placing the bow by the tree, she said, "I'll show you some tricks, but first we must retrieve the arrow—it is valuable."

By the time the sun approached the horizon, Noël had actually achieved some competence, and after dinner, they sat by the fire enjoying more warm calvados. Noël told her, "I wonder if I am the first Canadian taught to shoot by his wife."

She rose and slyly took his hand, "Come to bed, *Monsieur*, your secret is safe with me."

Three days later, Jacques-Henri sat rocking in Noël's chair when Noël returned home from working on the fort. "Tomorrow good day to hunt," he stated with authority. "One hour before sun—bring bow, no gun." Rising abruptly, he returned to his camp.

As directed, Noël dragged out of bed before the sun, donned his deerskin clothes and boots, took his bow and reported to Jacques-Henri's Indian camp with trepidation. The native residence continued to grow with the addition of a smoke house and another hut, the purpose of which remained a mystery. Jacques-Henri was waiting in front of the house-hut. Seeing Noël, he rose and motioned for him to follow.

"How will we see?" Noël asked.

"Moonlight," The Indian replied.

"But there's no moon," Noël noted. Jacques-Henri merely shrugged and moved quickly up the new clearing next to the creek. As they passed the beaver pond, it began to snow. When they reached the pasture, it was snowing heavily.

Noël viewed this as an obstacle but his guide curtly ordained, "Snow good." At the back of the pasture, their clear path vanished, and although the sun was breaking on the horizon, the snow kept visibility poor. Noël was amazed at the ease and speed with which his friend moved in the forest. An hour later, the sun was up and the snow was diminishing. Jacques-Henri stopped at a small clearing by another beaver pond, declaring, "We wait here." Moving into the cover of the forest, he perched on a fallen log.

Noël whispered, "Shouldn't we look for deer?"

"No," was the authoritative response. "Deer come to us."

As they sat silently in the forest, Noël wondered why the deer would come to them. Jacques-Henri began to point quietly to things Noël would have never noticed if alone. First was a giant nest, high on a tree across the clearing. It seemed empty, but suddenly a white head appeared as a massive bird stood and flew off. Jacques-Henri whispered softly, "Eagle." The bird circled overhead before it dove to the beaver pond, leaving with a large trout. Jacques-Henri continued to point, as Noël became astounded by the wonders of nature that were all around him—wonders to which he had previously been oblivious. Finally, they heard a rustle across the clearing as a deer came into view, beginning to feed off the ground. Noël went for his bow, but Jacques-Henri shook his head, causing Noël to realize it was female. His friend had told him, "Only kill mother deer if you are starving."

Eventually a buck with antlers joined the female. Jacques-Henri nodded yes and Noël took his bow. It was hard to tell who was most surprised, Noël, Jacques-Henri or the buck when the arrow found its mark. The female bounded off, and the wounded buck turned to follow, giving Noël just enough time to land another hit before the buck, too, disappeared into the woods. Jacques-Henri rose slowly, "We will follow, he will not get far."

Jacques-Henri led him to the site and pointed to the naturally occurring secret on the ground, "Salt lick. Deer comes to you." Noël wondered why his friend was so calm when the buck was escaping. When they started to follow, he understood why his friend had called the snow *good* as he could follow the trail of blood and the hoof prints easily. They made their way along until they came upon the wounded buck lying in the trees. Jacques-Henri knelt behind it, "Don't stand by the legs," he cautioned, making a cut on the animal's neck releasing a fountain of blood. The buck was soon still.

He then cut along the abdomen and the entrails spilled onto the forest floor. Reaching inside he removed the heart. Handing it to Noël, he instructed, "Eat."

Noël was aghast but took a bite of the warm muscle. Jacques-Henri took a bite as well and painted blood on his friend's face. "You *real* Indian hunter now," he decreed.

Jacques-Henri cut a long, straight branch to which he tied the carcass's legs allowing them to carry it back to Beauport where Jacques-Henri went straight to work on it.

Teaching Noël as he went, he expertly skinned the beast and hung the hide, proceeding to cut the meat, systematically removing and organizing the cuts with the precision of a master butcher. He saved the marrow and bones while collecting other organs. When finished, Noël fully appreciated the wisdom of his wife's decision to invite the family to join them. Finally, he took the antlers and hung them over Noël's door.

"Your first kill," he announced, "good medicine—make wife fertile."

Sunday the entire population of Beauport gathered for a picnic in the yard of Jean Guyon. With five married couples, eighteen children, nine single men and three natives, the forty people could still not fill his large riverside yard. Their purpose was twofold: first to celebrate seven months since they had bid farewell to France, a time and place that now seemed forever and a world away. Second was a sendoff for Noël Morin, who was leaving the three-man bachelor quarters for the upper town of *Québec*.

"*Monsieur* Giffard has asked me to move to a cabin with a shop in the upper town to renew my old career of carriage maker. To begin with, I shall build simple carts, but as Giffard points out, next season our new cattle will be strong enough to pull." With a widened smile, he added, "Of course, I know you will all be sad to abandon the carrying and hauling of everything manually that we have come to cherish."

Everyone laughed and raised a cup. Fortunately, another of the new farm hands had an extra talent—brewing ale.

The musicians played while everyone danced. Eventually the late hour and falling temperature typical on such a crystal-clear night began to dampen the revelry as the Beauport community headed to their homes. When Noël and Françoise arrived at their cabin, Jacques-Henri was standing at the end of the rise studying the bright, moonlit Canadian sky. Noël and Françoise joined him. "What do you see?" she asked.

He remained silent for a while before replying, "Big snow—two days"

"How do you know?" Noël questioned.

Shrugging, he only smiled, replying, "Just know," and headed to his camp.

The following morning was sunny and warmer as the men set off to build the fort. When Noël returned in the evening, his wife asked, "Have you seen Jacques-Henri today?"

"No. Why do you ask?"

"Well, I went to speak with Félicity-Angel this morning and no one was there. The entire camp is closed up. They haven't been around all day." Stirring her pot of porridge in the fire, she added, "It's just odd for all three to have gone and not said anything." There was still no sign of the Indians the next morning as the men braved the new cold front and headed to work on the fort.

The snow began at midday much as the last few snowfalls of the season. Until now, a three-inch cover had been most impressive to those raised where any accumulation was noteworthy. This storm, however, began to build in the afternoon and the men returned the canoes to Beauport by dead reckoning. Plodding through the foot-high snow, they made it back to their homes. Once inside Noël removed his coat and warmed himself at the fire.

170

When he described the storm to his wife, she laughed, "You have seen nothing, as yet!" adding, "but Jacques-Henri and his family are still gone. I'm beginning to worry."

"I wouldn't," he replied, inspecting dinner on the fire, "I think it is they who need to worry about us." They turned in early, snuggling against the cold as nature roared outside their door.

In the morning, Noël was up with the sun, opening one of their few small window shutters. Jacques-Henri had stretched thin, oiled animal skins over each opening which gave them some protection from wind and weather while allowing in some light although little visibility. "Everything is white," he reported, heading to the door. Pulling it open, he discovered a two-foot layer on the porch. Retiring to the interior, he told Françoise, "It's at least two feet deep, and still snowing—but not heavily"

Françoise looked up from the fireplace, spoon in hand, "I doubt it's going anywhere. Come in and eat. Believe me, you will have adequate opportunity to see snow."

Once he had eaten, he donned his coat and boots. Before he opened the door, he asked, "Do you hear dogs?"

"I didn't hear anything," she answered.

"I'll go see." A few minutes later, Noël burst through the door along with a pile of snow. Before Françoise could complain, he gasped out of breath, "There is a pack of wolves at Jacques-Henri's!" Before she could reply, he had pulled his musket from the hearth and returned outdoors. Cautiously creeping through the snow, he held his weapon at the ready, beginning to wonder if this was a prudent act. He could hear the wolves and when he turned the corner, he saw them! He also saw Jacques-Henri scratching one behind the ears. As Noël approached, they gathered about him and sat.

"Don't need gun," the Indian told him. "Don't even need bow."

Noël stood with his mouth agape. "Where did you get wolves?"

"Not wolves—Indian dogs."

"Dogs?"

Jacques-Henri shrugged, "Part dog."

Noël remained confused, "Which part?"

Jacques-Henri laughed. "You funny. Dog lives in village in summer. I take in winter for sled."

"Sled?"

Jacques-Henri pointed to a low, narrow vehicle on skis. "Goes on snow."

"Did you meet the team?" Noël looked up to see his spouse. The dogs immediately came to her and she raised her hand magically causing them to sit. "Can we go for a ride?" she inquired.

Jacques-Henri gave a low fluttering whistle, and the team lined up in front of the sled. He attached each to a small harness while Françoise showed Noël how to sit at the back of the sled with her in front of him between his legs. "Cozy, is it not?" she purred. Jacques-Henri stood on the back and gave a low whistle causing the team to leap into action.

Noël's greatest thrill had been sailing small boats in heavy wind. This was beyond that pale—it was beyond any thrill he had or had considered. As the wind whistled around him, the snow flew from the skis and the scenery passed by at an unbelievable pace. Noël wondered if falling from a cliff could be faster than this. Passing the first beaver pond, they came to the pasture, making a round trip that returned them toward home. Arriving at the Indian camp, Jacques-Henri said calmly, "Not bad. Snow will be better next month—now time to work."

Suddenly Noël remembered the firewood they had cut and left along the clearing. Now he understood why Jacques-Henri had insisted they wait until winter to move it. They gathered the neighbors who Jacques-Henri stationed along the path to load the wood, which he and the canine wood haulers would bring to each of the houses until each home was in the shadow of an enormous pile of winter fuel.

CHAPTER 21

Winter continued to close in on the community. The *habitants,* as residents were known, continued to travel from Beauport to the city three days a week, but the voyage, simple in good weather, was becoming more challenging. Increasing formation of ice in the rivers, in addition to cold and snow, made daily canoe passage more difficult by the day. Work on the city, however, had proceeded beyond expectations, and at the end of the day, the *Général* himself came to address the Beauport workers.

The founder of *Québec* was looking older and slower by the month. Although muted, his enthusiasm and optimism remained. "Men," he began from the porch of the fort headquarters, "I believe we can take pride in all our accomplishments to date. The fort is now a true fort—

174

capable of defending against whatever comes. The church and the *Habitation*," referring to his house and offices, "are sound, and we have enough housing in the city to secure all our new arrivals as well as the first wave expected in the spring. Therefore, I am suspending the mandatory three-day work detail. Those of you who are able are encouraged to come when possible to work on finishing touches."

With this he signaled a soldier who went to the new flagstaff and raised the blue flag with three gold fleur-de-lis carried by Champlain on his first voyage to *Québec*. The *Général* stood on a bench, raised his aging fist, shouting, "*Vive le Québec—Vive le Canada!*" Workers and soldiers alike cheered wildly until Champlain disappeared into his office. Then they did the only thing Frenchmen would do in this situation—retired to the taverns to toast the *Général*.

Étienne Forton had recently enlarged his liquor stock with some concern, fearing that a hard winter could slow his business. As the throng gathered at both locations, however, he realized this would certainly lower his excess product while improving his finances. Seated with a group of Beauport residents, Noël Langlois observed, "In spite of his enthusiasm, the *Général* is looking slower and weaker."

Noël Morin looked around and answered quietly, "*Monsieur* Giffard told me the *Général* has just received sad news. Most of you never knew Étienne Brûlé. As a boy, he hid aboard one of Champlain's first ships and sailed to Canada. The *Général* took him in like the son he never had. Later he went to the frontier to work with the Indians and became a valued interpreter." He paused to take a drink before continuing, "When the Kirkes came, Brûlé stayed to interpret for them. The *Général* took it poorly. When we returned from France, we heard he had gone far west with the Huron. Only yesterday, news came that Brûlé died one or two years ago. He was an obstreperous lad and apparently fell out with the Huron who killed him. Rumor is they burned him alive. The *Général* never forgave him for joining the Kirkes, but this news hit him to the soul. I think he still looked at the lad as the son he never had."

Eventually paying the largest tab in *Monsieur* Forton's history, they headed home to prepare for winter.

Québec: December 25, 1634

"I can scarcely believe we are going to church for Christmas day mass," Françoise told her husband while pouring his breakfast porridge. "The early years I lived in Canada, it was simply too cold. The cabin was filled with drafts and snow leaked through causing drifts inside. Last year in *Mortagne* I thought would be my last Christmas celebration."

"Apparently our new buildings are more secure," Noël declared as he sat to begin spooning in his porridge. "Aren't you eating?"

"I just don't feel like it," she confessed. "But you should hurry. Jacques-Henri is going to help us get across the river, and we should not be tardy."

Once he finished, they donned their deerskin boots and coats made by the Indians to ward off the frigid temperatures. The holiday dress of Perche was generally not adequate in Canada, but today, as they exited onto the porch, they encountered a fine morning. The sun was out and the wind calm, providing a better day than the past few. Following the well-worn path, they walked to the riverbank. Jacques-Henri had taught them to always use the

176

same path for each destination, barn, fields or other cabins, keeping the paths packed down and easier to use.

Plodding west along the bank, they encountered their neighbors making the same trek. Jacques-Henri had moved the canoes closer to *Riviére Saint-Charles* where the ice was not so treacherous. Here Pierre Boucher, who had become a skilled canoeist, joined Jacques-Henri and Félicity-Angel to ferry the community to the city where they hiked another well-worn path to the upper town and church. The bell was ringing as the Beauport group arrived a bit late, but the congregation waited as they represented a sizeable segment of the parish.

Young Hélène Desportes-Hebert and her mother-in-law stood at the church door, distributing decorative ribbons to each woman to adorn their deerskin coats. A fireplace, recently installed by Jean Guyon, improved the interior of the sanctuary. Once all were present, Father Lalemant began.

Following the canonical portion of his sermon, he added a rare, personal note. "It has now been ten years since I arrived in this wild and wonderful land to serve God and its people—both those newly arrived and those who have lived here since time out of mind. At times things were bleak and often it seemed we could fail, but I never lost faith in our cause. Thanks to *Général* Champlain, those who preceded him and those who followed, we have seen in the past several months, progress and accomplishments unexpected a short while ago. As I gaze down the path of life, I see our way is clear and our cause is just. Today we celebrate the birth of the Lord. Let us give thanks and pray for continued success. Vive *Québec* and God bless Canada."

Exiting into a blessedly sunny day, the pioneers gathered in the square to socialize. Étienne Forton opened his inn and those musically inclined brought out their instruments. As the sun began to set, the Beauport residents made their way to the canoes and were halfway home before the weather changed abruptly. Struggling to pull the canoes up to safety, they began the trek home in a whiteout. By the time they reached their homes, they were exhausted, and Noël and Françoise dined on porridge that had been simmering on the coals before falling into bed.

In the morning, they finished the porridge. Françoise seemed to tolerate breakfast until a short while later, she had to run for the chamber pot. "Are you ill?" her husband asked. "No," she replied with authority. "Then what...?" he queried.

Realizing her man was clueless, she revealed, "I'm pregnant." His mouth dropped as he asked, "But, how...?"

"The usual way," she answered, adding with a sly smile. "Do you remember what we have been doing each night?" She rose to stretch, suggesting, "See what it's like outside."

Going to the door, he struggled. "It's stuck." Pulling with all his weight, he opened to a wall of white. Snow was as high as the door. "Oh my God..." he whispered as he slammed the door shut, producing a loud thud. Reopening it, he realized the snow had drifted as high as the door but was not as deep—it was, however, almost waist high.

Beginning to don her boots, she said, "Get dressed, we shall go out and see." He looked with concern, "But what...?"

"I'm not ill," she declared, "and now that my stomach is empty, I'm fine. I will be able to eat at midday."

He began to dress with misgivings when they heard the barking as Jacques-Henri approached, carrying his wife and son in the dogsled. "Come out," he shouted. "We need weight."

178

Finally dressed, they worked their way through the porch snow to the sled. Once they were seated, Jacques-Henri cracked his whip and the dogs took off. Deep snow made the ride much slower, but the depth of the fluffy white added to the thrill. Jacques-Henri explained he needed to ride along each trail to reestablish it.

By midday, they had accomplished the goal and stopped at the Indian camp. Jacques-Henri barked something to his son in Algonquin, and the boy entered the second hut Jacques-Henri had built. Noël looked inside seeing the boy fanning the flames of a fire pit that had been simmering in the center of the hut. Surrounded by large rocks, it was not long before the rocks were very hot, and the boy began to pour water slowly, producing an enormous wall of steam.

Françoise took her husband's hand. "I know what to do," she said coyly, beginning to shed her clothes. "Get undressed," she ordered—"everything off." Her man was shocked, having never seen his wife naked outdoors in the daylight, not to mention in mixed company. When they were both nude, she led him into the hut. "Sit here," she ordered. Soon all five were around the fire bathed in hot steam. Soon Félicity-Angel produced a plate of cooked meat with a wonderful sauce. Passing it around, they began to dine.

Eventually Noël said, "I'm getting very hot." Françoise took his hand and guided him outside. "No problem," she decreed, as she pushed him into the snowdrift and rolled on top of him. Exhilarating did not do justice to the sensation. Once cooled, they returned to the steam bath. As the sun sank lower, they doused the rocks, letting the fire smolder down. After thanking their Indian friends profusely, they dressed to return home, where Françoise recooked some of Félicity-Angel's meat adding a dish of potatoes and onions.

When they retired, she crawled in naked next to her husband. "Take me," she whispered softly. "But isn't that…" he began to reply. "No," she replied with authority, "not until the very end." It had been a day of discovery for Noël Langlois.

CHAPTER 22

Québec wilderness: February 15, 1635

Moving silently through the forest as only a native could, Jacques-Henri led his troop of three men and two boys in his constant quest to turn French artisans into hunters. His cadre of neophytes was yet not approaching his level of stealth, but they were improving and Jacques-Henri was an eternal optimist. Each of the three men brought their rifles although Jacques-Henri continued to insist they use the bows. The two boys, Pierre Boucher and young Jean Guyon, called *Jeano* to distinguish him from his father, came armed solely with the native weapon.

Now three days out, they were camped along the shore of one of the area's many spectacular lakes, and yesterday Noël and Gaspard had brought down two respectable deer with their bows. Today they hiked to the north end of the lake where Jacques-Henri had promised even better luck. Trudging through a four-inch layer of powder overlaying two feet of frozen snow, they enjoyed the first sunshine of the hunt sparkling playfully off the ice-covered lake. Rising winds brought down swirling clouds of fluff from the dense evergreen forest.

Suddenly and silently, Jacques-Henri stopped. Raising his hand, he pointed. What had been hidden to the neophytes in the cover of nature was now evident—a magnificent ten-point buck. Motioning to the boys, he indicated it was their turn. Young Jeano took the first shot landing his arrow in the side of the animal's chest. Before it could bolt, Pierre hit it in the neck, quickly loading another arrow, hit a third strike that caused the beast to stumble to the snow.

Jacques-Henri patiently instructed the boys in bleeding and gutting their kill before giving them a bite of the heart, painting their faces with blood, and finally allowing them the privilege of hauling it to the camp. The remainder of the day consisted of spectacular views, missed chances of more game, and ended with ice fishing on the lake to catch enough fish for dinner and breakfast.

Sitting under the stars and warming to the campfire, Jacques-Henri regaled the lads with tales of Indian lore, while Gaspard played his jew's-harp. Suddenly Jacques-Henri stopped the lecture and motioned to Gaspard to be silent. It sounded like the crack of a breaking stick, but soft.

"The wind," Noël whispered, but his friend held his finger to his lips, while he stealthily reached for his bow. They sat in silence until another crack, then another and suddenly it was there—in front of them. The giant black mound of fur moved casually toward them. They had seen black bear foraging at the fort dump, but nothing like this.

It was enormous. Its sudden roar only served to make its image larger. Jacques-Henri shot an arrow directly into its chest, which just enraged the creature more. Jacques-Henri hit it again, causing the bear to strike him with its paw, sending him flying off his feet. As he dropped the bow, his students realized they had just seen their hero bested by nature.

The bear came to Noël who could now smell its pungent breath. It rose to its full height—almost as tall as Noël. It approached with a roar and a loud crack as it fell upon the hapless *habitant*. Lying under the crushing weight, Noël realized it was now still as he heard commotion from his comrades, who rolled the carcass over. Getting his bearings, he focused on young Pierre, holding his father's musket. Having crawled behind the beast as it swatted Jacques-Henri, the boy had found the weapon and landed a shot squarely in the base of the monster's neck.

Québec: the following day

With their men away, Françoise, Nicole and Félicity-Angel decided to take advantage of the beautiful winter day going to town for needed supplies. The ice had forced the canoes into storage, but it was now thick enough to cross safely on foot. Félicity-Angel, however, suggested they relax and take the dog sled. Slicing their way through snow onto the thick ice by *Riviére Saint-Charles,* Françoise and Nicole screamed with exhilaration.

In town, they ran their errands, stopping to gossip with the upper town wives who were also out enjoying the respite from blizzards. Eventually they made their way

183

back to the patiently waiting dogs and repeated the thrill of the ride.

Knowing her husband would not be home until tomorrow, Françoise decide to stroll to the barn where she found Xainte Cloutier and her children taking their turn at tending the animals. Offering assistance, Françoise slopped the pigs and milked two cows, skills she had not learned in France. From there she visited the frozen beaver pond. Turning toward home, she sensed someone else at the pond, but upon investigation, saw no one.

Accelerating the pace of her stroll, she quickly made it down the creek where she saw Nicole coming from the backhouse. Waiting for her friend, she gazed down river and had a glimpse of a man in *voyageur* dress standing by the stored canoes. From a distance, she could only make out a knot of dirty red hair protruding behind his *voyageur* hat. Turning to see Nicole, she asked, "Do you know who that man is?"

"What man?" her friend asked. Françoise turned back, but he was not there.

"Oh, I thought I…" embarrassed—there was certainly no one down there, Françoise said, "I must have just been dreaming." Returning home, she looked around the room, and secured the door with the large wooden brace. After heating some leftover porridge for her supper, she went directly to bed, her sleep burdened by dreams of phantoms, and sounds outside the house. In the morning, she opened a shutter to another sunny day. *What a baby I am,* she thought as she opened the door—only to find footprints in the fresh snow on the porch. In a panic, she took her bow and crept slowly around the porch surprising young Nicolas Boucher.

"Excuse me, *Tante* Françoise," he began. "I knocked but there was no answer. My Ma said I should see if you needed help with anything today." Both relieved and embarrassed, she smiled, "Yes, Nicolas. I have biscuits in here I need help eating."

By the time the men returned the following day, Françoise had recovered from her demons and saw no more phantoms. Jacques-Henri had cut flexible branches and made sleds to pull their bounty from the wilderness more easily. Unfortunately, the dogs had stayed home with the women so the men did the pulling. They were, however, pleased to find the method much easier than carrying the load.

Once they had displayed the abundant cuts of meat wrapped in the hides—with the bearskin being the highlight, Jacques-Henri announced, "Now make ice cave."

Unclear on the concept, Jean Guyon asked, "Shouldn't we smoke the meat first?"

The guide replied simply, "No—ice cave."

Happily, they now had access to the dogs, and Jacques-Henri loaded four stone hatchets in the sled and led the men onto the frozen river. Surveying the surface, he selected a position and chopped a hole as he had done up north to fish through the ice. He continued to cut more ice, however, removing the blocks and loading them onto the sled. Leading the dogs back to his camp, he removed a birch bark cover from the ground exposing a large, round hole.

"Dig hole when earth is soft," he explained before he began to line it with the ice blocks. Once his neighbors had the idea, some of them went home, returning with metal tools. Skeptical at first, Jacques-Henri rapidly saw their advantage in cutting ice blocks and soon they had ringed the entire *ice cave* with ice. After lowering the deer meat to the bottom of the hole, he explained, "Continue to save meat all winter—stays good all summer."

As the Indian pulled the cover back over the *cave*, Pierre Boucher said, "You forgot the bear meat."

Sticking out his tongue, Jacques-Henri made a face, "*Ce ne vaut pas le peine.*" Pierre took this to indicate bear meat was not an Indian delicacy, and when Félicity-Angel cooked and served it to the families that evening, Pierre realized it was not.

The following day, Pierre helped Jacques-Henri begin to clean and treat the hides. When it was completed, the Indian presented him with the bearskin, explaining, "For saving our lives." Young Pierre could scarcely contain his pride.

Beauport: Two days later

"Noël! Wake up!" Shaken from his dream of shooting bears, he sat up, hearing the pounding at the door. Leaving the comfort of their warm and snug Indian blanket made by Félicity-Angel, his bare feet hit the frigid wooden floor. Cracking the door, he saw Jacques-Henri, who shouted, "Come quick!" while pointing to the side of the porch. Subjecting his feet to the snow cover, Noel followed his friend in the brutally cold, star-lit night to the side yard. The problem was apparent. Flames shot like a tower on this

186

windless night, straight up into the sky, making them easily visible over the trees and blessedly unlikely to spread.

Pierre and his father met them. "It must be Drouin and Bélanger's place," Gaspard told them. Looking at Noël's lack of footwear, he ordered, "Get dressed and meet us there—quickly." Turning to his son, he added, "Pierre, go alert the others—hurry!"

Pierre headed to the homes while Jacques-Henri and Gaspard headed toward the flames. Returning to his house, Noel quickly dressed while explaining the dilemma to his spouse. She arose, covered herself with a large shawl and went to stoke their fire. "Bring them back here. They'll be freezing."

Leaving immediately, Noël headed past Jacques-Henri's camp, hoping there would still be someone with whom to return. The tenant farm was only a few hundred feet away from the Indian camp. Once on the cleared path, Noël could see the log cabin engulfed in flames, which were already beginning to subside for lack of fuel. Fortunately, the log cutting for building had removed trees closest to the cabins. Jean and young Jeano Guyon were there along with Zacharie Cloutier and his two oldest boys who had just arrived. They were all relieved to see Noël's tenants, shivering but intact. Eventually Marin Boucher and Pierre joined them.

"Praise God there is no wind," Gaspard said. "Noël, why don't you and Guyon take these two to your place to get warm? We will stay here until it is safe—then join you in the morning."

Noël led the two men who, dressed only in their nightshirts, were speechless from the cold. Stumbling along, they fell twice before reaching the Langlois cabin. Françoise opened the door and they entered, two blue

187

ghosts in nightclothes. "Dear God!" she exclaimed, "You look half dead."

"M-more than half," Drouin stuttered. She brought them in, and Guyon said good night.

Removing her large shawl, she covered the two refugees. "Come close to the fire," she ordered as she turned to stoke the flames. Bending to add another log, she realized she was open in the back as her gown fell to the floor. Retrieving it quickly, she said. "Excuse me!"

Drouin answered with his frigid stutter, "At-t least w-we k-know we are still, a-alive."

Françoise retreated to a corner of the room and rapidly dressed before returning to tend the fire. Having placed water earlier in the over-hanging kettle, she poured four cups, adding a shot of calvados to each. "Drink this slowly," she ordered.

A short while later, color began to return to the men's faces, and Bélanger announced in triumph, "I *am* going to live." Pointing to Françoise's bed shirt laying on the bed, he added with a twinkle, "And Madame, you are most definitely excused." Although still embarrassed, she was glad to see they had not lost their French-Canadian sense of humor.

Françoise poured another round and suggested, "We have this large Indian blanket. Perhaps we could all squeeze in for warmth."

Drouin smiled for the first time, "Thank you, but I have had enough excitement for tonight."

Just then, they heard a knock. Noël opened the door to Pierre Boucher with a large fur, explaining, "My mother thought the men could sleep on this." He laid his treasured bearskin on the floor. Not understanding the cause for laughter, Pierre excused himself.

✢

The following morning Gaspard called, finding the two bachelors alive, well and enjoying the first real breakfast they had in Canada, including a strong hot beverage Félicity-Angel had taught Françoise to brew from a ubiquitous black Indian root. Françoise invited him to sit and poured a cup of the black-root tea.

"I see you men survived the night," he began.

"Yes," replied Robert Drouin. "In fact if we had known how hospitable it was *chez* Langlois, we should have burned our cabin months ago."

Lacking Françoise's humor, Gaspard simply nodded, "I see. At any rate, I have already spoken to Cloutier, Guyon and my brother. They suggest we find you temporary quarters at the fort; however, we want you back as soon as possible. I believe we shall have even greater need of your services."

Standing to look at the fire, he continued, "We added these stone fireplaces to the family homes as a means of avoiding the very problem you had. We had little difficulty as we have three masons, and stone was not an issue as our grounds are littered with fieldstone. What we cleared away while cutting the trees more than filled our needs. Once winter breaks and we start on the fields, we can collect all the stone. Moving it with the help of Morin's carts and our new livestock we can begin to build true Normand stone houses." Returning to the table, he continued. "I am going today to speak with *Monsieur* Giffard—I can escort you men to the fort at the same time."

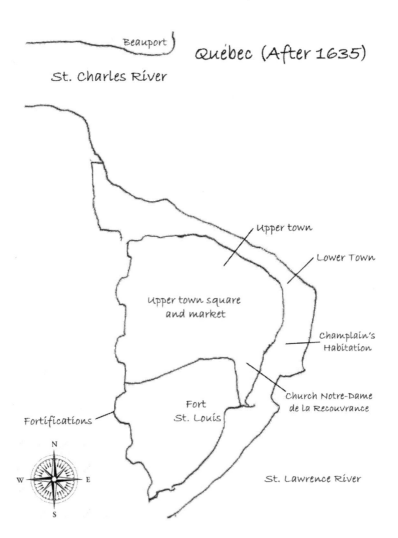

Beauport

St. Charles River

Québec (After 1635)

Upper town

Lower Town

Upper town square
and market

Champlain's
Habitation

Fortifications

Church Notre-Dame
de la Recouvrance

Fort
St. Louis

N
W — E
S

St. Lawrence River

CHAPTER 23

Perched in his favored spot, wrapped in a shawl, the old man watched the ice move. Had a painter captured this image, he may have titled it _Melancholy._ The old man, however, was anything but. Placing an acorn on the flat rock, he coaxed the squirrel forward. It took the nut, but instead of bolting off to safety, it began to gnaw the shell on the spot. The squirrel enjoyed the outing as much as the _Général._

Pointing over his head to the palisade surrounding the citadel, Champlain boasted, "Now we have a strong fort, equipped with cannon, munitions and soldiers—enough to do the job." Pointing down and to his left, at the upper town, he told his four-legged friend, "And down there the townspeople are planning to celebrate—do you know what?"

The squirrel merely cocked his head in a questioning posture. "The ice is leaving. Each year we celebrate the breaking of the ice, because we know it means springtime is on its way and we have again won our annual struggle with the forces of nature." As the animal finished the nut, Champlain placed another on the rock while pointing straight down and across the river to Beauport. "And there is the ultimate lifeblood and future of our society—*les habitants!* Those families and their children along with others who are soon to arrive..." he looked around before adding quietly, "They, and *not* the Jesuits—*nor* the Company of 100 Associates, will make this a great colony, perhaps someday a great country..." He looked again before he continued, "They will someday be as powerful as the church—maybe more so." He crossed himself quickly, just in case. Standing, he offered another acorn, "This is the last, *Mon Petit*, and I fear I must go. The revelers will expect a speech."

As he wandered into the upper town, the parishioners were just exiting the church where Fathers Lalemant and LeJeune had just celebrated a short mass for the occasion. Born a Huguenot in Brouage, south of La Rochelle, the converted Champlain did not mind missing the occasional service and knew neither of the two Jesuits would dare call him out on it. The citizens were filling the square, Étienne Forton's men were bringing out tables and the local musicians had begun to play. The timing of the impromptu event was determined more by movement of the ice than by dates or temperature, and winter had not entirely loosened its grip. Yet the sun was out and the temperature tolerable although snow banks remained on the periphery of the square. The citizenry did call for a speech and the *Général* stood on his favorite bench.

"Again the people of *Québec* have shown they are stronger than even the great northern winter as we look forward to better weather—along with the arrival of more ships with more goods and more fellow citizens. *Vive la Canada!*" As he stepped down with care, people cheered, though it was clear their leader's strength was failing.

If the French-Canadians were experts at anything, it was having a good time, and while the musicians played, the people danced and as Étienne Forton served, they ate and drank. When the sun approached the horizon, however, they headed back to the relative warmth of their homes in either the upper town or Beauport, realizing they were approaching their first real growing season.

Beauport: April 1635

Springtime arrived with a vengeance—the vengeance of births as the livestock began to produce offspring. Although this was anticipated and valuable, the *habitants* of Beauport had failed to fully appreciate their collective lack of experience. Fortunately, the three laborers sent from the work crews to help farm were capable, but they were soon overwhelmed. Noël and Jean Guyon went to apply to *Monsieur* Giffard for additional staff, returning with three more workers who were thrilled to leave the heavy labor to an activity they enjoyed—farming.

The Beauport *habitants* pooled their building skills to provide three small cabins for the six tenant farm hands, while these farmers went to work on agriculture and animal husbandry. By the end of the month, the collective animals had produced three new cows, one bull, two hogs, four sow, six sheep and two new goats. This, of course, also produced a good deal more work.

Along with caring for the animals, they had also hoped to extend their planted fields—as well as collect fieldstone for Gaspard's planned home improvements. To this end, they had taken delivery from Noël Morin, a cart and a plow to be pulled by their draft animals. Their most experienced hand, Jean Barry, son of a Normand farmer, explained this was not so simple.

"Cattle can pull carts and plows, but this skill does not come naturally. They must be trained."

"Well," declared Gaspard, "We must train them."

Barry scratched his chin, "It's a bit more complicated." Drawing in the dirt with a stick, he told them, "The best is an ox."

Noël decided it was no time to hide ignorance. "What's an ox?"

Jean Barry smiled, "The closest we can get to an ox is a castrated bull."

Marin Boucher said, "But if we castrate the bull…"

Barry finished for him, "You get no more cattle. At least not until your young bull is a few years older. You can use a goat, but the goat is not nearly as strong. The cow takes a while to train and you lose some of her ability to provide milk and new calves."

As Jean Barry had suggested, training the cow to pull was time consuming, but eventually they prevailed and the furrows began to appear in the pasture where Barry began due to the relative absence of stumps. Stones, on the other hand, were not absent. The men regularly filled the cart and delivered the stones to one of the homes. Once plowed, they began to plant, waiting until all frost was gone before beginning the crop that was foreign to all—*Maize*. Jacques-

Henri explained, "*Maize* is the mother of all our crops, but sensitive to cold."

Two days hence, Jacques-Henri announced the birth of puppies. Ultimately, three of the Indian dogs produced litters, and he distributed them among the five families with a few left over for the workers.

CHAPTER 24

<u>Beauport: May 1635</u>

In addition to farming and building, good weather brought the return of shipping. "Tell me again about your voyage," Françoise asked as she helped Noël with his buttons.

"It is upstream, to this place called *Trois-Rivières,*" he explained.

"Are there really three rivers?"

"No," he answered, "Only one, *Rivière-Saint-Maurice.* As it enters the *Saint-Laurent* from the north, it has three channels—hence the name."

"And why are you going?" she asked.

"Last year, the *Général* sent this man, LaViolette, to found an outpost. I'm bringing him supplies as well as Father LeJeune."

"Why is *he* going?"

"I suspect to start a mission. I hear there are many natives there."

"Well, I hope he stays," she said with authority, "I like Father Lalemant much better."

"I don't know about that," he told her, adding, "Pierre Boucher has asked to go and LeJeune said he could."

"Don't leave him," she ordered, "I worry about LeJeune with boys. I don't see why priests can't get married like everyone else."

He laughed. "Spoken like a woman who did not grow up in the church."

"Well... When will *you* return?"

"I'm not certain. It should not be long—maybe a week." Patting her enlarging abdomen, he added, "I'll certainly be back before the baby."

A whining from the floor caused Françoise to stoop picking up the new female puppy. "At least I'll have Tutu to keep me company."

He took his bag and they exited to find young Pierre waiting on the porch. He jumped to attention and saluted, "Ready to sail, *Mon Capitane!*"

The threesome walked to the canoes and Françoise paddled them to the city. "Are we taking the barque?" Pierre asked.

"No, just the large shallop."

Depositing her men at the docks, Françoise and Tutu returned to Beauport to inspect the farming. Behind her cabin sat an enlarging pile of fieldstone for her proposed Normand-style home. Beyond the Indian camp, she scarcely noticed the charred remains of Drouin and Bélanger's abode as it disappeared into the foliage. Next, she came to the area cleared to provide lumber for building, now occupied by grazing livestock unhampered by the

197

ubiquitous stumps. The stump-free pasture was next, already plowed and planted with crops, where Jacques-Henri was helping to sow maize. Just before the pasture set a new small cabin to shelter their new farm hands. Her property housed the talented Jean Barry and another Normand from Rouen, Jean Ameline called *Rouget*, which served as name enough for him.

Sitting to rest on a fallen log with Tutu in her lap, she marveled at the enterprise. She had been particularly amazed when Noël told her he was the *sous-seigneur*, and although Giffard controlled the land, Noël's parcel would someday reap rewards possibly making Françoise and her husband well-to-do land barons. Today, however, they were still dirt-poor farmers. As the sun reached high in the sky, she returned to her cabin with her new companion right behind her.

After a bowl of leftover breakfast porridge, she and Tutu went to tend the kitchen garden next to the cabin. Once finished, she returned to the house where sitting on the porch, she threw a stick for the puppy to retrieve. Françoise had never had a childhood, let alone a pet, and she was enjoying the new dog immensely. Once Tutu tired of the game, they went inside. Opening the shutters overlooking the porch to let in some air, she told her new pet, "I'm going to lie down, *Petite*. Growing a baby is tiring—try not to bark."

Puppies are not necessarily obedient and soon Françoise was awakened. Tutu was barking at the window. Looking up, Françoise saw the face—the awful face, with an eyepatch and dirty red hair under an equally filthy *voyageur's* hat. She screamed and the face disappeared. Leaping up to close the window, she saw Félicity-Angel on the porch. Slowly she opened the door to find her friend alone. "Was there a man here?"

Félicity-Angel looked about, "I didn't see one. I was coming to visit and heard the scream, but saw no man."

Sighing, Françoise said, "Please come in. I think this pregnancy is making me crazy." The women shared black-root tea and discussed the farm. Françoise told her friend about the visions of the disappearing man.

"I think our minds are cluttered when we are with child," the Indian told her. "I saw things when I carried Jacques-François." She did not mention her own current pregnancy, but invited Françoise to dine at the camp, which she accepted gladly.

Sitting around the small fire, eating Indian-fashion with her fingers, she told Jacques-Henri about the face. He gave his typical shrug, "*Voyageurs* are around this time of year, but many will be leaving soon. We may not see them until their return in late autumn or sometimes the next spring. They are odd but generally harmless. I have rarely heard of one interfering with *les habitants* without a good reason."

After dinner, Françoise returned to the house. In spite of Jacques-Henri's reassurance and the warm night, she locked all the shutters, pulled the table in front of the door and allowed Tutu to join her in bed.

Fleuve Saint-Laurent: two days later

Pelting spring rain and high west winds tested Noël's skills as he approached his destination. Due to poor visibility, he was only a few hundred meters away when he first saw the three mouths of the *Rivière-Saint-Maurice* entering the waterway. Noël told himself he would have found it alone but was relieved by the presence of *Monsieur* Bergeron who had been to the outpost before. Father LeJeune remained dry below decks, but young Pierre Boucher had donned his foul weather gear and was standing fearlessly beside Captain Langlois. As the two-mast shallop neared the dock, Noël chose prudence and had Bergeron lower the sails. His two other crewmembers then took the long oars and brought the boat in nicely in spite of the foul weather.

Bergeron threw a line to the dockhand and the men stowed the sails, while the craft was being secured. Stepping ashore, Noël headed to the small harbormaster's hut. This structure had existed for several years, but construction of the small fort and palisade, which Noël could scarcely see on the rise due to the poor visibility, had only commenced with the arrival of LaViolette less than a year before. The grizzled harbormaster validated Noël's papers, reporting, "I'm surprised you made it, Captain—rugged weather for May. But my Indian says tomorrow will be better. I don't know how them rascals tell—but they're right most of the time." Returning Noël's papers, he continued. "Commander LaViolette is up at the fort—he's waitin' fer you. If it's okay by you, I'll get some men to start unloadin' the goods."

Noël agreed and headed back into the rain and up toward the fort. Pierre was waiting outside the door and accompanied Noël to the palisades still under construction. Always filled with curiosity, he asked Noël, "How long has this been an outpost?"

"I was told," Noël began, "it is quite old, at least as old as *Québec* itself."

"How can that be?" the boy queried.

200

"As far as I know, this has been a stopping place since the very earliest days of the fur trade." Pointing up the *Rivière-Saint-Maurice*, Noël explained. "You see, most of the furs from the north country come down that river."

In spite of the foul weather, they had a reasonable view from the entry to the fort, revealing the three small islands formed by the three mouths of the river. No guard stood at the gate and they simply made their way up to a door labeled, *Headquarters*. Entering the small office, they discovered its solitary occupant, a distinguished gentleman in officer's dress. *"Bonjour Capitan,"* he greeted them, standing and offering his hand, "I am Commandant LaViolette. You must be Captain Langlois."

Noël affirmed the question adding, "And this is Pierre Boucher, a member of my crew." Pierre, not yet fourteen, looked older—and acted much older. He glowed as the commandant offered his hand.

"Captain Martin speaks highly of you, sir," LaViolette told Noël, who answered with a smile, "Captain Martin is married to my sister, sir."

LaViolette laughed, looking out the door, "I see my men are unloading. Hopefully we shall have the fortification sound by the snow." Returning to his desk, he said, "I was told you were bringing a Jesuit."

"Yes, Father Paul LeJeune. He is on the boat, unless he has left to visit the Algonquin village."

"Our native population is returning," the Commandant told him, "mostly from the Abenaki Tribe. A few years ago, the Iroquois ran them out. Those demons come down the Iroquois River that flows from the Five-Nations area. Once we began to re-establish the fort, they went home, so the Algonquin tribes are now returning. They welcome the Black Robes—that is what they call the Jesuits. I only hope

201

the missionaries do not cause any trouble. Sometimes the Jesuits try too hard to change the native culture. In addition, I'm told that a few years ago they brought the plague with them."

Making their way back to the dock, Noël and Pierre found LeJeune. "I am off to the Algonquin Village," he announced before adding, "Would you like to come with me, Pierre?"

"Oh yes, Father!"

Noël looked pensive, but the boy told him, "My ma said I could."

Noël knew this would not sell well with *his* wife, but agreed. LeJeune reassured him, "I'll make certain he is back here when the next shallop comes in a few weeks." Noël watched them walk off before heading back to the dock. At least the weather was improving—as the harbormaster's Indian had predicted.

He reached the dock just in time to see a group of large *voyageur* canoes heading up the *Rivière-Saint-Maurice*. The harbormaster was watching intently. "There goes trouble if you've ever seen it," he told Noël.

"Isn't it just a team of *voyageurs?*" Noël questioned.

"Them ain't *voyageurs*," he said in disgust, "They's *coureurs-de-bois*—outlaws!"

"Why doesn't someone stop them?" Noël queried.

"Everyone's afraid to. First of all, they gotta be caught. Right now, they's just goin' fer a ride. You gotta catch 'em with furs or tryin' to trade. Anyone that tries with that crowd is never seen again, unless it's layin' in a ravine or floating home to *Québec*—face down." Pointing to the lead canoe, "See that ugly mother?"

"With the dirty red hair and the eye-patch?"

"That's him. Calls himself Half-face. Meaner than a snake. No one trucks with him. They says he got half his face burnt off fighting with a Mohawk—and he *still* killed the Mohawk."

Noël watched them travel upstream at an impressive rate until they were out of sight, and returned to his shallop.

CHAPTER 25

T olling as mightily as it could, the small church bell signaled the end of mass as the citizens of *Québec* exited into a perfect sunny day with a mere whiff of westerly breeze barely disturbing the ubiquitous maple trees. Étienne Forton stood at the ready with tables from his upper town inn, and some of the ladies had brought baskets from home to contribute to the traditional post mass community *repas*. Nearing the end of her pregnancy, Françoise waddled her way to a table with Nicole.

"It seems everyone is here today," Nicole noted. "It's what I love about this time of year." The five Beauport and the seven upper town families attended, along with a few military officers, some tradesmen such as Drouin, Bélanger and Morin, as well as the interpreters, Tardif and Nicolet.

The day laborers and enlisted soldiers tended to gather in the lower town.

"I also love the long days," Nicole remarked, "just like we had in Perche."

"Noël says it is because we are at the same latitude—whatever that means," Françoise replied.

"Then why is it so much colder here in winter?" her friend questioned.

"I asked Noël about that, too," Françoise answered. "He said something about sea currents—I don't know why a sea current would matter. Neither place is near the sea."

Nicole laughed, patting her friend's enlarging abdomen. "But you have more important things to concern yourself with. How long is it now?"

"Mathurine say she thinks less than one month. I'll be glad to have it over with."

Nicole nodded, "This will be the second birth since we arrived. The *Général* says we need many more offspring to grow the colony."

"Well, I am doing my part—and so have you," Françoise said laughing. Looking about at the energy mass of children in the square, she added, "We seem to have brought a lot of children with us."

"Yes," Nicole responded, "but the problem is that almost all the women are in this square as we speak, and there are many eligible men about—soldiers, laborers and single tradesmen. I wonder how they will ever find wives." Leaning in, she whispered, "Gaspard said some of the men have made enquiries about the older girls," beginning to count on her fingers, "Marie Guyon and Marguerite Martin are oldest and only 11. Louise Couillard and Françoise Pinguet are 10, and Anne Cloutier and Marguerite Couillard 9. Hélène Desportes was only 14 when she married, still three years older than our oldest girls, and 14 would still be very young for a bride in France."

Étienne's helper brought the ladies two glasses of cider. As Françoise sipped hers, she related, "Félicity-Angel is pregnant and due soon after me, but we don't count the Indian children as colonists. Jacques-Henri insists I attend her birthing. When she had Jacques-François, I was there but did nothing. He still credits me, however."

"You were the one to finally deliver Remie Giffard," her friend reminded her.

Françoise laughed, "Yes, by falling on her and almost killing her, the baby and myself."

Nicole touched her glass to Françoise's, "It worked, did it not? *Santé*."

While the tables were cleared, the musicians began to play, and the pioneers of this city in the wilderness danced, drank, visited and relaxed on their day of rest. Eventually the sun neared the horizon, and saying goodnight, they left for their homes. In spite of her condition, Françoise continued to paddle the canoe. Once inside the cabin, Françoise climbed into bed saying, "Make love to me tonight."

Noël turned in suspicion, "But how...?"

She merely smiled. "Come, I'll show you. Both Nicole and Félicity-Angel gave me advice. I think we'll try Félicity-Angel's first." Noël awakened as the first rays of light hit the window. To his surprise, his pregnant wife was already making breakfast. He arose with a new respect for her and her Indian friend.

Beauport: July 18, 1635, 5:00 AM

"I think it's time."

206

Noël rolled over and replied to his wife, "No it's not. The sun isn't even up."

"No," she replied, "It's *time*."

Suddenly opening his eyes, he jumped out of bed. "What do I do?" he shouted beginning to pace.

Propping herself up in bed, she directed, "Get dressed and help me up." Noël jumped into his clothes with a speed not seen since he encountered the bear. As he pulled her to standing, she said, "Oh..." Looking down, a flood of light pink fluid splashed off the floor. "I think you had better go get Nicole. On your way back, tell Félicity-Angel. She wanted to be here and probably knows more than anyone."

Her husband bolted out into the gray summer morning, heading toward the Boucher cabin. Soon he returned with the two women. "What do I do now?" he asked.

Nicole took him by the arm and walked him to the door. "Why don't you go help Gaspard?"

"What does he need help with?"

Pushing him gently out the door, she answered, "He'll find something."

Standing on the porch, he saw Jacques-Henri approaching. "I stay and guard house," he said with a degree of authority. As Noël started toward Gaspard's, the Indian sat cross-legged in front of the door, motioning to Noël, "Go."

In the house, the women had positioned Françoise in bed. Nicole felt her abdomen. "You have dropped and the position is good. Hopefully this won't take long."

Félicity-Angel took over and rubbed a brown salve on her perineum. "Easy out," she explained.

Soon Françoise had contractions, then pains followed by bad pains, but she only cried out twice. Félicity-Angel soon said, "Head coming," and deftly put her small-calloused hand under the child's chin, guiding it out. She rotated it slightly until the shoulder appeared, then the next shoulder, and suddenly the screaming infant was free but for its umbilical cord. Nicole was shocked to see no sign of tearing. The Indian handed the child to its mother. "Nice big son," she announced. "Give him breast, he ready." The two ladies delivered the after-birth, dealt with the cord, and cleaned up the area.

Nicole opened the door for air and almost fell over the seated Jacques-Henri who looked up questioningly. "It's a boy," she told him. "You may go see."

Entering, he came to the bedside to see the newborn aggressively sucking. "Good eater, he will be strong. What is his name?"

Françoise had given little thought to this, yet she suddenly opened her mouth, stating something she had never vaguely considered, "Robert—it was my father's name." Once things were under control, Nicole left to tell the neighbors and return with Noël who looked much worse for wear than his wife. She also spread the news she had discovered the community's official mid-wife.

Québec: July 20, 1635

Françoise was beginning to get around but was not bothered with chores as her friends all pitched in to help with Beauport's second Canadian-born Frenchman. Noël had spent yesterday recovering from his shock with work in the kitchen garden. Today he was returning to the neighborhood chore of house building. The new stone structures were already habitable at the homes of Jean

Guyon and Zacharie Cloutier with work finishing at Gaspard Boucher's.

As Noël stepped onto his porch, he was greeted by a young man from the harbor. "Captain Langlois," the lad said, "I have been sent to fetch you to the harbor. A ship from France has arrived but became mired outside of Île d'Orléans. You are required to go free it." Noel returned for his captain's gear, explaining the situation to the ladies who became very excited. This would be the first ship of this season. Anticipation was high as to what and whom it would bring.

Monsieur Bergeron greeted him at the harbor with the large shallop ready to sail. The far end of Île d'Orléans was just twenty miles from the city. The downstream current would help, but they were hindered by a northeast wind, requiring continuous tacking of the shallop. Once they were away, Bergeron explained. "They have their own river pilot, but unfortunately he came too close and went aground."

It took over four hours to reach their destination. As Noël checked the situation, he observed, "The pilot came too near the downstream end of the island and is aground on the sandbar—hopefully not too far aground." Climbing aboard by the ship's rope ladder, he met with the captain. "We will try to pull you free," he explained, "but it depends on how hard aground you are." Returning to the shallop, he put in all six large oars and picked the six strongest men from his crew and the ship's crew to row. Unfortunately, the ship would not budge.

"We will have to unload the passengers," he informed them. Since the ship was very close to the island, disembarking was easy. With crew and passengers, there were about eighty people, among them the sailors, several

209

soldiers, a few Jesuits and about fifty civilians, mainly laborers. As they disembarked, Noël saw a familiar face—a friend from Perche he had not seen for several years. "Côté! Jean Côté!" he called. After exchanging greetings, Noël needed to return to work, and the passengers celebrated on the solid ground of the island with the assurance their destination was a short distance away.

Even with the passengers ashore, the boat would still not move. Fortunately, the wind shifted suddenly to a brisk southwest breeze. Noël raised the sails of the shallop and along with the oarsmen, they broke the ship free to the wild cheers of all. As the passengers boarded, their smiles showed they realized their two-month ordeal was ending. Bergeron told Noël, "My pappy used to say 'sometimes it's just as good to be lucky as smart'." Noël, however, was happy to accept the congratulations from the ship's captain for his skill. Once all were back onboard, he saw that night was falling. "I am afraid we must wait until morning," he explained to the ship's captain.

At first light, he weighed anchor and began the journey to the city, slowed by the continuation of the southwest wind that had freed them yesterday. Approaching the harbor, they were greeted by an excited citizenry of *Québec*.

Once his paperwork and other duties were completed, Noël rowed back to Beauport and his wife and family. Along the way, he realized that although the ship had brought more citizens and workers, it had brought just one family and only one single woman, further increasing the gender imbalance of the colony.

CHAPTER 26

September 1, 1635:

Beauport had become a hive of activity. *Monsieur* Giffard had given new land grants, called *sous-concessions*, to Robert Drouin, François Bélanger, and Noël's old friend, the newly arrived Jean Côté, designating three sizeable strips to the east of the current five *sous-concessions*. The artisans of Beauport were back once again to land clearing and house building. All five of the original residents now enjoyed solid fieldstone houses and were attempting to construct three more for their new neighbors before the big snow. In addition, Giffard had allowed each of the now eight *sous-concessions* to take on more tenant farmers from the nearly 300 new colonists.

Dividends would now be paid to the *sous-concession* owners, the *sous-seigneur* like Noël, who took a share of Giffard's rents. Only two of the new *sous-seigneur* would live the bachelor's life. Just as Noël had come with Françoise, Jean Côté had come with the ship's solitary single woman, Anne Martin, not related to Abraham Martin or Noël's sister, but a woman from Côté's home area. The two had decided to come to the new world, planning to marry in the autumn. Bélanger and Drouin, however, remained desperately in the wife market.

Other additions to the colony were two notable immigrants now housed in the upper town. Pierre Delaunay was a member of the 100 Associates and single. Phillipe Amiot was from Picardy, northeast of Paris, and brought his wife and two children—both boys. Now, at the end of the shipping season, and after six ships and 300 new colonists, the colony had only added one unmarried woman, Anne Martin—already spoken for.

When the day's work was over, Noël returned to his new stone palace—at least Françoise thought it was—where she sat comfortably on a porch rocker nursing their new son. Sitting on the second rocker in a very un-Indian position, Félicity-Angel nursed her new addition, Henri-Makya, born three weeks after Robert Langlois. Father Lalemant had originally balked at the name at baptism but gave in to the persistence of Jacques-Henri, who insisted his son have one *proud Algonquin name.* He did not share with the priest its meaning, *eagle hunter.* Since Henri-Makya's birth, the two mothers were inseparable, dreaming of the day their sons would play, hunt, and fish together in this wild place.

Noël sat on the edge of the porch, soon joined by Jacques-Henri and seven-year-old Jacques-François. When Noël asked how the wives' day was, Françoise responded, "We walked down to the pasture. It is certainly expanding with your new workers."

"What did you do with the babies?" he asked.

212

"Carried them *papoose*," she said, referring to the Indian carrier.

"Aren't they heavy?"

"Not in the *papoose*. We plan to start working the gardens with them next week."

Trying to digest this news, he asked, "And how were things at the pasture?"

"Well…" she replied, "We thought the men were not getting along. They seemed to fight and argue about everything—even the silliest things."

"Now that you mention it," Noël observed, "The workers on our building sites seem to be out of sorts. It seems odd. Everything is going well, the weather is good and things are certainly better than they were when we arrived just one year ago."

Jacques-Henri said simply, "Women."

"But," Noël countered, "there are no women."

"No women—*is* problem." The group was silent until Jacques-Henri continued, "Man with no woman unhappy—unhappy at home *and* at work."

"That's fine," Noël countered, "but how do we solve it? There are no women."

"Find woman."

"But where?"

Jacques-Henri rose and pointed west, "Algonquin village."

Noël remained silent while his friend continued. "Some years ago, Iroquois make big raid and war on Algonquin. Many braves killed. Now village has many lonesome women." With a smile he added, "These women act just like your men."

"But, what about…?"

Jacques-Henri anticipated the question. "Indian women are not like French. May go with man or not. If not happy, just leave."

Françoise got the picture, but asked, "You mean not get married?"

Jacques-Henri shrugged, "Indian woman does what she wants. Maybe get married, maybe not. To the west, many Indian women marry the *voyageur*. Jesuits marry them if baptized. Maybe have child, maybe not. Maybe stay together, maybe not."

Françoise related, "When I was with the Algonquin village, there were some women married to the *voyageurs*. Sometimes they had children—they called them *Métis*. A few people in *Québec* today are from such marriages. Maybe it is an idea. How would we… invite them?"

Jacques-Henri sat back down and said, "Just ask."

While the *sous-concession* holders and workers of Beauport attacked the harvest, the five women of the community met to discuss the prospect of mingling between the male colonists and the female natives. "I have spoken with Father Lalemant," Nicole began. "He understands the problem and agrees—within rules according to church doctrine, of course. First, no sexual activity outside of marriage, and secondly, marriage only between couples both baptized within the church. He also says they must get married at the Algonquin village chapel. He will not, however, object to socialization between single adults."

"Does that include the women not in the church?" Mathurine Guyon asked.

Nicole smiled, "He did not forbid it. I thought it best not to dwell on the issue."

The ladies laughed and the meeting took on a social level with giggling at all the possible ways this could go. Actually, Lalemant, although a stanch steward of the church, was nonetheless a realist, a realist who had spent some years in the colony among the sexually deprived immigrants and the equally deprived native women in the village. He could see the possible good effects of this plan for the natives, Frenchmen and the church.

The women decided to proceed cautiously, beginning with the single men in Beauport. The original ten workers, now called *habitants*, because they had their own small portions of a *sous-concession* called *habitations*, not to be confused with Champlain's home and office spelled with a capital H. The newer workers, called *engager*, were each assigned to work on one of the five original families' larger *sous-concessions*. The women had planned to delay the scheme until the end of the active harvest, but Jacques-Henri disagreed. "The sooner you control needs, the better their work."

Noël and Gaspard met with the *habitants* and *engager* who were in favor of the plan—with a bit of uncertainty. Jacques-Henri began by taking a few men to the camp during their time off. Soon the native women were coming to Jacques-Henri's camp to visit. Jacques-Henri explained with satisfaction, "For years Algonquin women married *voyageurs* who passed through villages, but now we have men and women coming in *each* direction—works better."

The first worker to take the plunge was *Rouget*, who now lived on one of the two *habitations* on Noël's land. He married one of Félicity-Angel's cousins, a *Métis* woman, Marie-Bernadette. Not only did she come to care for his house and his needs but accompanied him to the fields each day as one of the strongest and most efficient workers. Françoise could see that the plan was going to work better than expected.

By the end of the harvest, a few workers were married and many others had an *arrangement*. The attitudes of both the Frenchmen and Algonquin women had improved greatly. Noël and Gaspard reported these changes to *Monsieur* Giffard who suggested they meet with Champlain.

The *Général* met them cordially. "I have always supported marriage with the natives," he told them, "In the early days we had many unions. Unfortunately, more often than not, the Frenchmen disappeared into the forest with their native women—rarely seen again. Their offspring were generally raised as natives." The old man rose slowly from his seat with the help of his cane and walked cautiously to look out a window. "Hopefully now, we can use this to produce new *habitants,* particularly *habitante* women. *Monsieur* Giffard, I want you to spread this idea to the other *concession* holders as well as to the men who work in the city or the fort."

As they left the *Habitation* office, Noël said, "The *Général* seems to be showing his years,"

"Yes," Giffard agreed. "He hardly uses his left side at all. It is sad—he was such a giant in his day."

Québec: November 17, 1635

Its construction finally completed, *Notre Dame de la Recouvrance* was large enough to hold most of the city and today nearly filled for the wedding. Jean Côté and Anne Martin had made many friends since their recent arrival, and several workers attended with their new or future Indian wives and some with their native concubines. Father Lalemant, always more liberal than LeJeune, added a welcome to the new couples along with his usual festive wedding mass.

As winter approached, there had been a few two-inch snowfalls. Today began sunny but turned ominous during the ceremony, and the *Québécois* exited into an early blizzard. Outdoor celebrating being out of the question, they squeezed into Étienne Forton's two facilities for a toast or two before heading home.

When the Langlois family finally reached home through the blizzard, Françoise removed young Robert from his papoose and began stoking the fire in preparation for dinner. Once they had dined and put the baby to bed, the two sat facing the fire on their porch rockers, which moved inside in winter. Françoise poured two cups of hot water, adding calvados. Handing one to her husband she said, "With all the new men in Beauport and all the different jobs, I'm confused about who is who and what does it mean."

Noël sipped his drink. "Sit down and I'll try to explain—it is a little complicated. The King owns all of *Québec*. He has hired the Company of 100 Associates to govern it. They collect rents and pay some to the King.

They keep the rest. They have divided the coast north of the city into large areas like Beauport. They call each a *concession*, but think of it as a city in France. The Beauport riverfront is about one hundred-eighty *arpents* (six miles) long and extends at least that far back into the wilderness. The Company has given it to Giffard to handle. He is the *seigneur* who collects rents and pays the Company some of it. In turn, he has given large parcels to us, the original settlers. Once we were here, they decided to make us *sous-seigneur* and our land parcels are *sous-concessions*. Think of them as *areas* of a city. As the land is farmed, we pay rent to Giffard and keep the rest."

He rose for another drink and continued, "When *Rouget* and Barry arrived, they were sent to be our tenants. Now that they are successful, we have given them parcels of our Langlois *sous-concession* to farm. They pay us rent. Their properties are called *habitations,* think of them as farms in France. *Rouget* and Barry are called *habitants*.

Françoise interrupted, "But isn't a *habitant*..."

"Yes," he continued, "*habitant* also means a farmer and *habitation* also means a place to live, like the *General's* house and office is called the *Habitation*. It is confusing, but these are the terms they use. Lastly are the workers, like our new men, who are called *engager*. They are tenants on our land who have agreed to work for three years, after which they can return to France or try to buy their own *habitation*. Actually, everyone who came, beginning with us, signed such a contract, but we were more fortunate as we were first. This may make us a great deal of money— for us and our children."

She stood and took his hand, "I guess I understand, but you are correct, it is confusing."

Winter descended with its usual fury, but the colonists were prepared. Making and maintaining paths, hunting and ice fishing became routine as the pioneers improved their skills. All eight Beauport *sous-concessions* now boasted a fieldstone house, and all the *habitants* and *engager* were housed in cabins. Many of the *habitants* had an Indian woman, and *Rouget* and Barry had each married *Métis* women at the Algonquin Village Chapel. Attitudes in both the French and native camps had improved.

There were many more hunting parties, but due to the endless nature of the wild in all directions, five hunting parties could embark at the same time from the same place for a week and never hear or see each other. Braving the elements, most people tried to get to mass in the city each Sunday. Only one dark cloud hovered over the community—Champlain had fallen ill in late autumn and remained bed ridden, unable to move one side. In spite of the prayers of both the French and native populations, his prognosis remained grave.

Christmas day began blessed by one of the first clear days of the winter. The typical joyous atmosphere of the season soon ended, however, by the words of Father Lalemant, "This morning *Général* Samuel Champlain has gone to find his heavenly reward." All joy of the season disappeared as *Québec* sank into mourning. The great man—the Father of all Canada and all Canadians, was dead. The church remained silent with the exception of the tiny bell, and the congregation passed at the end into the snow-covered square. The people of Canada knew they could and must continue the work and the dream of the great man.

❖

"The snow has subsided," Françoise told her husband, "I'm going to take a short walk. Robert is asleep." Putting on her warm deerskin boots, coat and hat, she opened the door to a one-foot drift on the previously swept porch. Trudging along with Tutu marching behind in her footsteps, she felt the first sunshine she had seen in days and continued on the path to the vegetable garden and eventually the barn. A light snow hung on the trees and the newfound sunlight sparkled on its way to earth. Two red cardinals in a maple tree called to her with their haunting staccato call.

Reaching down, she patted her dog's head, now a simple task since she had grown into a mighty sled dog like her parents. Coming to the end of the garden, she heard a rustle in the thicket. Tutu barked and a large buck appeared, bounding off toward the pasture. The dog began to follow but stopped with a gentle command from her mistress. Approaching their new barn, Françoise gazed though the perfect setting along the path in the woods. It took a moment before she saw him.

Fifty feet down the path, he stood motionless, in the same *voyageur* garb, filthy hat, ratty red hair and eye patch. He, too, had a dog much like Tutu but more wolf. Both dogs made moves but stopped with soft words from their masters. Françoise stood immobile, not knowing what to do. Had it not been for his dog, she would have stood her ground or turned back to the house, but now she could see how any move could bode badly.

Both stood motionless for at least three minutes when a gust of wind brought a cloud of snow from the trees. When it cleared, he was gone without a sign. Considering her options, she moved ahead and when close to his position, realized the blown snow had covered any sign of footprints. In fact, it was difficult to say if there had ever been any. Looking around carefully, she saw nothing, turned, and hurried back to the house—again uncertain if this was real or imagination.

CHAPTER 27

Québec: June 11, 1636

C areful, sir, it would be a shame to arrive just to tell them you have drowned."

Charles stood, pulling himself back inside the rail of the ship. "Have no fear, *Monsieur* Delisle. I assure you I can swim. Why only two years ago I swam across the Seine and back, just above the Cathedral, with no difficulty. I was merely admiring the purity of the water here— certainly better than the Seine."

Delisle smiled, "I believe my chamber pot is often clearer than the Seine."

Charles gazed along the coast, "And regard this land— pure, unspoiled, filled with the most luscious trees on earth. I tell you when I first received the assignment, I thought I was being sent to Hell, but the more I see it, the more I see the opportunities—and the adventure." Walking over to the ship's wheel held by the river pilot, who had joined them a few days earlier, Charles called out, "You, pilot. What was your name?"

"Langlois, Excellency, Noël Langlois."

"Yes, how long have you been here?"

Trying not to take his eyes off his job, Noël replied, "Two years, sir. I came from Perche."

"Ah, I heard many of the first families were from there. What is your impression of this place, *Monsieur* Langlois?"

"Well, sir," Noël begin with caution. "It is a wild place and the winters are hard, but I have come to embrace it."

"I suppose it is even more rugged than a rural area such as Perche." Noël remained silent while Charles continued, "Are you married, sir?"

"Yes, sir."

"Children?"

"One, sir, a son born last year."

"Very good," Charles concluded. "And when should we arrive?"

Pointing to the upcoming fork in the river, Noël told him, "This is *Île d'Orléans*. It is about twenty miles in length, and the city is just beyond it. With the long days, and if the weather holds, we should be in the city well before sunset."

"Good," Charles stated before wandering back to the rail.

Charles Huault de Montmagny was named Governor of New France in January, months before France received word of Champlain's demise. Born in Paris 53 years earlier, Charles had descended from aristocracy and advisors to the King since Henri II. Trained by the Jesuits, he was an engaging personality and gifted administrator. *Québec* could have fared much worse.

"Excuse me, sir," said his secretary, "You said you wished to review some of these documents before landing. If we do it now, you will have time to return above deck when we near the city."

Montmagny looked longingly at the countryside, "Very well, *Monsieur* Piraube," he agreed while heading to his cabin.

The change in administration could not have been better timed had it been planned years in advance. Samuel Champlain had been an explorer and adventurer. He had traveled this land for many years, investigating all its advantages and peculiarities, finally hacking out a small foothold at the perfect location, *Cap Diamant*. Now, when the foothold was marginally secure, it was the ideal time for Charles de Montmagny, a skilled organizer who knew how to build and grow a colony—the perfect choice to establish Champlain's dream permanently.

Two hours later, Delisle entered the ship's office. "Excuse me, sir, the pilot says we will soon come into view of the city."

Charles jumped from his seat, "Come, I do not want to miss this."

Returning to the rail near the pilot, he said to Noël, "The waterway has become quite narrow."

"Yes, sir," Noël replied, "we are in the northern channel around the large *Île d'Orléans*. The river stays relatively narrow beyond here."

Looking ahead, Montmagny exclaimed, "My God! Is that a waterfall ahead?"

"Yes sir—Montmorency Falls."

Charles went closer to the rail, "If we have the skill and tools to do it, we could put a formidable mill here—it would put any mill in France to shame."

Eventually the city came into view. Montmagny swooned, "I see why the *Général* chose this place. What a formidable position!" Looking off to the north side of the *Saint-Laurent,* he questioned, "Are those houses across from the city?"

Noël replied, "Yes, sir. That is Beauport. I live there."

"How do you travel there from the city?"

Noël told him, "Usually by canoe."

"Yes, I've heard of those. Are they that effective?"

"Quite effective, sir—once you get the hang of it."

Montmagny looked on. "Those houses are stone. It looks like Normandie. I thought everything here was of logs."

"We have some masons from France, sir, and a good deal of fieldstone,"

As they approached the docks, they could see a sizeable gathering for the arrival. Once they landed, Guillaume Couillard, Abraham Martin, Giffard, as well as the Juchereau brothers and Father Lalemant greeted them. Once introduced, Charles told the Jesuit, "Let us go directly to the church to sing a *Te Deum* to give thanks for our safe voyage. From there I want to go directly to the fort."

Later upon leaving the church, the group began the climb to the fort where they met a color guard with Commander Brasdefer. "Welcome to Fort Saint-Louis, Excellency." Extending his hand with a ring of keys, "Here are the keys to the fort."

Accepting them, Montmagny merely nodded, before looking about him, saying, "I believe one of our first chores should be rebuilding this structure with stone. I hear you have masons and plenty of stone here." Pointing ahead and beginning to walk, "Come show me around and we shall share thoughts on improvement."

225

By 11 p.m., the sun was setting, Charles de Montmagny was home in his new quarters at the *Habitation* and Noël Langlois home with his wife and son. Québec had awakened this morning with uncertainty of its future and was now retiring filled with optimistic enthusiasm.

Beauport: June 24, 1636

With Robert in *papoose*, Françoise made her way home along the coast through the bright June sunshine. Her neighbor, Perrine Boucher had given birth to another Françoise only two days before, and this had been Françoise's first visit.

The Indian-*habitant* relations were working better and better. Only in the middle of winter did Françoise realize *most* of the eligible native women were *Métis*, meaning half-blood, usually the product of a *voyageur* and a native woman. This served to the colony's advantage in two ways. First, the *Métis* women were less valued by the tribe and therefore more available. In addition, they had *softer* features that appealed to the *habitants*. She would learn, however, to expect fewer children from these women as the Indian culture favored nursing well into early childhood, which prevented frequent pregnancies. As she tried to adjust her papoose to accommodate her own enlarging abdomen, she wondered if nursing longer was worth considering.

At any rate, the plan was working well. Attitudes improved and work became more productive. This came at a good time, when the colony needed the *sous-seigneur* artisans to work on the stone reconstruction of the fort, leaving all the farming work for the *habitants* and *engager*.

226

❧

Sunday, the citizens of Beauport loaded their canoes for the city and a special mass. After his death at Christmas, the colonists had buried Champlain in a makeshift winter grave. With the return of good weather, they had just moved his body to a proper tomb next to his beloved *Notre-Dame de la Recouvrance*. Father LeJeune returned to give the eulogy for his old friend after which there were no dry eyes among the parishioners leaving the church. Well into her last trimester, Françoise told Noël, "Perrine and I are going to *Monsieur* Forton's for a cider and a rest. You can go visit with the men."

Abraham Martin was already expressing an opinion when Noël arrived. "It was a grand sermon, but it still irritates the devil out of me that neither the King nor that maniac, Richelieu, sent any word of sympathy or gratitude." Pulling on his white beard, he added, "They even had his replacement chosen before hearing of his death."

"I agree, Abraham," replied Giffard, "but had they realized his worth, they would likely have stolen him back to Paris."

"At least they have sent a viable replacement," added Jean Guyon. "We are already beginning the foundation of the new fort. Governor Montmagny says that eventually he will send a team down here to turn the church into stone. We were lucky to control that small fire early this winter, we may not be so fortunate next time."

"Perhaps we could get some heretic to turn it to stone—like Lot's wife," Martin said with a hearty laugh.

227

"Think you have your scripture confused, Abraham," Noël pointed out. "I believe that was a pillar of salt."

"Well, whatever," chuckled the white-haired seaman. "Tell you what, lads, let's stroll down to the lower town to have a pint at the *Terre Sauvage*—like the old days."

Once seated at Étienne Forton's venerable old shed, Giffard continued, "I hear Governor Montmagny has already started the engineer, Bourdon, drawing a new plan for the city, with real streets and crossroads—like Paris."

"I sure as hell hope it smells better than Paris," Abraham Martin added. "When I was there in '29, it smelled worse than my backhouse in summer."

As Forton's bartender brought a tray of beer, Guyon pointed to a rough building across the way. "I hear those three Gagnon brothers, who came with their widowed mother from Tourouvre at the end of last season, have started a general store over there. My wife tells me they are doing a brisk business."

Gaspard broke his silence. "Now that we have more men with Indian and *Métis* women, we have more business."

"I still think we will need more than the Indians to really get going," announced Martin. "Look over there." Pointing to Montmagny's ship being loaded to return to France, he continued, "See all those young men? They are some of those laborers who came with Champlain in '33. Their three-year term is up, and I hear more than half of them are returning to France."

Noël looked across, "Is that right? *Monsieur* Giffard?"

"I am afraid so, Noël. I did not know that was common knowledge. The Indian women are helping, but if we cannot get more eligible French women, we are not going to expand as we should."

When Noël returned to the upper town and his wife, his young son was taking some cautious steps between the mothers. As he watched with the smile of a proud father, his wife whispered in his ear, "It is a good thing—I don't know if I could papoose two at once."

Beauport: September 3, 1636

Having taken a day off from carpentry in the city, Noël had spent it as *sous-seigneur,* inspecting the work on his *sous-concession.* Returning home, he found his pioneer wife hard at work over dinner with two-week-old Marie-Nicole in papoose and Robert playing on the floor with a ball fabricated by Jacques-Henri. No sooner had he kissed his wife and new daughter and begun to play ball with Robert, there was a knock at the door.

Opening to a soldier in uniform, he decided to step out. When he returned, Françoise asked, "Who was it?"

"A soldier from the fort," he responded. "He asked that I meet with the governor tomorrow morning."

"About what?"

"He didn't say, but I can hardly imagine why he wants to see me."

She smiled without interrupting her stirring over the fire. "Maybe he heard you are the smartest man in the colony—not to mention the most handsome."

"I doubt it. I suspect it is nothing, but we shall see," he told her, kissing her on the forehead at the same time as Robert's ball hit him squarely in the back of the head.

229

At first light, Noël canoed his way to the lower town dock and began to walk to Montmagny's office in Champlain's old *Habitation,* examining along the way the works in progress on streets, paths, and old buildings. Entering the *Habitation,* he was surprised to be whisked immediately to the governor's office. Montmagny stood immediately, asking Noël to be seated. The new leader of *Québec* was taller than Noël. He retained all his long gray hair, tied in back, and as he paced about the room, he was clearly in excellent physical shape.

"Thank you for coming, Captain Langlois. I have a project in mind and need assistance. It struck me that you may be just the man." The governor paused. When Noël did not respond, he continued. "I believe I would like a tour of the area before winter. I would like you to accompany me." Noël remained silent, as well as confused, while Montmagny went on. Looking at a map of the *Saint-Laurent* valley, he declared, "I would like to begin at this *Cap Tourmente,* and continue upstream—inland, to this *Île de Jésus.*"

Noël swallowed hard at the magnitude of this voyage. Trying not to stutter, he admitted, "Actually, sir, I have not been that far upstream myself."

"That is all right. What I am interested in is your skill and integrity. I do not want to travel with those who wish to tell me what I am seeing. I want to see it for myself and make my own decisions."

"Well, sir," Noël began, "would you like to take the large shallop?"

"Not at all. I want to go in one of these Indian craft—canoe, is it? It seems like the correct way to see the real country. Why don't you pick your crew and review it with me?"

Noël thought quickly, "Actually, sir, the natives are the best people to guide the canoes—and us as well. If you want to avoid people who will try to influence your decision, then I suggest Captain Abraham Martin, a few soldiers, a priest and an interpreter, perhaps *Monsieur Tardif*."

"Captain Martin will do," Montmagny agreed, "but the interpreter, I think, is too opinionated—and no priests."

"I know an Indian who is a skilled canoeist and good interpreter," Noël offered, "and I also know a young man who is better with a canoe and the Algonquin language than I. He would also be very discreet."

"Good and *two* soldiers should do. I would also like to take my secretary, Martial Piraube." Returning to his desk, he turned to Noël. "Put it together and we shall depart in three days—at dawn."

Noël stood, trying to keep his jaw closed while the governor added, "That will be all, Captain."

Noël headed to the dock where he found Abraham Martin. When he arrived home, he went to see Jacques-Henri and then, young Pierre Boucher.

Cap Tourmente to Ile De Jesus (Montreal)

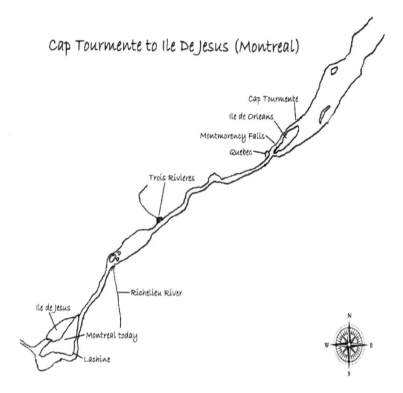

Cap Tourmente

Ile de Orleans

Montmorency Falls

Quebec

Trois Rivieres

Richelieu River

Ile de Jesus

Montreal today

Lachine

N
W   E
S

CHAPTER 28

<u>*Québec*</u>: September 7, 1636

Well before dawn, Noël, Jacques-Henri and Pierre Boucher had three canoes at the lower town dock where two soldiers and five native paddlers joined them. Soon they saw Montmagny and his secretary approaching with the unmistakable white-headed Abraham Martin bringing up the rear. Noël was pleased Montmagny and his secretary had taken his advice and wore leather clothing. Though not fashionable, he knew they would soon appreciate it.

Surveying the meager luggage in the canoes, Montmagny questioned, "Do we have adequate provisions?"

"Well, sir," Noël replied, "we have equipment for camping and some basic rations. The natives prefer to forage for food along the way to minimize weight."

"Then that's how we will do it!" the governor exclaimed. "I want to see the local ways."

Jacques-Henri introduced the five paddlers, two of whom had native names, before explaining to the governor, "We will have the end positions on each canoe. Noël, *Monsieur* Martin, and Pierre will be center paddlers while the soldiers and officials may sit where they please."

Noël was relieved when the two officials managed to board without capsizing, and they headed downstream into the northern channel around *Île d'Orléans*. Soon they came to an area of high granite cliffs where they found the breathtaking Montmorency Falls, descending from what seemed forever, crashing violently to the earth as they entered *Fleuve Saint-Laurent*.

"We must stop here," Montmagny ordered. Once the Indians had beached the crafts, the governor stood, looking up at the magnificent force of nature. "Let us climb to the top," he suggested.

Noël frowned, "It is quite a long hike, sir."

Undaunted, Montmagny declared, "Well, we shall have a go," and the entourage began the trek. As they proceeded, Montmagny continued to look for opportunities to harness the force with a mill wheel. By the time they reached the top, he had considered a few. Noël was impressed they had succeeded in climbing and had a new respect for Montmagny along with sympathy for Piraube who appeared ready to die. From their panoramic perch, Montmagny admired the view, asking about various areas while Piraube tried to recover. Eventually they headed down and continued alongside *Île d'Orléans*.

"When Cartier saw this place," Martin related as he pointed to the mainland coast, "he was impressed with its beauty and declared, '*Quel beau pré*', referring to the

234

beautiful meadow. Since then it has been known as the *Beaupré* Coast." As they approached the downstream tip of *Île d'Orléans*, Noël suggested they make camp.

Beaching the canoes at a clearing on *Île d'Orléans,* they proceeded with military efficiency as each Indian and colonist knew their role. Jacques-Henri started a fire while two of the other Indians helped set camp and the remaining three disappeared. By the time the camp was set, the three returned with a large deer, already bled and gutted.

"My God!" said Montmagny, "when I was a lad, we hunted near Fontainebleau. We would be lucky to get two such deer in a year—and we had guns!" Soon the natives had the creature butchered and were cooking it all.

"We will never eat all that," Piraube said.

Martin laughed, "Don't worry, we shall eat it eventually."

Settling in to eat, they told about their own lives. Montmagny was the third son of a wealthy aristocratic family near Paris. Due to the position of this birth, his family had him trained in the military and eventually named to the *Compagnie de la Nouvelle-France* in 1632. Piraube had a similar birth in a less wealthy family and was educated in the law. Since lawyers were illegal in New France, he became a notary, charged with the legal affairs of the colony. It was clear he was not the outdoorsman his superior was.

The Indians arose to break camp at first light. Piraube remained snoring under his cover but Montmagny was nowhere to be seen. Noël was becoming worried until he saw him strolling toward the camp. "What a wonderful morning!" he exclaimed, "I found all manner of wonders on this island."

Martin said calmly, "Perhaps it would be better to take one of the soldiers or Indians with you on a hike."

"Why?" Montmagny asked, "Are there renegade savages?"

"Not likely," Martin answered, "But there are bear, wolves, mountain lion and the occasional wild boar—oh yes, and the snakes."

The governor's demeanor changed as he simply replied, "Oh."

Following breakfast, they pushed off the *Île* heading downstream until they came to another prominence surrounded by a rocky beach, crowded with seagulls. A few ragged cabins sat along a small river where a small shallop sat moored to a smaller dock. As they beached the canoes, Nicolas Pivert wandered down to greet them. One of the early settlers of the colony, he and his wife had come from Normandie in 1623. He showed Montmagny around his lonesome domain of *Cap Tourmente*, explaining that its name came from the sudden and violent storms that frequented the area, often without warning.

Saying farewell to Pivert, Montmagny ordered the men to head back upstream to begin their long voyage. "I visited Acadia and Tadoussac on the trip in from France. Now I want to see what treasures you have hidden on the interior." They returned through the southern channel around *Île d'Orléans,* providing a better view of the southern shore of *Fleuve Saint-Laurent*. Passing *Québec* with the high cliffs shielding *Cap Diamant* and the fort on the south, the governor remarked, "My God, is this wonderfully defensible! When our stone masons have finished, it will be the most impenetrable fortress on earth!" Continuing upstream, they watched the majesty of Canada revealed beside them. When Jacques-Henri deemed they had done enough, they made camp.

Autumn was approaching, and with it nights that were darker and colder, causing the Indians to build a greater fire where the men heated the leftover deer and visited. Addressing the Indians, Montmagny told them, "I am particularly interested in your thoughts—about your land, your people, your history, and particularly about your relationship with the French." Impressed by the grasp of French language these men revealed, particularly the two men who lacked Christian names, Achak and Machk, he listened patiently. While the evening progressed, Noël realized the governor asked intelligent questions, but more so, that he was an astute and gifted listener, allowing the natives to speak their minds at their own pace without interruption.

Two days later, they landed at the docks of *Trois-Rivières*. While they secured the canoes, Commandant LaViolette greeted them. Once they were on land, another larger group with much larger canoes docked beside them. "Benoît and Bernier!" exclaimed Martin, then addressing Montmagny, "These men are successful fur traders. You may wish to visit with them."

The governor had heard of these men from his aides. "Yes," he answered with enthusiasm. Turning to LaViolette, he asked, "Commandant, is there somewhere we could meet with these gentlemen?"

"Yes, Excellency, we have a tavern in our small fort. We can dine there as well." The offer of food and drink was enough for the *voyageurs* who proceeded to the fortification where they broke into groups. Montmagny, LaViolette, Benoît, Martin and Noël sat at a table while the

237

rest of the crews gathered at the bar. To the surprise of some, Montmagny invited the Indians, but Jacques-Henri told him they would camp outside.

Again, the governor proved himself an astute listener, as he was educated on the ways of *Québec's* premier industry as well as its problems. At the end of the evening and the discussion, the drinking continued. LaViolette invited the governor to his quarters, but to his surprise, Montmagny told him, "I prefer to camp out with my men." Piraube, however, readily accepted the offer of inside quarters. Before they retired, Montmagny asked Noël and Abraham, "Tell me more about this *Half-face* Benoît mentioned."

Martin scratched his ample beard, "Well sir, he has been around several years. His team works totally outside the law."

"Why isn't he stopped?"

More beard scratching. "He is slippery and evil, and you must remember this is a vast wilderness. Frankly, he has become a legend."

"Still seems as something could be done," the governor concluded, "but I must say I learned a great deal tonight."

The next day found them entering a wider expanse of the *Saint-Laurent* known as *Lac Saint-Pierre*. At the end of the 'lake', they made camp on the south shore at the mouth of the Richelieu River, so named by Champlain for his clerical nemesis. Ironically, it drained waters into the *Saint-Laurent* from the only body of water named for the founder of Canada, *Lac Champlain.* As they ate, Jacques-Henri explained. "This river had been known as the Iroquois River because it flows from land of the Iroquois."

"I have heard a little about these people. Jacques-Henri, tell me about them."

Jacques-Henri pulled out two pipes and a sack. Offering one to Montmagny, he started, "Need pipe for this." Looking up at the cloudless night of stars, he lit the pipe, blew a ring and began. "Two people, different language—like French and English. Different land, different ideas, different life. Sometimes friend, oftentimes not." Montmagny began to cough, Jacques-Henri said, "Not so much smoke—strong tobacco." With a smile he added, "Iroquois tobacco—the best."

Montmagny looked surprised while Jacques-Henri merely shrugged and continued, "Iroquois village in one place. Wood cabins, grow crops—like white man." Blowing another ring and pausing, he finally continued. "Algonquin live everywhere. Live in tent. Move with season, move with hunt. Pick vegetables and berries from forest, and take game from forest. Algonquin believe all land belong to all men. Iroquois disagree."

The discussion went on into the night. Eventually all were asleep but Jacques-Henri and the governor. As the sun began a glow on the horizon, Jacques-Henri concluded, "Algonquin can live with white man—Iroquois cannot—will not. They may seem friend sometimes, but only seem." Montmagny went to sleep on the most profound thing he would learn—something he would not fully appreciate in his lifetime.

As the voyage progressed, the *Saint-Laurent* took a rather sharp bend to the south, eventually turning sharply due west. Pointing to the northern shore with a small mountain in the background, Martin explained to the governor. "When Cartier saw this, he said, '*Quel mont royal!*' declaring it was a Royal Mountain. One cannot go beyond here in a shallop—you shall soon see why."

As they proceeded west, the current increased and waves built. Soon they could see the wildest water Montmagny had ever seen. The Indians beached the canoes and hiked to see a wide river of endless, ferocious rapids. "Here Cartier said," Martin related, "'This must be the way to China.' Hence, he called it *Lachine*. Unfortunately no one has found China over here and the rapids prohibit anything but portage."

"The *voyageurs* talked about that," Montmagny recalled, "Must they carry the canoe far?"

Abraham laughed, "You don't want to know how far. However, this might be a good place to camp."

That evening Montmagny engaged Pierre, "You haven't had much to say this trip, young sir."

Pierre looked at his feet, "*Monsieur* Martin told me if I spoke, he would cut out my tongue."

"I see. What if I give you clemency?"

Pierre smiled, "What would you like to talk about?"

The governor sat back and listened to a teenager's view of the wild.

Doubling back in the early morning rays, the canoes followed the shore of the island that would one day be Canada's greatest city. Turning north they came to the small branch of the *Saint-Laurent*, which formed the north side of the larger island and separated it from *Île Jésus*. Jacques-Henri told Montmagny, "There been small Huron camp here. I believe Jesuits have set a mission there."

The governor was confused, "Now who are the Huron? Are they Iroquois or Algonquin?"

Jacques-Henri smiled, "Hard question. Huron speak like Iroquois, but hate Iroquois more than anyone." Shrugging, he added, "I guess they are own tribe—odd people."

Freed of the contract of silence, Pierre Boucher added, "I lived with the Huron for a while with Father LeJeune. They were very pleasant. They behave like Algonquin but sound different."

In early afternoon, Jacques-Henri pulled the canoes onto a beach on the southern shore of *Île Jésus*. Pointing to a small path he explained, "Leads to village." They had not gone far when they encountered an emaciated figure in a black robe, motioning for them to stop. "Come no further!" he gasped with his voice breaking. "Pox! All dead—Go! Go!"

Before Montmagny could ask a question, Noël had grabbed him, pulling in the direction of the canoe. The entourage double-timed it back to the beach where they quickly boarded the canoes and headed back towards *Québec*. Once they were well off shore, Abraham Martin explained, "The pox is much like the pox we have occasionally in Europe. Natives are particularly susceptible. There have been devastating outbreaks in various camps over the years. Sometimes brought by *voyageurs*—more commonly by missionaries."

After they had landed for the night, three Indians, Achak, Machk, and a Christian native named Jacques-Denis organized to find food. Montmagny asked to accompany them and was ultimately granted permission. He borrowed a musket from one of the soldiers, but Machk took it, returning it to the soldier, "Gun no good—hurt ears."

Montmagny had learned debate at this point was fruitless and followed empty handed. Very soon, they

241

encountered a sizable female deer. Montmagny expected an arrow, but Jacques-Denis shooed it away, "Do not kill mother deer." The governor had just received the first of many lessons in Canadian conservation. Not much further into the forest, the natives came to a silent stop. Montmagny surveyed the trees before he finally spied the prey, camouflaged in the thicket—a monster. At least twice the size of any deer, it had a rack of antlers of size and structure he had never seen.

Machk landed the first arrow, and his companions fired in turn, hitting the hapless creature no matter which way he turned. Ultimately, it fell to the ground. The natives bled and gutted it with surgical precision, and tied the carcass to large sticks to carry. The three natives planned to carry it but, to their surprise, the governor volunteered to help. Returning to the camp, Montmagny wondered if he would die on the spot of fatigue, but he had impressed the natives—more than he would know.

As he inspected the animal, Jacques-Henri told Montmagny, "Caribou, not so big as moose but," touching his thumb to his index finger and kissing them as he had learned from his French neighbors, "the best taste."

After dinner the men smoked (Iroquois tobacco), and Montmagny asked Jacques-Henri about the episode at the Huron camp. Taking a long drag on his pipe, he gave his typical shrug before explaining. "White man's pox very bad. Sometimes kills whole village. Some people blame black robes. Also one reason Iroquois hate white man." He was silent the remainder of the evening.

Continuing their return trek the next afternoon, they passed another group of *voyageurs* traveling in the opposite direction at an impressive rate of speed. Both groups ignored one another. "Who were those men?" Montmagny asked.

Abraham answered quietly, "Half-face."

"Why did we not arrest them?" he asked with an astonished tone.

"Bad idea, Excellency." Abraham replied, "*Very* bad idea."

CHAPTER 29

Québec: April 10, 1637—Seven months later

I'm going to bring it in at the end of the dock, Bergeron. I suspect it will be safer there." Noël brought the shallop in with surgical precision as Bergeron jumped the small shelf of ice with the mooring line. Once the boat was out of danger, Noël stepped ashore. "You can handle it from here, Bergeron. I need to report to the *Habitation*. If we have a job for tomorrow, I'll stop and tell you on my way home."

Making his way to the office, he said hello to the workers building roads, two in the lower town and three in the upper town. Entering Champlain's old offices, he went to the harbormaster to deliver his manifest. He and Bergeron had taken five soldiers from the fort to reinforce the new facility at *Trois-Rivières*. As the clerk filed the documents, he told Noël, "I have a message for you to see

Monsieur Giffard before leaving. He is in the Company office—and here is your manifest for tomorrow. Some supplies to *Cap Tourmente.*"

Noël pocketed the manifest while entering the office to find Giffard talking to Secretary Piraube who had almost recovered from the trip in the fall. "Oh, good, Langlois. Please have a seat. I have some rather good news." Noël certainly preferred good to bad news, but though he had a good relationship with Giffard, he did not entirely trust him. Giffard took a document from the desk. Handing it to Noël, he asked, "Do you know what this is?"

"Some sort of property document?"

"Yes. You see the Company met with me, and they are very pleased with the progress on the Beauport *sous-concessions*—especially yours and one of your neighbor's. This document gives you the rights of the property in perpetuity. Do you know what that means?"

"A long time?"

"Yes," agreed Giffard, "at least your lifetime and possibly with the option to pass it to an heir at your death." Leaning forward, Giffard continued, "What this means is no one can take it from you. Now, I remain the *seigneur* and our relationship does not change other than your improved security. The way things are going, I feel it is safe to say you are going to become a wealthy man. Now one of your neighbors has also had this good news. We would expect the other *sous-seigneur* will eventually have the same offer, but please don't say anything until I tell you." Giffard took the document, folded it into an envelope and presented it to Noël, bidding him good day.

Stepping into the bright spring sunlight, Noël was pleased but confused. After stopping to tell Bergeron of tomorrow's assignment, he headed for the canoe dock.

Approaching his home, he was not entirely surprised to see Zacharie Cloutier sitting in one of his rocking chairs. Looking at the envelope in Noël's hand, Cloutier said, "I thought you would be the other lucky soul." Noël took the other seat while Cloutier continued, "Don't worry too much about keeping it quiet. All the Beauport *sous-seigneur* have heard the news as well as all the spouses. Word is that everyone will have this soon."

Cloutier was the oldest of the Perche immigrants and Noël considered him the wisest. "What do you make of this, Zacharie?"

"Actually, it is simple. First, it is to our advantage and will probably become to our *great* advantage. This is not, however, a charitable token of the Company's good will. Remember the date."

"The date?" Noël questioned.

"Three years after we signed our three-year contracts. The Company is just beginning to turn a profit and it may well continue to grow. But only if the land produces. If one, two, or God-forbid, all of us Percheron decide to return home, it could ruin the Company.

"In a few years, when they have more settlers, it will not be so crucial. This land in perpetuity will be for us and perhaps a few more, but no one after the Colony is on a solid footing. Fortunately for us," waving his hand over Beauport, "we will be in a position to run our *sous-concessions* as the lords of the manor did in France, but we will continue to be a fortunate few." Standing, Cloutier finished, "How does it feel to be the lord?"

Noël laughed, "So far, not bad."

"I must go," Cloutier said as he headed down the steps and then with a smile, "Say hello to her ladyship for me."

Noël entered his house to Robert jumping into his arms while Marie-Nicole sat on the floor chewing a doll made by Félicity-Angel. Françoise put down her stirring spoon and saw the envelope. "Did you get one, too?" she asked cautiously.

"Yes, how did you know about it?" he asked.

"Everyone knows, even the upper town families."

"I suppose we should be cautious," he told her. "It looks good but I wouldn't spend any money yet." That evening they discussed possibilities well past their normal bedtime, both realizing they were facing a future neither had ever dared to expect.

The next morning, Noël rose before the sun and headed to the docks. "We are only going to *Cap Tourmente*," he told his wife. "If the wind and weather are fair, I should be home tonight or tomorrow at the latest." Kissing her goodbye, he patted her abdomen, "Your ladyship is beginning to show."

Approaching the shallop, Noël was surprised to see a familiar white-headed figure sitting on the rail. "How does it feel to be lord of the manor?" Abraham Martin asked as Noël boarded.

"I guess everyone does know," Noël answered.

"*Québec* is a small world, my friend." Martin told him, "But congratulations, some families in the upper town already have such a contract—it gives one security." Looking around, Martin continued in a lower voice, "That is not why I am here. I should warn you that the governor did *not* take my advice about our old friend Half-face."

Lowering his sea bag into the hold, Noël simply replied, "Oh?"

"You know those soldiers you transported to *Trois-Rivières?* Well, they are charged with stopping Half-face if he tries to head up the *Saint-Maurice.*" Noël frowned while his large friend continued. "Worse still, he has sent three small squads to hunt him out. I hope these men know what they are up against. Half-face will stop at nothing. I thought I would tell you so you can keep your head up and not get in the middle of anything."

Bergeron appeared and began to cast off, while Noël responded, "Thank you, I will, but we are only going to *Cap Tourmente.*"

Martin stepped onto the dock and waved, "Bon voyage."

Back in Beauport, Françoise had finished breakfast and, putting Marie-Nicole in her papoose, went to the Indian camp followed closely by Robert and Tutu. Leaving Robert to play with Henri-Makya, she told Félicity-Angel, "I'll take Marie-Nicole and Tutu. I want to weed the vegetable garden and dig up all the old carrots."

She was nearly finished with her chore when Tutu began to growl. Looking around she saw nothing and told him to be quiet. The dog lay down but soon began again. Looking out, Françoise thought she saw *him*! Squinting in the sunlight, she could almost make out the *voyageur* hat and red hair. Françoise raised her spade to use as a weapon while Tutu took off into the woods. Françoise called her to no avail. She was ready to turn and sprint for the Indian camp when her dog began to return at a slow trot, arriving at her feet where Tutu proudly dropped a large hare, its neck now broken. Françoise sat on an old log, scratching her dog's chin and congratulating her. Having the pet's attention, she told her, "It's been almost a year. I thought it was over. Every time I think I see him, I am alone, and at the end he is never there. I must be crazy. Maybe it's the pregnancy." Then thinking, she added, "That's it! Each time I've been pregnant—I think." She rose to finish her chores, returned to Jacques-Henri's camp, and spoke no more about the episode.

A sudden thunderstorm delayed Noël's return and Françoise made certain the house was secure. In the morning, she asked Marie Guyon to help her with some chores—more for companionship than assistance. As they began washing the floors, Marie told her, "*Tante-Françoise,*" (all of the children from the five original Perche-Beauport families had taken Pierre Boucher's habit of referring to the wives as *tante* or aunt,) "I have exciting news, I am to be married this summer!"

Françoise stopped her scrubbing. She knew the question of marriage of the oldest French girls was a topic, and that Marie at 13 was among the oldest, but... "Aren't you a bit young, Marie?"

Marie stood, "I have had *my monthlies* for a year—and look." Putting her hands under her breasts, she pushed up on her enlarging bosom.

"Well..." Françoise said, "Who is the lucky man?"

"*Monsieur* Bélanger."

Françoise thought François Bélanger was probably between 25 and 30. He was from an area of France close to

Perche and was now a *sous-seigneur*—she could do worse. "What does your father say?" she queried.

"Papa thinks I'm young, but says it is the way things will be in Canada. He knows *Monsieur* Bélanger will be able to take good care of me. I think we are going to be rich!"

Françoise congratulated her, thinking, *Thank God by the time my children are this age, things will be more normal.*

That Sunday after mass was the first picnic of spring and the five Perche-Beauport wives met under a giant maple tree. Needless to say, marriage was a topic. In addition to Marie Guyon, Anne Cloutier, not quite 12, was to wed Bélanger's old roommate, Robert Drouin. Not to be outdone, the upper town was also to have two weddings of young girls.

On the way back to Beauport, Nicole told Françoise, "Just between you and me, I hope my girls don't marry so young. What would it be like not to have a childhood?"

"I wouldn't know," Françoise replied, "I never had one."

Two months later, Beauport had a double wedding as both young girls were married on the same day to the two former roommates, joining their mothers as wives of Beauport *sous-seigneur*. Two months after that, Françoise gave birth to her third child whom she named Agnes-Anne, after her mother.

Following dinner, Noël sat by the fire in one rocking chair while Françoise rocked young Agnes-Anne in the other. Her carpenter husband had improved their quarters by adding a separate bedroom where Robert and Marie-Nicole were now asleep and a loft as an eventual bedroom for their growing family.

"Is that a knock at the door?" she wondered.

"I'll see." Noël went to the door and cautiously opened it a crack. "Come in," he said, opening it wider to admit a snow-covered Abraham Martin. "Whatever brings you out tonight?"

Martin hung his coat by the fire, standing there to get warm. "I had some information I thought you should know." Looking at Françoise and the baby, it was evident he wanted to speak to Noël alone.

"I'm just going to bed," she announced, "I'll finish nursing in the bedroom." Entering the room, she shut the curtain but stayed close enough to listen.

Noël poured two glasses of calvados and the men sat near the fire. "You remember the three squads the governor sent to find our *coureurs-de-bois* friend?" Noël only nodded as Martin continued, "Well, only one has returned so far—empty handed." Taking a long drink, he continued. "They found another squad today."

"Where were they?"

"Well up *Riviére-Saint-Maurice.*" Martin answered.

"What were they doing?"

Lowering his voice, Martin said, "Hanging from trees—gutted and skinned like beaver." Françoise swallowed her scream as he continued, "All but one. They only found his head. I hope His Excellency will listen to me next time."

251

Their voices became whispers as Françoise put the baby in her small crib and climbed into bed, covering her head to muffle her sobs."

CHAPTER 30

At the height of fall splendor, Beauport's maple trees revealed their finest reds and golds, illuminated by the brilliant autumn sun. "Keep them in line, Tutu." Françoise called, leading her brood to the vegetable garden. Noël told her she could now have one of the _engager_ help her with the chores, but today was perfect for gardening and she enjoyed it too much to share. The fact they had reached this economic status was reward enough for her. When they reached the garden, she carefully surveyed the periphery. She had not had seen her phantom for more than a year, only an occasional shadow in the corner of her eye, but she was now convinced it was all her imagination—almost convinced.

Turning to review her troops, she ordered, "Robert, you can help me dig the carrots. Girls, you can collect pretty leaves." Pointing to a nearby pile, she added, "just the best red and gold ones. Marie-Nicole, you show Agnes-Anne how to do it. And, Tutu, you keep them all here." Though bred as a sled dog, Tutu was female, and a natural herder of small beings. Once Françoise was confident Robert could harvest the carrots without breaking them, she began to dig potatoes.

In balance, 1638 had been a good year for the colony. Ships arrived periodically with needed French goods, animals, and people. The people, however, continued to be mainly male *engager* with only the occasional family and rare single woman. There had been some marriages with natives along with some co-habitation, but as Robert Giffard had predicted, *Québec* still desperately needed French women. In addition, as more *engager* finished the third year of their contract, there remained a steady stream of men, who seeing no personal future in Canada, returned to France.

Animal breeding, on the other hand, was going well with good balance of sexes. Each *sous-concession* and many of the *habitants* had enlarging animal populations as well as their own cart, crafted by the extremely busy Noël Morin. Each *sous-concession* now owned an ox. A major new convenience for the Beauport residents was a wooden bridge across the narrows of *Riviére Saint-Charles*, making dry-land passage to the city possible.

Once Françoise had the produce she needed loaded in her wooden wheelbarrow, she ordered her troops, "That's all for today, children. Marie-Nicole, put your leaves in here and we shall head for home. We must be ready for dinner when your father arrives."

The new enlarged bell tolled as the parishioners exited Champlain's church into a tolerable autumn day. A gentle breeze from the south tempered the overcast sky while Noël and Françoise strolled with their children, admiring the many recent improvements in the city. "These streets remind me of Mortagne," Françoise observed, "even the names like Saint-Louis and Sainte-Anne. The stonework on _Château Saint-Louis,_" referring to the name of the fort, "will make it look like a duke's fortress in the French countryside. Hopefully, someday the church will look like Notre-Dame de Mortagne."

Glancing down at the lower town, she added, "With the repair of the old _Habitation,_ even it looks like a respectable building. I heard they are going to begin a small hospital on the north side." Looking up at the sky, she suggested, "I don't think it's going to rain, let's go to _L'Auberge Oie Bleue_. Everyone will be there."

Approaching Étienne Forton's establishment, she told Noel, "I see the men have gathered outside for something. I will take the children inside with the ladies and you can see your friends."

Entering, she saw the wives of the _sous-seigneurs_ of both Beauport and the upper town gathered around a few tables while the children played on Forton's new dance floor. Leaving her offspring in the midst of the youthful pandemonium, she pulled up a chair with her neighbors at what appeared to be a serious conversation.

She did not need to inquire. As she sat, Nicole Boucher said, "Françoise, did you hear what happened in _Trois-Rivières?_"

"No, why?"

"Wasn't your husband just there?"

"Yes, he only returned last night. Why?"

Remie Giffard explained, "We heard two men were killed there this week—by *Iroquois!*"

Françoise could sense the trepidation in the words. "He didn't say anything to me," she answered.

"Well," said young Hélène Hebert, "I suppose we shall have to wait for the men to hash it out and find out when we get home."

The two groups remained at their indoor or outdoor stations as the day wore on. The men quickly switched from beer to straight calvados and the women from tea to wine. Eventually Xainte Cloutier suggested, "I believe we should go break up the men and go home before dark."

The other Beauport families rode their carts to the city over the new bridge, but the Langlois family had arrived by canoe. As Françoise paddled the craft home, her husband said nothing about news from the interior.

After dinner, Françoise put the children to bed and joined Noël on the rocking chair by the fire before asking, "Did you go to *Trois-Rivières* this week?"

"You know I did."

"Well?"

Noël sipped his black-root tea before saying, "I thought the men had promised not to discuss this with the wives."

She almost smiled, "You fail to consider the influence of wives."

"Well, it seems last week a few Iroquois came up the Richelieu River and made their way to *Trois-Rivières.* They attacked the fort, but the soldiers sent last year by Governor Montmagny drove them off. Unfortunately, two local men were killed in the ruckus."

256

"Did you know these men?" she asked.

"No."

The following evening found Françoise and Noël again in front of the fire. She rose and returned with calvados. "I don't understand this trouble with the Iroquois."

Noël accepted the beverage and replied, "No one does."

Pouring her own cup, she sat, "You can do better than that."

Noël sipped his drink, staring into the fire. Eventually he began, "Here is how I understand it. Long before the Europeans, the natives trapped animals for their furs. Early French explorers discovered this and began to trade European goods for furs to take to France where these furs were rare and valued for their quality. This trade involved Algonquin, Huron and Abenaki. As exploration increased, furs became a lucrative business."

Taking a sip, he peered into the fire. "Around the same time, Dutch and English explorers arrived at lands to our south where they remain today. They too discovered the furs and began a similar industry, but in the south, the trade was with the natives of that region—the Iroquois. Things were stable then, the industry small and furs in abundance."

He stood and stoked the fire, organizing his thoughts. "As more Europeans came, the demand for furs increased. The tribes moved farther inland for more furs. Eventually the Iroquois had to turn north, encroaching on Algonquin land. The Iroquois had occasionally been hostile to Indians of our region, but something is now making this a larger problem."

Françoise was now very intent on the story, "What is that?" she asked.

257

"The English are coming in greater numbers and starting to drive the Dutch out. The English had always distained the Indians and the Dutch are taking advantage of this."

"What are they doing?" she questioned anxiously.

"Something we shall regret forever—giving the Iroquois guns. This is starting what Abraham Martin calls, *the Beaver Wars.* Now the Iroquois are invading Algonquin land more and more."

"I don't know why they can't get along like the Europeans," she exclaimed.

Her husband laughed, "I guess they didn't teach European history in the convent. I'm off to bed."

Françoise lay awake long after her husband began snoring, thinking to herself, *I used to see voyageur phantoms, now it will be Iroquois phantoms as well.*

CHAPTER 31

Always a hotbed of rumor, *Québec* hit a new high in late June as tales—from those considered *possibly true* to those considered *absolute fact*—filled the conversations in the square. Many involved the topic of nuns. Since the days before the Kirke brothers, opinions varied from, "we must have nuns" to "what would they do in this wilderness?"

Since the arrival of the Perche families, however, the need for *religieuse* to aid the Jesuits in education and to provide healthcare had become a popular opinion. Some word of possible arrival of nuns filtered through the society from time to time, but now it seemed to be real. With the arrival of the first ship of the year came a vague message that a group or groups of sisters were being assembled to come to Canada. Estimates of numbers ranged from two to

259

twenty. All other details were equally obscure, but rumors put their arrival at the end of June.

As always, a crowd attended the arrival of each ship. They waited anxiously as the usual stream of male workers, occasional families and the rare woman disembarked, but no *religieuse* appeared. Word finally arrived at the end of July that the ship, *Saint-Joseph,* had arrived in *Fleuve Saint-Laurent* carrying two groups of nuns and it would be in *Québec* any day.

Excitement in the colony always reached a high when a ship was expected, but this time enthusiasm was at a peak. Abraham Martin had piloted the ship to the eastern end of *Île d'Orléans* where they stopped for the night of July 31. Determined to make the arrival special, Governor Montmagny dispatched Noël in a shallop to bring the nuns to the port on the morning of August 1. When the shallop rounded the western tip of the *Île,* the crowd was ready.

Montmagny had limited spectators at the lower town dock to officials, upper town families and Jesuits. Others, including the Beauport families, viewed the event from above where the upper town overlooked the *Habitation* and docks. In spite of the late stage of her current pregnancy, Françoise attended with the others. Weather had been fair all week, although today dark heavy clouds hung low while a north wind blew ragged white puffs beneath them, a worrisome sign of an impending storm.

Noël brought the shallop to the dock perfectly in spite of the brisk wind, and *Monsieur* Bergeron hopped smartly to the dock with lines. Nicole Boucher had just obtained written information on the passengers from Father LeJeune. "There are two groups," she read aloud, "The nuns in the Black are Ursuline, like we had in *Mortagne.* They are the

260

teaching order. The group in gray is Augustinian. They will run the hospital."

The three Augustinian nuns left the shallop first, "Their benefactor," read Nicole "is the Duchesse d'Aiguillon." She then explained, "Gaspard says she is the niece of Cardinal Richelieu, and has more money than the King—but no intention of visiting Canada." Next, followed three nuns in black, led by a woman in secular dress. "These are the Ursuline who shall run the school," Nicole noted, "Their leader is a lay sponsor, Madame de la Peltrie. She is also rich," looking to Françoise, she added, "and comes from Alençon very near where your husband was born. I suspect that is her in the dress." These women appeared ragged, staggering on the gangplank—a phenomenon recalled by all who had made the passage. Following behind came six Jesuits. Finally, a young girl in the dress of an Ursuline novice and a large nun in black followed, hauling bags—they appeared bright and alert. "It says there are two *religieuse* who are helpers. Those must be the two."

The nuns and Jesuits knelt and ceremoniously kissed the ground of *Québec*. Some required help rising before proceeding to the upper town for a short service. The citizens were thrilled when the sky began miraculously to clear as they approached *Notre-Dame de la Recouvrance*.

When the women had a better look at the nuns, they could not help remarking on their appearance. "Nuns are always so proper," said Xainte Cloutier, "but these are emaciated and disheveled."

"Probably a difficult journey," replied Mathurine Guyon, "I don't think we looked any better." The entourage then proceeded to the fort while the women of Beauport headed home.

The following morning, Nicole was at Françoise's door. "A soldier came by this morning and told me the governor is having some people to speak with the new nuns. He requested that you and I attend."

"Why me?" Françoise asked. Patting her abdomen, she added, "I don't know if I can waddle that far today."

"I am certain you can make it," her friend encouraged, "and it is particularly *you* they want." Françoise looked puzzled while Nicole added, "Apparently they heard of your teaching experience in Mortagne and your feats at midwifery."

Françoise shrugged, "I hope they are not disappointed."

"They won't be," Nicole said. "We can take the canoe. I can paddle." Then smiling, "They are meeting at the *Habitation*, so you will not have far to waddle."

Arriving at Champlain's old workplace, they were surprised when the soldier on duty whisked them promptly into the office, where they met the leader of the Ursuline nuns from Tours. Marie Guyart, now known as *Marie de l'Incarnation*, appeared to be about 40. She remained a bit disheveled but her severe nun-like façade had returned. She seemed to know a bit about the two women, particularly Françoise's experience in Mortagne as well as the Algonquin village some years before.

"Do you speak the native tongue?" she asked Françoise.

"Not well, Sister." Aside from her friends back in *Mortagne*, nuns still frightened Françoise. She tried, nevertheless, to remain poised. "But I *can* communicate."

"That is better than we can do. I believe you would be of great help to us." Looking at Françoise's middle, the nun added, "You do seem a little... *delicate* at the moment. When are you due?"

"Soon, Sister—very soon."

"I see, well, we should meet once you are over your confinement. Is this your first?"

"No, Sister, my fourth."

"Oh," the nun simply muttered, "over how many years?"

"Four, Sister."

Seeing the nun was a bit uncomfortable with the topic, Nicole asked, ""How did you find your voyage, Sister?"

Marie de l'Incarnation's demeanor turned more severe, "Dear Lord, it was awful. I am certain it was the worst crossing ever. We had storms, one after another—the waves tossed the ship about and some actually came onto the deck! My bed clothes became totally soaked."

"Yes, the storms can be fierce," Françoise agreed.

"That is only the half of it," the nun continued. "We were attacked by pirates!"

"Oh, dear!" Nicole said with a frown.

"Yes—Spanish pirates. They boarded our ship and looked about. I feared they were about to ravage the sisters. Fortunately, the captain managed to scare the demons off." The Beauport women remained silent while the sister added. "Then worst of all, we came upon a *mountain* of ice—larger than the ship! I believe the captain called it an *iceberg.*" Placing her hand on her chest and catching her breath, she went on, "We ran right into it. It is a miracle we did not drown." She crossed herself before continuing, "Yes, it was a desperate voyage—but for the benevolence of our Savior, we would all have certainly perished."

Next, they met Madame de la Peltrie, the wealthy benefactress of the group. Not much older than Françoise, she was pleasant but carried the air of one born to privilege.

263

Lastly were the other two Ursuline nuns from Tours, both in their early twenties who seemed quite nervous. Proceeding to the next office, they met the women in gray, the Augustinian sisters from Dieppe. All three were in their twenties but had an air of confidence and expressed great interest in the maladies of the area and getting to work.

Leaving the offices, Françoise and Nicole virtually ran into two women readying the cabins by the *Habitation* to temporarily house the nuns.

"My God—Sister Marie-Claude!" screamed Françoise.

The portly nun lifted Françoise off the ground, while hugging her to her ample bosom, declaring, "I prayed to God each night you would still be here." When she released the embrace, Sister Marie-Claude observed Françoise's abdomen, "Oh dear, I hope I did not injure you."

"You could never hurt me, Sister Marie-Claude, but how did you come to be here?"

"It is a bit of a story," she reported looking around. "We are nearly finished here. Let us go to the bench by that tree and visit."

Sitting beneath the giant chestnut tree, Françoise began, "How did you…"

Sister Marie-Claude took over. "When you left, I was taken with the idea. I also took your old job of helping with the students. When I learned there was talk of an Ursuline mission, I journeyed to Tours and offered my services. At first they were not interested; however, I persisted and finally they agreed to take me as a worker to help my friend here." Putting her hand on her slender young helper, she explained, "This is Charlotte Barré, she hopes to enter the sisterhood." As shy as Sister Marie-Claude was bold, the diminutive teenager merely whispered, "Hello."

264

"We heard you had a frightening voyage," Nicole reported.

"Oh, on the contrary," chortled the portly nun, "It was wonderful in all respects—terribly exciting. We had the most excellent storms—perfectly thrilling. We pitched, tossed and were constantly sprayed with water. Then some waves actually came over the boat—what an adventure!"

"We heard there were pirates," Françoise added.

"Oh yes! How exciting they were! They behaved as though we should be petrified, but I saw they were Spanish and knew pirates or no, Spaniards are Catholic and not about to harm nuns. They left without a fight. Then there was an iceberg!"

"That must have been terrifying," Nicole observed.

"*Au contraire*! I was only disappointed we could not come closer."

"Were you terribly cramped on the boat?" Nicole queried.

"Oh my, no!" The nun said with a chortle. "How could you be cramped on such a boat?"

"Well, with the other passengers."

"Oh didn't you know?"

"What?" Nicole questioned.

Again with the laugh, "When we arrived in Dieppe, the ship did not have enough space for Madame de la Peltrie's furniture. So she hired the *Saint-Joseph* for us."

Finally, Sister Marie-Claude put her hand on Charlotte Barré's shoulder, "Well, my young friend, I suspect we should finish our chores." She gave Françoise another bone-crunching hug and the women returned to the dock. On the way home, the two Beauport women laughed at the different viewpoints of the voyage and marveled that anyone was wealthy enough to hire their own ship.

One month later, Françoise gave birth—another daughter. She could not be faulted with failing to supply females to the colony. She named her Marguerite.

In Canada, the pendulum of life and death often swung swiftly, and a few days later the church bell chimed for the death of Guillaume Hebert who came to Canada as a boy. His was the first French family in Québec, and later he had married the first French person born in Québec. Now Hélène Desportes-Hebert was alone with three children under three years of age. Widow Hélène was 19 years old.

CHAPTER 32

C areful, Sister," Françoise cautioned the nun as she boarded the canoe, "remember, stay low and hold both sides." *Marie de l'Incarnation* entered successfully followed by Françoise with Marguerite in *papoose,* and then Jacques-Henri, who paddled the canoe from the back.

"Dear God," said the nun as they entered *Fleuve Saint-Laurent* bordered on either side by Canadian autumn magnificence, "Could paradise be any lovelier?"

Françoise had reported to the makeshift convent at the *Habitation* two weeks after the birth of her daughter. The nuns had already made a temporary classroom and had acquired two female students, one native and the other French. The two younger *religieuse* staffed the class while

267

Marie de l'Incarnation set herself trying to learn the native tongue with the help of Françoise. It was here Françoise suggested a trip to the Algonquin village before winter descended. At first, the nun had concerns, "What will you do with young Marguerite?" she asked.

Françoise grinned, "Bring her, Sister—Canadians must be strong to survive."

With Jacques-Henri paddling, the trip was less than half a day. On entering the village, the nun was filled with questions and enthusiasm. She immediately took a tour of the tents, huts and common cooking facilities as well as the one prominent log cabin, built by the Jesuits to serve as a school for boys, a chapel for mass, and Indian or *Métis*-French weddings. Françoise was impressed at how quickly Sister Marie learned as she developed a reasonable fluency in Algonquin as well as an appreciation of the native ways. Toward the end of October, Jacques-Henri suggested they head home before the first big snow.

Françoise and Sister Marie had generally fallen asleep each night as soon as they lay in their tent, but this last night the nun sat up, asking. "When you were first here, were you married?"

She had learned bits and pieces of Françoise's early life from the stay, but had never actually asked. On the other hand, Françoise had gained a new respect for the sister during their visit, in spite of her early opinion following the nun's description of the voyage to *Québec*. Instead of skirting the issue, Françoise decided to be perfectly frank and related her life from the early days in the slums of Paris to Guy and her early life in *Québec*—avoiding no detail. At the end she concluded, "So you see sister, I have not always been the upstanding woman you may have thought me."

"It seems to me you are a remarkable woman," Sister Marie replied in the darkness. "Allow me to tell you my story."

"My father was a baker from Tours. A hard man, he treated me roughly, marrying me off in my teens to a silk worker who treated me worse than my father—very much like the violent behavior and sexual indiscretions you described. We had a son, to whom I gave little love. My husband's business failed, and he died—I was 19, my son two. Forced to live with my sister, I worked for her husband serving men along the wharfs of the Loire River— even Huguenots. They did worse to me than my late husband."

She paused to dry her eyes and regain her composure as a wisp of moonlight, sneaking through the top of the tent, now muted the darkness. "I abandoned my sister *and* my son when I was 26 and he was eight. I went to the Convent in Tours, and he ran off to the wharfs in Blois. Sometime later, he stormed the convent with other boys, crying, 'I want my mother back!' I did nothing—not even acknowledge him. Eventually he was sent to live in a monastery, and I took the holy orders. Since that time, I have strived to make up for my past."

With that, she lay down and covered herself, explaining, "So you see, my friend, I, too, am not as pure as I may seem." Françoise lay down as well, cuddling Marguerite, lost in her thoughts of the past—and future.

At daybreak, Jacques-Henri pushed the canoe downstream with two passengers who had formed a secret bond—a bond that would last a lifetime.

As Jacques-Henri expertly guided the canoe into the *Habitation* dock to deposit the nun, three friends greeted them. Nicole Boucher, Xainte Cloutier, and Mathurine Guyon were obviously upset. "Thank goodness you made it home safely, Françoise," Nicole announced while the nun crawled cautiously from the canoe. Now thinking of the tragedies that could have occurred in her absence, Françoise merely looked puzzled, anxiously asking, "What?"

"One week ago," Nicole began, "three of the *engager* went hunting in the forest behind Beauport. When they did not return, two of our men went to search for them. They found them not far from our pasture, dead and *scalped!* They said it was an Iroquois attack. We have been praying for your safe return ever since."

After depositing *Marie de l'Incarnation* safely at the *Habitation*, Françoise and Jacques-Henri hurried back to Beauport. She was relieved to find Noël at home with the children. "These three men lived together in a cabin on Marin Boucher's land." Noël began, "I only knew them in passing. When they told Marin they were going hunting, he suggested they take a guide from the Algonquin village. Apparently, they said they had no need. They were not going far, and only for the day." He stood, walking to the door and opened it, peering out before continuing, "When they did not return after two days, Marin and Zacharie Cloutier went looking. Apparently they were less than a mile north of the pasture when they found the bodies."

"And they were—scalped?" She whispered, as though it would be less awful.

"Apparently," he replied.

"How did they know it was Iroquois?" she asked.

"I guess Iroquois arrows are easy to identify."

She looked questioningly at Jacques-Henri, who replied, "It's true."

Noël declared, "It is worrisome this was so close to the farms."

Jacques-Henri added, "Yes—and odd. I will go investigate." He slipped out the door and was gone. Françoise and Noël tried to go on with dinner as nothing had happened, fooling no one. She gave a synopsis of the trip before the couple retired, with the door heavily barred and Noël's musket nearby.

It was not until two days later that Jacques-Henri reappeared with Achak and Machk. Noël knew both men well from the voyage with Governor Montmagny. "We went to area beyond meadow where these men were discovered," Jacques-Henri explained. "It was apparent they were not killed there—no blood. There was a trail from where bodies were dragged, and we followed it— deep into high country. One-day walk—more for Frenchman. Farther than I have taken any Frenchman to hunt. These three made their camp in a small box canyon— perfect place for ambush—closed in, no visibility, no way out."

He then pulled an arrow from his pack. "The Iroquois killed and scalped them before they knew it. They pulled bodies all the way back to be easy to find—make statement, scare people." Showing the arrow to Françoise and Noël, he explained the identity of the Iroquois arrow.

Sitting, he continued, "I have plan. These two men," pointing to Achak and Machk, "will bring their women and set camps at each end of Beauport. With my camp in between, no Iroquois will come close. You should be safe in town. Any men want to hunt should take one of us."

Françoise kissed him and his two friends, "Jacques-Henri, you are too kind."

He smiled, "For you. You help my woman give me strong sons."

Françoise knew she had done nothing special but decided she would no longer discourage the idea.

Québec: January 9, 1640:

In the wilds of Canada, there was little time to dwell on massacres, and marriages could not always wait for springtime. Barely three months since the death of her husband, the bell of *Notre-Dame de la Recouvrance*, tolled again for Hélène Desportes-Hebert. Noël Morin, one of the single men with money, property and a successful trade, had made his move.

"When I saw you on our way back to France in 1629," he told Françoise in confidence, "I thought of asking you, but when I heard you were going to see Langlois, I knew I had little chance. Had I known women would still be so scarce now, I might have tried harder."

Today, however, he was satisfied. Although Hélène came equipped with three small children, her family had money and position in the community—and she was still quite young. They would live in her pleasant house in the upper town.

Typical of a second marriage, the congregation was small and the service short. The few attendees left the ceremony trudging through the snowdrifts across the square to *L'Auberge Oie Bleue* where Étienne Forton was happy to see the business in the dead of winter. Françoise had left all four children in the capable hands of Félicity-Angel while she attended on the arm of her husband without a papoose and as far as she knew, *sans-fetus*. Attempting to prevent pregnancy for a while, she continued religiously to nurse young Marguerite.

The colony was hoping to continue with its many projects, the convent school and hospital construction began while the long awaited conversion of the church to stone sat waiting in the building *queue*. Unfortunately, the next few weeks of constant blizzards put an end to all optimism as one of the worst winters in memory descended.

The Beauport residents hunkered down for the duration. Fortunately, their shelters were sufficient, and they had laid away adequate supplies of food and fuel. Unfortunately, the severe weather frequently made hunting and fishing impossible. The primary activity was working to keep some paths and the chimneys open. Travel to town even for mass, was generally out of the question. However, as always happens, the sun finally came out and the ice eventually began to break.

Beauport: June 15, 1640

Stopping to watch the bird, Noël remembered the day Jacques-Henri had shown him his first eagle. This one was circling, looking for prey, when it suddenly disappeared below the tree line, only to reappear with some manner of woodland rodent in its talons, heading back to its nest. The spring had been as fair as winter had been brutal, and Noël

273

had taken the day off from piloting and building to visit his *habitants* and *engager.*

Sous-seigneur had proved to be more work than he had imagined. There were now four *habitants*, each with his own *habitation* to farm. *Rouget* and Jean Barry each had a *Métis* wife and each wife was with child. These two men also claimed one *engager* each to help in their fields. Noël's two more recent *habitants* remained in the wife market and were farming alone. In addition, Noël's land had four *engager* working for him.

Coming to the rise before the river, he could see his family sitting out front, enjoying the day. As he came closer, he realized Jacques-Henri's twelve year-old son, Jacques-François, was showing his brother, Henri-Makya and young Robert Langlois, now both five years-old, how to shoot the bow. Their mothers, along with Jacques-Henri sat nearby, cheering them on. As Noël approached, Robert came running, "Pa, I shot two arrows right in the circle!" Taking his father by the hand, he pulled him to the tree where Jacques-Henri had carved a circular target. Pointing to the tree, he continued, "Jacques-Henri said I am almost as good as Algonquin, and even *better* than Iroquois."

Noël laughed, "But, are you better than me?"

His son replied, "Mama said, *she's* even better than you."

"Well, you had better go practice more," his father told him, "until you are better than Mama. I am going to sit with the adults."

He plopped down next to his wife, as she asked with a smile, "How is the lord of the manor?"

"Tired," he replied, "I never thought it would be this much work."

"Remie Giffard told me," she began, "her husband said, 'soon the *sous-seigneur* will each need a manager'."

He stole a sip from her black-root tea. "I don't know about that."

Jacques-Henri stood and looked around. "Smoke..." he said.

"I don't smell anything," Françoise observed.

The Indian looked around with his nose in the air. "Upper town," he declared, pointing.

They all looked in that direction and Noël said, "I see it, a little black smoke... Oh, oh, I see a flame."

Jacques-Henri took his arm, "Come—find out." They sprinted to the canoe, and racing across the river, they ran to the upper town just in time to see the smoldering church burst into a ball of flames. The crowd of onlookers with buckets and blankets backed away. A sweat-covered Abraham Martin came to Noël and put down his bucket. "I guess that's it."

"What happened?" Noël asked.

The bearded mariner shrugged, "Someone saw smoke and called for help. We took buckets from the well and tried to douse it like we did with the small fire a few years ago, but it was too far gone..."

Suddenly the roof collapsed, along with the wooden bell tower. In half an hour, it was over. *Notre-Dame de la Recouvrance* had been reduced to ashes.

Finally, the battle-weary firefighters took to their only remaining refuge, *L'Auberge Oie Bleue,* where Étienne Forton was ready to quench their smoke-parched thirst. Noël's neighbors, all in attendance, had been working on the two current building projects. "I am over at the *Hôtel-Dieu,*" said Gaspard, referring to the hospital project on the north side of the upper town. "There is already a small clinic there and the nuns will work from it for now. We should have this completed this year. They do not want much because they eventually plan to move closer to the natives."

"The Ursuline Convent, in the center of the upper town, where I am working," Marin Boucher added, "is going to be a much bigger project. It will probably take two or three years. The problem with both projects is they are mainly wood for now, and we just saw where that gets you."

"I'll tell you one thing," they looked up to see Father Jérome Lalemant, who had been listening, "We are going to rebuild the church in stone—no matter how long it takes." As he pulled up a chair, he called to *Monsieur* Forton, "Étienne, I think I need a beer." As Forton delivered the brew, Lalemant, who had replaced his uncle, Father Charles Lalemant, set a small book on the table. "Fortunately I had this book of records with me. Unfortunately, the rest of the church documents have just disappeared in smoke." Opening the book while taking an un-priestly slug of beer, he reported, "Since the return in 1634, there have been twenty-one marriages. That is…" thinking for a second, "three or four weddings a year on average. In spite of our attempts with native women, there is a long list of *engager* scheduled to return to France again this year. Our population has gone up, but by the end of the year, we will still only be about 300 souls. We *must* find a way to bring more French women!"

As the group broke up, Abraham Martin convinced Noël and Gaspard to continue in the lower town. Entering the *Terre Sauvage,* they were greeted by the sole two occupants, the *voyageurs* Benoît and Bernier. Extending his meaty hand, Martin said, "What brings you rascals to town this early in the season?"

As usual, Benoît answered, "We went in early this year so we could come back early to get a jump on next season. Been in the Huron country, just got back to see you lose another church."

Martin nodded, "how are things out there?"

"Not so good, Captain. Don't know what we'll run outta first—beaver or Huron."

Bernier choked a giggle as a round of drinks arrived, and Noël asked Benoît, "What do you mean?"

"Didn't hardly see a beaver in the Hudson River Valley—all trapped out by the damn Iroquois. Almost same with the Huron, *pest* gotta lot of 'em. They say they lost two outta three people in the last three years. Now the Iroquois is comin' their way for the beaver. Last Huron village we was at, Iroquois killed about a third of the braves in a raid—just three days ago."

Gaspard was obviously upset, "My boy, Pierre is leaving with the Jesuits in several days—to go to the Huron country."

"Probably not so bad, yer honor," Benoît replied, "the Iroquois usually don't truck with the black robes. I'd tell 'em to bring a gun, though."

Gaspard was not satisfied, "What about this *pest?*"

Benoît drained his beer, "That's what I call it, yer honor. Some call it pox, measles, plague or epidemic. Seems to be over now. Three bad years in a row, but nothin' this year. I suspects all the black robes that carried it have died. It's them Jesuits what brings it, way I sees it."

Not expecting any more consolation, Gaspard asked, "Why do they call it the Hudson River?"

Benoît drained his second beer, "Well, yer honor, back thirty-some years ago, there was this guy, Hudson, Englishman I think, but come with the Dutch. Explorin' down there—same time as Champlain up here. Things got named fer him."

"Have you seen this Half-face?" Noël inquired.

"Didn't see his sorry ass for two years. Word was someone finally killed the bastard. But them Hurons told us they just saw him. Say he was trappin' down in Iroquois and Dutch country but now that the beavers run out, he's headed back here." The beer continued to flow until Bernier fell asleep. Abraham Martin returned to his land behind the fort while the two Beauport men returned home—with several new worries.

CHAPTER 33

Beauport: June 17, 1640, two days later:

At daybreak, Françoise left the children with the ever-ready-to-help Félicity-Angel and headed to the canoe. Pierre Boucher was waiting, as she knew he would be. Soon to be 18 years old, he was every bit a man and had become one of *Québec's* most talented pioneers as well as translator.

"After you, *Tante* Françoise," he directed, helping her to board before taking the helm in back. Now even more skilled than she, Pierre was the best canoeist in Beauport after Jacques-Henri. Arriving at the *Habitation* before classes began, they each helped one of the two young nuns translate their lessons for the day. The school now had three native girls from the area and two French students. They hoped to have a small dormitory at the end of the season where they could board girls from the Algonquin village.

Pierre's Algonquin was far superior to Françoise's but he was to go inland next week with the Jesuits to the Huron missions, and Françoise hoped to learn as much from him as she could. Finishing at the temporary convent, they made their way to the north side of town and the makeshift hospital. The three Augustinians had turned their facility into a functioning hospital where Sister Marie-Forestier greeted them at the door. In her early twenties and the youngest of the three nuns, she seemed to be in charge.

Taking Françoise and Pierre on a tour of the small facility, she walked them down a row of cots, explaining, "We are seeing mainly injuries." Pointing to the first patient, "This man has an abscess where he cut his leg four days ago." Françoise winced as Sister Anne-le-Cointre opened his boil with a red-hot knife to the screams of her patient. Sister Marie added, "Hopefully, next time he will not wait until it is infected."

Coming to the next cot, there was a man having his arm wrapped. "This man," Marie-Forestier informed them, "fell from a ladder and broke his arm. Sister Marie-Guenet has set it and is applying a plaster." They continued down the small ward as the nursing-nun described the other patient issues. At the end, she invited them, "Come into our office."

The *office* was a miniscule room with one short bench that barely held Françoise and Pierre. "We are relatively busy," she told them. "We have had two deaths, one from a fall and another man brought in having drowned in the river. Fortunately we have not seen any epidemic ailments." Addressing Françoise, she reported, "You had asked about training in the native language. We are interested, but unfortunately, none of the native people choose to visit us. *Marie de l'Incarnation* told me of your visit with her to the native village last autumn. I wonder if we could take one to meet some of the tribal leaders and explain our facility."

Québec: June 24, 1640

One week later, Françoise rose before the sun, which is quite early in *Québec* on one of the longest days of the year. She kissed her husband and children goodbye, gave instructions to Félicity-Angel, and left for the canoes with Jacques-Henri. Traveling to the docks, she was in time to kiss Pierre Boucher farewell as he departed with Father LeJeune and four of the new Jesuits for the Huron mission. Before they were out of sight, Sister Marie-Forestier appeared with a small sack.

"I'm ready," the young nursing-nun announced. Jacques-Henri helped her board, and the threesome embarked for the Algonquin village. Charmed with the surroundings she was filled with questions of the countryside. Once they were well beyond the city, she paused, and Françoise asked her, "How did you come to be a nun?"

The young *religieuse* replied in a very matter-of-fact style. "I was born in Dieppe. My family was quite well-to-do. My mother had promised the Virgin to give a daughter to the church, and when I was eight, they took me with a bag of money and deposited us both at the Augustinian Convent in Dieppe."

"Do you see your family often?" Françoise inquired.

With no emotion, the girl answered, "I never saw them again." Françoise was speechless.

Soon Sister Marie-Forestier saw a magnificent animal on the bank. She gasped, "What is that?"

"Moose." replied Jacques-Henri, who proceeded to explain the giant of the Canadian wild to the nun. The topic of the Dieppe convent did not come up again. As they approached their destination, the nun asked, "How do you think these people will view me?"

Jacques-Henri broke his silence, "You will have difficulty convincing them to use your service. Tribe feels it can care for its own." Sister Marie-Forestier only nodded.

Soon they arrived at the village. Due to their early departure, it was still morning. The usual cadre of residents came to the shore to see who had arrived. They knew Françoise, and Jacques-Henri introduced the nun before the natives invited them to take a tour of the village. Near the end of the tour, there was a commotion inland. Jacques-Henri rushed to it with a few braves. Returning quickly he told the women, "Iroquois attack. Braves wounded."

Soon braves were carrying damaged brethren. As they laid them on the ground, the young nun began to evaluate them. "This man is critical," she told Françoise, "his upper leg is wounded and bleeding badly. He must have a damaged blood vessel. He will bleed to death in a few minutes if we cannot stop it!" Putting her hand on the gushing wound, she looked around. Not seeing what she needed, she tore open the top of her habit. Underneath she wore a binder, which flattened her breasts. Quickly removing it, she used it to fashion a compression dressing, immediately halting the red geyser.

282

Hastening to the next man with an arrow in his arm, she felt the back of the arm, saying, "The tip is right here." Carefully she pushed the arrow through the back, and breaking the shaft, removed it in two pieces to avoid further injury. She then sacrificed another piece of her habit for dressing.

The third man had an arrow in his abdomen. She broke the arrow leaving a small amount protruding, telling Françoise, "This will stop it from toggling and causing more damage. I will need to remove it later." The next two men were dead. She merely used her hand and gently closed their eyes, whispering a short prayer. As she progressed, she removed arrows and dressed wounds with morsels of her diminishing habit while the tribe watched in wonderment this young *religieuse*, tending the wounded in a torn dress with her blood-soaked bosom exposed to the world. Soon two native women brought a pile of ragged cloth to make more dressings.

Once they were finished with the first round, the women took her to the riverbank, submersing her in the cold *Fleuve Saint-Laurent*. They removed the remainder of her habit and washed off the blood. When she stood, they covered her nakedness with a native dress. When she returned to reevaluate the warriors, the women brought native poultices and salves. She began a second round, applying them as needed along with more secure dressings.

When all the critically wounded were tended, she addressed the broken bones. With her direction and the strength of the other women, she set and immobilized them as best she could. She then returned to the man with the arrow in his abdomen. "I need a very sharp knife and an assistant." Françoise volunteered and Jacques-Henri offered his knife. "Is it sharp?" she asked.

283

Jacques-Henri touched it to his finger producing a spot of blood. "No knife sharper," he boasted.

She gave Françoise two cloths, demonstrating, "Hold these on either side of the wound." Françoise complied and the nun made a longitudinal incision over the wound. "Pull the skin edges apart," she ordered as she cut deeper. Finally, she put her finger in the wound, releasing a gush of combined dark red and bright red blood. Françoise was queasy but held to her task. "Praise the lord, it has not penetrated any organs," the nun announced. Taking the shaft in her other hand, she carefully withdrew the tip. "Now apply a great deal of pressure," she told Françoise. "And hold it for a while." Once the bleeding diminished, she placed a wick of cloth in the wound and sat the man up, wrapping a poultice around his abdomen.

As the evening sun was setting, the crisis was under control. The natives had made a shelter near the fire pit with a cot for each non-ambulatory, wounded warrior. Sister Marie-Forestier reevaluated each one and the tribe posted a woman to watch them through the night. While the nun was occupied, Françoise asked Jacques-Henri, "What do you know about the attack?"

Giving his typical shrug, he answered, "Apparently random attack. These men went to hunt close to village. Iroquois happened by. They were small group—attacked and ran."

"Will they come back?" she asked.

"Not likely—small band."

They rejoined the sister as the tribe prepared for a village dinner around the fire. Sister Marie-Forestier, sat in her native costume and watched, mesmerized by the fire, the singing, and dancing. The food, eaten with fingers, was excellent as a man related the events of the day in

284

Algonquin, then in halting French. After dinner, the *religieuse* checked her patients by torchlight and retired to a small tent with Françoise.

Françoise told her, "You were fantastic. I believe you have won the allegiance of the tribe in one day—quite a feat." Looking across in the partial darkness, brightened slightly by the dying fire and the crescent moon, she asked, "How did you learn all that?"

"I read some, I've seen a little. In truth, I have never actually done it before."

Françoise jaw dropped, "That can't be true."

Marie thought for a while, before responding, "When my family left me at the convent, fourteen years ago, I did not look at it as an opportunity, but rather a cross I was to bear. I frankly did not bond with the convent in Dieppe. When this opportunity arose, I did not take it to come here—rather to leave there." Looking out the tent opening, she concluded, "I should go check the patients."

When she returned, she reported, "Some of the dressings needed change or reinforcement. Blessedly, they are all surviving at this point." Returning to her cot, she remarked, "This dress is very comfortable. I am certainly grateful they had it."

Françoise smiled, "I thought you looked fine bloody and bare breasted—like a Viking."

"Oh dear. You must promise to never tell a soul—but will the natives say something?"

Françoise chuckled, "Most native women go without a top in good weather. They probably hardly noticed it."

Now the nun was stifling a giggle. Finally, she became serious, "As I said, I was not particularly anxious to come here, but now—I feel that I was born to come here. Today was certainly the best of my life. In the convent, I would go to sleep hoping to wake up in a new life. Suddenly I feel as

285

that has happened. I can scarcely wait for tomorrow." Eventually they fell asleep. Françoise only awoke twice— when Sister Marie went out to check her patients.

The threesome stayed four more days, until Sister Marie-Forestier deemed her patients healthy enough to remain in the village, but she asked the Chief if the more seriously wounded could come see her in one or two weeks. The Chief readily agreed. After they had pushed off from the shore on their way home, Jacques-Henri told her. "One week ago, Chief would never agree to that."

Françoise had not eaten breakfast the last two days. When Marie asked about it, Françoise simply blamed it on the excitement. They both, however, suspected it was more than that.

CHAPTER 34

Françoise used her first two days back in *Québec* to organize the home front. Fortunately, between Félicity-Angel and her neighbors, there was actually little to do. The house was clean, the children in order, and the garden tended. Not having been to town other than to deliver Sister Marie-Forestier to the convent, she did not know how much was known about the Iroquois attack until she had a visit from her neighbor.

"We were all concerned when we heard about the attack at the Algonquin village," Nicole reported.

Realizing news not only traveled quickly in the city, but in the territories as well, Françoise thought she would downplay it so not to upset Nicole, who was doubtless worried about Pierre. "The attack was small and outside the village," Françoise told her, attempting to sound

287

nonchalant, "I only saw some of the wounded who were brought to the village."

"We heard the sister had many people to treat." Nicole replied.

"Well, yes..."

"We heard she stripped naked," Nicole added, "and made bandages from her habit!"

"Where did you hear that?" Françoise asked cautiously.

"Two of Félicity-Angel's sisters came to visit. They had the whole story."

Françoise recognized her assurance to the nun that the Indians would not spread the tale, was a bit overstated, and she answered. "Oh, nothing like that, she just used a few... pieces of cloth."

It seemed Nicole liked her version better, but she dropped it, saying, "I only hope Pierre is safe. I don't know why people can't get along." Noël rescued Françoise as he arrived home and changed the topic to *sous-concession* management, causing Nicole to excuse herself with, "I will see you at mass tomorrow, Françoise."

In the morning, Françoise readied her troops and led them to the wagon. Now that everyone was ambulatory, the wagon suited the family better than the canoe. Since the fire, the community celebrated mass at the Jesuit chapel, *Notre-Dame des Anges*, and as the congregation exited to visit in the square, Françoise saw Sister Marie-Forestier. Waiting to approach the nun alone, Françoise asked how she was. "Just fine." the nun replied. "Everyone heard about the raid and they have been very kind with their... congratulations."

"Oh, good," Françoise replied, relieved. "They didn't mention the..."

"My nakedness? Why yes, every one. They have been, however, most kind and understanding. I think I am a bit of a celebrity." Françoise's jaw dropped as the nun put her hand on her arm, declaring, "Madame Langlois, I *love* Canada!"

Québec: July 4, 1640

Leading her brood to the Sunday picnic, Françoise encountered another nun. *Marie de l'Incarnation* bent to the level of Marie-Nicole, declaring with enthusiasm, "Oh, how you have grown! You will be ready for school soon."

The girl curtsied and replied, *"Oui, bonne sœur."*

The nun patted each of the children on the head before addressing Françoise. "I wonder if you could stop by tomorrow. We have a new student I think you should meet."

The *religieuse* did not seem to want to discuss it anymore, so Françoise simply agreed, continuing on to the square.

In the morning, Françoise enlisted Félicity-Angel for childcare before departing for the lower town, where the Ursuline nuns had just taken occupancy in a new temporary facility while awaiting the completion of the eventual grand convent in the upper town. *Marie de l'Incarnation* met her at the door and ushered her to one of the two small classrooms where Sister Marie-Joseph sat on a small chair in front of her two native students who sat on the floor. In the corner sat a forlorn native girl about eight years old.

Marie de l'Incarnation took the girl's hand and brought her to standing, staring sadly at the floor. "This is

Ouébadinoukoué." The nun said softly, before telling the child, "This is Madame Langlois."

The girl remained silent as the grave when Françoise said, "*aramikkassin*" which was as close to *bonjour* as she could muster in Algonquin.

Turning to Françoise the nun explained, "She comes from a village upstream of *Trois-Rivieres*. They are having great difficulties with the Iroquois—they massacred most of her family. There was no one to look after her, so they left her here."

Suddenly Françoise flashed back almost twenty years, when she was this terrified eight-year old, abandoned among a group of strange women. She gently put her hand on the child's forehead, brushing back her hair with a smile, but received no response.

"She has never been baptized." *Marie de l'Incarnation* explained. "Father Lalemant has agreed to do it tomorrow—I would like you to be her sponsor."

"Of course," Françoise answered, and then knelt, holding the child's face gently in her hands, telling her in her halting Algonquin, "We will take care of you, *Ouébadinoukoué*." The girl opened her almond eyes and almost smiled while Françoise gently embraced her.

That evening Françoise related the story to her family. "What will her Christian name be?" asked young Robert.

Surprised by such a question from her five-year-old son, she replied, "I don't know. What would you suggest?"

"Marie-Madeleine," the boy replied with the confidence of the Pope.

Stifling her laugh, his mother answered, "Marie-Madeleine it shall be."

290

Françoise reported to the Jesuit Chapel the following day with young Robert, his four-year-old sister, Marie-Nicole, and Nicole Boucher. Father Lalemant came out to speak with the group. "She knows no family name," he explained, "and we have no way of telling if she has one. We should give her one. What should it be?"

Without hesitation, young Robert called out, "*Chrétienne!*"

The prelate smiled, "Out of the mouths of babes—a wonderful idea, Robert. *Chrétienne* it shall be! What better name than the name of her new faith?"

After the service, Lalemant invited Françoise to visit for a while. Outside the chapel, they sat on a bench shaded by a large maple tree while the two Langlois children took the newly named Marie-Madeline by the hand, leading her to a rope swing attached to a limb.

"Have you given thought to the education of *your* children?" he asked.

"Yes, Father...some. They are still quite young."

"Since the arrival of the good sisters," the priest continued, "We have expanded the seminary to have a school for native boys who live there and a school for the French boys who can either stay or commute. Soon we can begin the same in the convent for girls. I can foresee a day when Canadian children are better educated than those living in France."

"I would need to discuss this," she replied, "with my husband, Father. They are still quite young."

"Yes, but even young children progress more rapidly when they can interact with others." He pointed to the three youngsters who were now playing together on the swing, and Marie-Madeline was laughing.

Eventually Françoise told him, "We should go, Father, we will walk Marie-Madeline back to the lower town." Heading down the old path to the lower town, which had now become a road capable of facilitating a cart, her two children walked on either side of Marie-Madeline, each holding hands with their new friend.

CHAPTER 35

Québec: August 1, 1640

Your operation has certainly prospered in just over a year, Sister." Françoise declared as Sister Marie-Forestier showed her the latest improvements at the *Hôtel-Dieu*.

"We could not be more pleased," replied the nun, "now we have our clinic, two treatment rooms and beds for ten patients. With our increase in patients from the city as well as natives, we will soon need to expand. As you know, we hope to eventually move closer to the tribes."

"Don't you fear the Iroquois?" Françoise asked.

"Yes, but one cannot be motivated by fear when God's work is at hand."

Françoise nodded, deciding not to press her opinion that the move was a dangerous idea. "I suppose I should excuse myself, Sister. I want to go see the convent project and need to get home."

"Yes," the nun replied, "and, as always, thank you for your generous help putting us in touch with the Indian population. You know it is a major part of our mission."

Françoise began her way south, toward the ongoing construction of the Ursuline Convent, reflecting on how her life had evolved from farm wife to wife of a *sous-seigneur* with enough help at home to allow her time to assist with local good works.

In a country noted for cold, today was stifling, as the clear sky left the sun unrelenting. She pulled her bonnet forward to keep out some of the glare. In spite of the heat, the men were hard at work, and she waved to Gaspard with a few other neighbors working on the structure. Looking toward the wall of the fort to avoid the glare, she saw it—it was him, the one-eyed man in *voyageur* dress! She had not seen him for two years, but there he was.

"Surveying the work, my dear?" The words shook her from her phantom as she turned to see Sister Marie-Claude.

"Oh, no, Sister—I mean, yes, I..." She looked back, but he was gone. "Sister, did you see a man over there, by the wall?"

"Why no," replied the plump *religieuse*, "I've been here all morning and seen no men other than the workers. Why do you ask?"

"Oh, it's nothing...what are you doing here?"

"I was asked to come check a few things for the convent. Actually, I was just heading back to the lower town. Will you walk with me?"

As they began the trek down, Françoise told her. "I have this vision sometimes of a man, but then he's *not* there."

"Is he handsome?"

294

"No, actually quite ugly—I think it is my imagination and means I am pregnant again."

"Oh, how wonderful!" Marie-Claude congratulated. After a few steps, she added, "I wish nuns could have babies, we could raise them in the convent. But I suppose then we would have to—you know, have *relations*." She chortled before continuing, "You know, I have a recurring dream about a man—don't ever tell the others."

"Is he handsome?" Françoise queried.

"Oh, my yes."

"What do you do with this man in your dreams?" Françoise added.

"Well, nothing—but I think he wants to." She ended with another chortle.

Coming down the newly enlarged path to the lower town, they saw an ocean ship at the dock. "New arrivals," reported the sister. Looking, with her hand shading her eyes, she added, "There is your husband in his captain's jacket."

Françoise peered down, "That's strange. He said he was visiting the tenants of the *concession* today." Approaching the ship, she called, "Noël!" He seemed oblivious, however. She came closer and said, "Wait, is that him?"

"Of course it is," said Marie-Claude, "don't you know your own husband?"

They went up to him and Françoise, said softly, "Noël?"

He looked at her and pointed to himself, "*Moi?*"

"Who are you?" she demanded.

Removing his captain's hat and bowing gallantly, he announced, "Captain Jean Langlois at your service, Madame."

"Oh my God! You are his brother."

"Whose?"

295

"Why Noël's, of course, he is my husband."

He came and looked into her eyes. "Impossible! No woman as beautiful as you would marry my ugly brother."

"I would so!" she exclaimed, "and he is not ugly—why he looks just like you!"

"Well, then," he said, stifling a laugh, "perhaps you could be gracious enough to take me to him. And you are…"

"Oh! Excuse me, I am Françoise…Langlois." She put out her hand, and he took it. When he released it, she jumped into his arms. "Welcome to Canada!" she declared.

When she let go, he added, "I believe I am going to like it here. How do I get to see my brother?"

Françoise pointed to her canoe, "We take *my* ship."

"I shall retrieve my sea bag and will be at your disposal."

When he returned, she told him, "I forgot my manners, and did not introduce you to my friend, Sister Marie-Claude."

He bowed to the nun, *"Enchanté, bonne-sœur,* I am pleased my sister-in-law keeps such beautiful company."

The portly nun chuckled and whispered to Françoise, "He is another pretty one." Then announced, "I must get back to the convent." Whispering again, "Come tomorrow and tell me everything."

Françoise took Jean to the canoe. "Hold on to the rails and stay low," she instructed.

"Madame, I am a ship's captain," he announced, "and *know* boats."

He stepped in, held the rail, but stood and lost his balance, spilling into the river like a cannonball. As he came sputtering to the surface, Françoise told him, "Like I said…"

When they reached Beauport, she beached the canoe and cautioned, "Stay low this time."

Noël was sitting on a rocker while the children played in the yard. He said nothing until his wife and brother reached the steps. "Have you been fishing?" he asked his wife.

"No." she said incredulously.

"It looks like you caught something," he suggested.

Jean walked up the steps and the brothers embraced. "I wondered if I would ever see you again," Noël told him. Stepping back, he added, "Do you have anything dry?"

"Oh you men!" said his spouse who took Jean by the hand, "Come, we have some things of Noël's. You must be the same size."

Noël took his brother to meet Jacques-Henri and his family while Françoise worked on dinner. Most of the work, however, was already done by Félicity-Angel, who had taken on the job as housekeeper, nannie, and *sous-chef*. Following dinner, the three adults sat on the porch and visited while the sun set. The younger of the two brothers, Jean had run off as a boy to work the shipyards. Working his way from cabin boy to captain over several years, he now held a high position in shipping. He had been almost everywhere, but never married.

"When do you go back?" Françoise asked him.

"I am not going to go back," he told her. "I think I'll stay here for a while—perhaps forever."

"But what about your ship?" she questioned.

"The first mate is qualified and due for a promotion to captain. They will be fine."

"What will your company say?" she wondered.

"They won't like it, but there is not much they can do. In addition, I am too valuable to fire."

"But where will you stay?"

297

He laughed, "Can I sleep in your room?"

Her jaw dropped, and Noël laughed, "She is not yet used to your humor."

"You mean I can't?"

"No." Noël said, "We have a room you can use, and soon we shall find something more permanent for you." Indeed the house had grown with the family, now with two children's lofts as well as a small second room for just such a guest.

In the morning, Noël took his brother for a tour of the *sous-concession* and the city, while Françoise left Félicity-Angel in charge and left to report to Sister Marie-Claude.

When the men reappeared in the late afternoon, the four children were playing in the yard while Françoise was indoors stirring a pot over the fire. "It appears you have been hard at work," declared Jean as he looked into the pot. "What have you prepared?"

Françoise tasted a spoonful, "Corn porridge with… ham and crushed walnuts."

"Don't you recall making it?" her brother-in-law asked.

"Well…actually Félicity-Angel made it while I was in the city."

Jean put his hand on his chest, "Dear Lord, my sister-in-law is the lady of the manor."

"Well…I usually…"

Jean interrupted, "Don't worry, my brother has already confessed that he is becoming an aristocrat."

"But, we are not…"

Both men laughed, and she went back to her stirring. "I explained our good fortune to Jean," Noël reported. "But what he told me is of more interest. Come out on the porch. It is too nice a day to stay in here."

The Langlois porch had grown along with the rest of the house and now held four rocking chairs where they sat, viewing the city and upper town farms. No more a field with shacks, *Québec* was taking on the appearance of a prospering village.

"Jean had some interesting men aboard," Noël began.

"Yes," Jean replied, "Two men, Dauversiere and Fanchamp, two *very rich* men. They had dinner in my cabin each night and discussed their plans. It seems there is a large island almost two-hundred miles upstream from here. They called it *Mont-Royal*. Currently its rights belong to a *Monsieur* de Lauson who was president of your Company of 100 Associates."

Françoise asked, "Isn't that the place you took Governor Montmagny when he arrived, Noël?"

Noël nodded, and his brother continued, "They plan to bring men next year to settle it."

Françoise stood, "Perhaps we should have refreshment." Disappearing into the house, she returned with three cups and a bottle of Calvados.

Tasting it, Jean remarked, "Not bad, but not up to the standards of Normandie." Setting it down, he continued. "Their plan, as stated, is to bring three communities to the island: priests to convert the natives, nuns to treat the sick, and nuns to teach the natives." He stood and went to the end of the porch, as if to find inspiration. "My lord, it is lovely here!" Turning, he added, "As the voyage continued, however, I realized they had other motives."

"What are they?" Françoise asked, becoming intrigued.

"We discussed it today and I believe Noël understands it better than I."

"As you know," her husband began, "Fur and fish continue to be the colony's major source of revenue from France. In addition, we understand furs are becoming scarce in our area and the traders are moving farther upstream and inland each year. By putting the trading post for furs on the island, the *voyageurs* will have less distance to travel, hence more time to trade and the industry will become much more productive."

Jean returned to his seat. "These men spoke to me just before landing and asked if I could take them to the island. Today when I discovered Noël's experience with it, I went to them and said Noël and I would do it. The problem is they are very secretive and want to involve as few people as possible."

Noël added, "I thought we needed someone with a bit more experience—and an interpreter. I suggested Abraham Martin and Jacques-Henri."

"That sounds workable," his wife agreed.

"Yes, but they are a bit suspicious of relying on a native."

"How will you get along without Jacques-Henri?" she questioned.

"They agreed to take Jacques-Henri," Noël explained, "if we could also bring you."

"Me?" she said in surprise.

"I was also surprised," he added, "but they felt if they had you to listen to Jacques-Henri, they would have more confidence that he was interpreting accurately."

"Confidence in a woman," she remarked, "what is the world coming to?"

"What is important," cautioned Jean, as he returned to the porch railing, "is secrecy and making certain no one knows what is happening, at least about the trade aspects. And remember, these are *very* powerful men."

That night, Françoise asked her husband "Wasn't there an epidemic when you were there before?"

"Yes, but I saw Benoît a while ago and he said there has been no *pest* in the past two years. He also said there are many fewer Huron."

Québec: August 15, 1640

At first light, Noël and Jean had the large shallop packed and ready. Due to the increased space, they carried more provisions than the voyage with Montmagny, realizing these two men required more tending. The men reported to Montmagny that they had hired the Langlois brothers for a simple sightseeing tour of the river. When Noël introduced the two men to Françoise, she was treated more as a courtesan than a member of the team, but she had known French *gentlemen* in Paris and let it pass.

The men had volumes of questions, however, as they traveled into the depths of Canada. Noël and Abraham handled them politely, while the Frenchmen ignored Jacques-Henri almost as much as Françoise. The first landing was *Trois-Rivières* where they met Commandant LaViolette. Noël introduced them as two Parisian businessmen who were taking a sightseeing tour of the area. When asked about the *Rivière-Saint-Maurice*, the Commandant told them it was *the gateway to the beaver trade,* although he did finally admit the volume was now diminishing. He explained that most of the natives were Abenaki. They merely nodded and avoided prying questions.

As they continued the voyage, Dauversiere had more serious questions. "What is the nature of the trade from this *Rivière-Saint-Maurice*?" he asked.

Abraham Martin replied, "It was once the main source of furs, but in the past few years, numbers have dropped—significantly."

When Fanchamp asked about the native tribes, Noël suggested they have Jacques-Henri explain. The men began irritated, but became more impressed as the discussion continued. By evening, they had acquired an inescapable respect for this odd savage although one of them constantly questioned Françoise about Jacques-Henri's accuracy and veracity.

Their next stop was at the mouth of a river flowing from the south. "This is the Richelieu River," Abraham instructed, "but it was called the River of the Iroquois."

"Are they not the bad Indians?" Dauversiere inquired.

Abraham asked Jacques-Henri to reply, and this time the French gentlemen did not object as Jacques-Henri embarked on a well thought-out description of the tribe, describing their bellicose ways while still showing a certain respect for their capabilities. "And how is the fur trade from this river?" Fanchamp queried.

Jacques-Henri answered by pointing his thumb down. "Gone—no beaver left."

The conversation went to the long-term relations of the Algonquin, Iroquois, French, Dutch and English, as well as the river's role in Iroquois attacks. By the end of the evening, the men had a better understanding than many

Québécois. "Why does the Governor not build a fort here?" they asked.

"Lack of resources," Abraham answered. "However, he does have plans for the future." Again, Fanchamp subtly questioned Françoise about Jacques-Henri's report.

Finally, they reached the island *Mont- Royal* and *Île de Jésus*. Noël explained his last visit and the reason for leaving suddenly. "And you are certain this plague is gone?" Dauversiere asked nervously.

Abraham Martin shrugged before answering, "As far as we know." The Frenchmen were not reassured. First, they visited the rapids of Lachine where Noël told them of the difficult portage. The Frenchmen were obviously impressed by the rapids. The next day they traveled back to the east, then west into a much smaller river between the *Mont-Royal* and *Île de Jésus,* ultimately coming to a fork. The arm to the south entered the Lachine rapids, but the arm to the west was obviously more easily traveled.

"Why not use this river?" Fanchamp questioned.

Abraham pulled on his white beard before answering, "The river to the east runs dry, and enormous portages are required beyond that point. It is called the Ottawa River for the tribes along its shore." Pointing south, he continued, "The rapids are part of *Fleuve Saint-Laurent*. Once portaged, it leads to an endless chain of rivers and lakes whose boundaries, if there are any, are unknown." Pointing with authority to the south, "Here, gentlemen, is the mother lode of furs for the next one-thousand years!"

From there they hiked a short way to a small native village. "Algonquin," Jacques-Henri explained, "friendly— my people."

The two Frenchmen were obviously skeptical—and frightened, as they were welcomed into the camp. After introductions, with Jacques-Henri translating for Dauversiere and Françoise for Fanchamp, they were taken to a large fire pit and invited to sit.

The evening commenced with eating, drinking, smoking, telling tales, singing and dancing. Due to the assistance of Françoise and Jacques-Henri, the men had an inkling of what it was about. As the evening wore on, their hosts assigned tents for shelter, and thanks to the drink and smoking, they slept soundly.

In the morning, they headed back to *Québec*, with a new appreciation of this wild land. They discussed very little with the *Québec* authorities, and the *Québécois* members of the crew swore themselves to secrecy. Four days later, the two men sailed back to France on Jean Langlois' ship, piloted by his former first mate.

CHAPTER 36

Beauport: February 22, 1641—Six months later

F ine son!" exclaimed Félicity-Angel, holding the screaming infant, still blood soaked with his cord dangling—attached to his mother. After showing Françoise her newest child, Félicity-Angel handed it to Sister Marie-Claude to wash and swaddle, while the native midwife dealt with the cord and placenta. When Félicity-Angel attended to the mother, the nun sat in a rocker, cuddling the noisy lad. Feeling the softness of her ample bosom, he instinctively began to suck.

"Not yet, my dear," Sister Marie-Claude told him, "alas I am not equipped." As if he understood, the baby stopped sucking and returned to howling. Eventually Félicity-Angel took him to return to his mother.

When Françoise's labor began in the early morning, Félicity-Angel sent her oldest son to fetch Sister Marie-

Claude who insisted on being called. Nicole Boucher took the young children to her house and Jacques-Henri took the men and older boys on a day-hunt. "This is easier without the other children," Françoise declared.

"Will you name him after his father?" Sister Marie-Claude inquired.

Looking into the infant's blue eyes, his mother replied, "I believe I will save that name for one of the next boys. This one I shall name—Jean-Pierre."

Winter temporarily loosened its grip on *Québec*, and two days later, Noël loaded his wife and new son, along with his brother and the other children, into the family cart, now equipped with snow runners. Arriving at the Jesuit Chapel, they met Sister Marie-Claude and Father Lalement who baptized Jean-Pierre Langlois. The boy's uncle and the nun stood as sponsors.

On the very same day, unknown to the people of *Québec*, another group of French citizens met at the Cathedral of *Notre-Dame de Paris*. They had named themselves *l'Association de Montréal*. Inspired by the report of Dauversiere and Fanchamp, they had chosen Paul de Chomedey, Sieur de Maisonneuve as their Governor, and before the altar of the Virgin, consecrated their proposed, *Ville-Marie de Montréal* with plans to send a founding company when the weather broke.

A mild winter allowed Noël to take his brother on short hunts, but now the weather was fair, and the two brothers decided to do an overnight hunt with the assistance of Jacques-Henri and Machk. At the last minute, they agreed to take Robert and Jacques-Henri's two boys as well.

"We should be back tomorrow night," he told his wife, "or the next day at the latest, if the hunting is good."

Giving him a peck on the cheek, she said, "Nicole and Félicity-Angel are taking the children to Nicole's sister-in-law's for a birthday—I can't remember whose, but it will be just little Jean-Pierre and me at home. It's a perfect time for a number of things I want to do around the house."

"I don't know what it could be," he replied, glancing around the room, "Félicity-Angel keeps it spotless."

"I know, but it is my house and... Oh, you wouldn't understand."

At nine o'clock, she lined up the three girls. "Marie-Nicole, make certain your sisters behave."

"Yes, Mama," she answered, "and can we take Tutu? She likes to play with the other dogs."

"I suppose, but be certain she behaves. Now go next door, Madame Boucher is waiting."

Françoise followed them onto the porch where Nicole was already waiting with her brood. Félicity-Angel appeared, and the entourage moved on. Returning to the house, Françoise nursed the baby and returned him to his crib. She dusted and swept, but as Noël had indicated, there was little to do. *I will do Robert's loft next,* she thought to herself, *it never stays neat for a moment.* She was not disappointed and had real cleaning to do. A few garments

307

thrown about could also use washing. Filling the wash-basket, she backed down the ladder to keep her balance.

Turning to set the basket down, she saw him—it was him! This was *not* her imagination. "What do you want?" she demanded.

"What I always wanted when I returned home, my dear."

He removed the filthy *voyageur's* hat and set it on the table. In spite of the years, he still had red curly hair. When she could see his undamaged side, it was unmistakably him. Previously, she had attempted to delude herself that it was not, but now there was no question. The damaged side was much worse than it had appeared from afar. His ear and eye were gone, and his skin had the consistency of a corpse one week dead. He pulled off his shirt, revealing a lifetime of scars. Approaching her, he grasped her upper arm with a filthy hand, which lacked one finger. His grip was no weaker for the loss.

Pulling out his long knife, he menaced it under her chin. "What would you like to do first?"

"You can kill me if you like but you'll get nothing!" she declared in her most defiant tone.

He backed away and laughed, his laugh was even more evil than it had been 13 years before. "I am not about to kill *you,* my dear." He walked to the crib. "Is this the latest edition?"

"You fiend, you wouldn't dare!"

He took the long knife and threatened the infant. "I believe you have forgotten what I dare do."

As he brought the knife up, she screamed, "No! I'll… I'll."

The baby began to cry, and Guy turned and laughed, "I know you will. Get undressed—NOW!"

She began to unbutton her blouse while she talked, saying anything, trying to give herself time to think. He came to her and ripped her clothes off. "Now would you like to start easy or painful?"

She began to sob as he took her with his vise-like hands and fell onto her. She could scarcely move under his weight, but he just lay there, on top, while she continued to sob. Suddenly he began to roll over and rolled right onto the floor. She shut her eyes and waited. Then she opened them.

"Jacques-Henri! How? Where..."

The Indian bent, retrieving his knife. It protruded from Guy's back, between his ribs where it entered exactly into his aorta. Jacques-Henri covered her with the dress, and said, "I told you what I would do if he ever came back. Go get cleaned and dressed. I'll take care of him."

Guy outweighed Jacques-Henri by at least 100 pounds, but the Indian picked him up like a feather and flung the body off the porch. Françoise went into her room where there was a washbasin with water. Shocked there was no blood on her, she washed quickly and put on clean clothes, rolling the damaged garments into a ball.

When she returned, the front room was in order and the floor clean. Jacques-Henri reentered, ordering, "Take the child and go to my camp. No one will bother you there. I will get rid of the body and return soon."

"But...where will you hide it? Someone may find it."

He laughed his usual casual laugh, which lowered her fears. "I am Indian—no one will find it."

Once in the hut, she crawled under a fur blanket and began to nurse her son. When she opened her eyes, she realized she had been asleep. Sitting up suddenly, she saw

Jacques-Henri, sitting cross-legged, watching over them. "Oh, I must have fallen asleep—what time is it?"

He shrugged, "Midday, perhaps later."

Sitting up, she said, "We should go home before the children return." Entering the house, she saw it looked as if nothing had happened. Putting Jean-Pierre in his crib, she turned to her friend. "I cannot thank you enough."

He shrugged, "You help my wife give me strong children."

She almost smiled. "What did you do with the…"

"It is gone. No one can find it. He is gone. This time for good!"

They went to the porch and sat in the rockers when she asked the question that had just occurred to her. "I thought you went with the men."

"I did," he answered. "But I have been watching for this man a long while. Every time I see him, he escapes. He was almost as clever as Indian—just more evil. I have sometimes seen him watching you, but could never catch him—only scare him off. Today I smelled him behind us as we left to hunt."

"Smelled him?" she asked.

He shrugged, "Indian gift. I walked with men until I knew they would not see him and told them I hurt foot, then turned back. By the time I arrived, he was in house. You know the rest." Soon the girls returned with Félicity-Angel and Tutu, filled with stories of the party.

Françoise was preparing dinner when the hunters returned the following evening. "How was the hunt?" she asked, trying her best to seem calm.

Noël dropped down in a rocking chair, "Not good, first Jacques-Henri hurt his foot and came back. We hardly saw an animal. I don't think anybody killed anything."

310

"Oh, I don't know," she responded nonchalantly, "I suspect somebody did somewhere."

After dinner, the hunters were ready for bed. Once her husband was snoring, she crept out and opened the door. The moonlight flooded the yard, illuminating Jacques-Henri, sitting cross-legged, under a tree while keeping watch. She returned to bed, said her prayers with an uncharacteristic enthusiasm and fell asleep.

A few weeks later, the family dined at Jacques-Henri's camp. Robert showed his Uncle Jean Jacques-Henri's collection of furs, displayed around his hut. "Jacques-Henri," the boy asked, pointing to a small specimen, "what is this new one?"

Jacques-Henri came and looked, "That is very unusual fur—from rare red weasel." Françoise was watching and she looked down to hide her expression. She had spent enough time at the Indian camps to know a scalp when she saw one.

CHAPTER 37

<u>Québec</u>: May 16, 1641

Françoise slid her canoe into the city landing. Every year there were more canoes as more *Québécois* bonded with the native craft. Securing it, she saw a small flotilla of canoes rounding the tip of the city as they arrived from the west. She decided to await their landing so she could tell Noël and the neighbors who had arrived. As they approached the docks, it seemed to be a mélange of Jesuits, natives, and Frenchmen. She recognized a few of the Jesuits but no one else.

Once secured, they headed to land where a bearded man in the flotilla waved to her. As he approached she screamed, "Pierre!" Running to embrace him, she exclaimed, "I scarcely recognized you." Fully a head taller than she, his hair was to his shoulders and his beard on his chest—clearly no longer a boy. "Tell me, how was it?"

"Interesting and exciting, *Tante* Françoise," he responded, at the same time that a soldier approached.

"*Monsieur* Pierre Boucher?" he asked, snapping to attention.

"That's me," Pierre replied.

"Message from Governor Montmagny!" the soldier announced, handing Pierre a paper as he saluted and marched away.

As mystified as Françoise was, he unfolded the paper. "It seems," he said as he read, "the Governor wants to see me—immediately!"

As Pierre headed to the fort where Montmagny now had his office, Françoise stood in amazement, thinking, *what did they do with that cute little boy?* Making her rounds of the convent school and the hospital, she made a few purchases at Gagnon's store before pointing her canoe toward Beauport.

Following dinner, Pierre came visiting with his parents. It was a beautiful evening, so Françoise brought an extra chair to the porch and fetched a bottle of calvados with five cups. Once all were seated and served, she asked Pierre, "What did the Governor want?"

"He asked about the voyage," Pierre began, "then he told me he was enlisting me in the army."

"When?"

"Right away," was his response. "He swore me in this afternoon, as a junior officer."

"How wonderful," Françoise replied with muted enthusiasm, "but why?"

"He wants me as his official interpreter."

"But what about *Monsieur* Tardif?" she questioned.

Pierre choked down his first sip of Calvados. When his eyes cleared, he answered, "The governor said I knew more

313

dialects, which is true, and that I don't have as many friends."

"What does that mean?" she puzzled.

Pierre merely shrugged but his father replied, "I believe it means he does not know anyone well enough that he would confide in them against *Monsieur* Montmagny's best interests."

"Not necessarily an easy job," Noël observed.

"I can handle it," Pierre said with the confidence of youth and took an adult swallow of the Normand liquor. "There is also the issue with the Iroquois. He believes my grasp of their language is greater than Tardif's—so do I."

"Did he mention Mont Royal?" Noël queried.

"Yes, quite a lot. It seems *l'Association de Montréal* is a newly formed group of clergy and businessmen. They plan to send a large group of men—and some women, to Canada this season with a plan to settle the place for converting, teaching and healing the natives. The Governor believes they also have hidden business agendas regarding trade. He hopes I can accompany him when they come—to keep an eye on their activities."

"Sounds like *espionage,*" Noël suggested.

Pierre stood, "Yes, well I should get to bed. I am due to report at midday." Looking to Françoise, he added, "*Tante* Françoise, I wonder if you could give me a tour of the convent school and hospital tomorrow morning?"

"Of course, Pierre."

"Good, I shall take my leave. Mother, you and father can stay and visit if you like."

As he headed to his parents' house, Nicole whispered, "Dear Lord, what have you done with my little boy?"

Gaspard said, "I don't think he was ever a little boy. This is certainly a man's job, and I am a little uneasy with

314

it. I see many pitfalls. However, I have thought that many times, and he has always been up to the task."

Noël stood to pour another round of calvados. No one objected.

Québec: May 17, 1641

Soon after daybreak, Françoise and Pierre paddled into the canoe docks. Françoise gave him a brief tour of the improvements to roads, buildings and other structures that had occurred in his absence. "We will work our way to the Ursuline Convent," she told him. "They have just left their temporary quarters in the lower town. The main convent is still under construction but they have nuns' quarters, classrooms, and dormitories enough to handle their current load."

Sister Marie-Claude met them at the door with a hug that only she could give. They toured both the completed and under-construction areas ending with the classrooms. The native class now had seven students including Marie-Madeline Chrétienne who was blossoming into a real student. The second room held four local girls, two boarders and two commuters. Françoise told him, "This autumn we are sending Marie-Nicole to the Ursuline school and Robert to the Jesuit school."

"I wish this was here when I was young," he said.

From there they headed inland to Sillery, a small community just west of the city where the new construction of the permanent Augustinian Convent and the hospital, called _Hotel Dieu_, was nearly finished. The clinic was busy and several inpatient beds occupied. "They started by the old hospital," Françoise explained. "However, a growing Algonquin community here in Sillery caused them to move

315

to be closer to the tribe. I still think it is a little dangerous to be this far out of the city."

When they finished, Pierre excused himself. "I must report. I will not be home regularly. The governor is having me quartered at the Fort."

Beauport: July 4, 1641

Noël and Françoise sat on the porch on this beautiful summer afternoon, having a serious discussion. "That's all I heard," Noël said, "I don't understand it either."

His wife stood looking to the west. "That's Gaspard's canoe, coming back from the city. Go see if he knows something."

Noël hiked along the shore and helped his neighbor beach his craft. "I heard a rumor today. Something about the Iroquois making peace overtures to Montmagny and him turning them away. I said, it can't be true, but wondered if you knew anything."

Gaspard put his end of the canoe down, saying, "Yes, I do know something."

As the men hiked up to the Boucher residence, Gaspard explained. "Pierre came by the Ursuline Convent today, where I have been doing some stone work. He said an Iroquois party came to the fort under a sign of truce. They spoke with the governor—Pierre translated. The chief proposed a peace."

"That sounds encouraging," Noël acknowledged.

"Yes, at first glance, but there were other conditions. The Iroquois wanted a certain portion of the fur trade—a large portion and exclusive trapping rights to certain areas."

"I see the difficulty," Noël responded.

"Yes, well, Montmagny refused—apparently in no uncertain terms. The Iroquois chief threw his sign of truce on Montmagny's floor and stormed out. Pierre thinks it looks bad."

"I see."

"Montmagny thinks so, too. He has sent troops out to blockade the mouth of the Richelieu River, stopping Iroquois travel. Pierre leaves with them in the morning to translate. I hope he will not be gone long. Furthermore, Montmagny plans to build an actual fort at the mouth in the spring."

When Noël arrived home, Françoise asked what he had learned. "Don't go north of our property or beyond the city without one of the Indians," was all he said.

CHAPTER 38

The usual bevy of ships had visited the port this year, bringing supplies, soldiers, workers, businessmen, a few families and fewer single women. Generally they departed for France with the usual cadre of *engager*, returning home after completing their three years without finding a satisfactory life. Today's late-arriving vessel was special. It held the long anticipated group for Mont Royal. A small group of men and some women disembarked, heading to the fort. The remainder stayed in port and spent the night on the ship.

Rumors flew as to what was happening until two days later, when Pierre Boucher visited his family. Meeting with the original five Beauport families, he told them, "I have been with the governor negotiating with these people. He has given me permission to discuss a few things with you—

and only you. He asks you to refer any questions from outsiders to the governor or me. This group plans to begin a village on the island and call it *Ville-Marie de Montréal.* Their leader is Paul de Chomedey, Sieur de Maisonneuve. They call him Maisonneuve, and he is to be the governor of the new settlement.

"A renowned statesman and soldier he comes with 35 men and 10 women: a few nuns, wives and one very wealthy benefactor, Jeanne Mance, who has ties to a group of wealthy ladies in France. As you may have heard, Montmagny is opposed to this plan and has offered *Île d'Orléans* in exchange. Maisonneuve flatly refused. Due to the late date, the group is going to winter here. Montmagny is not being hospitable, and I believe they are going to stay in Sillery."

The group did leave the ship and move to Sillery, near the Augustinian Convent. There was little interaction, other than constant rumors, until spring.

Québec: May 8, 1642

During the winter, Maisonneuve hired carpenters to fashion his own boat, an odd-looking flat-bottomed sailboat along with two smaller craft. Onto these, he loaded his group of 45 souls, including Jean Mance, three sisters of Saint-Joseph and seven other women who were joined by a late arrival, Madame de la Peltrie from the Ursuline group. Taken with the enthusiasm of Mance, she brought her furniture and fortune to aid this new endeavor.

Montmagny came in his own boat, bringing Father Vimont, who had replaced Father LeJeune as director of the missions, Pierre Boucher, a few soldiers, Noël to pilot, and Françoise and Jacques-Henri to deal with Indians. Noël had to sail slowly to stay behind Maisonneuve's odd crafts, but they eventually reached the island ten days later, choosing the point where *Fleuve Saint-Laurent* turned from south to west to disembark.

It was a pleasant spot where a small stream emptied into the *Saint-Laurent.* The shore was meadow, leading up to forest, alive with spring. When Maisonneuve and his people left their boats, they kissed the ground, while Montmagny came ashore begrudgingly to deliver the island on behalf of the Company of 100 Associates. Following a few stilted pleasantries, the *Québec* party boarded and sailed east, leaving the *Montréal* group to their construction. As they turned north and lost sight of the new colony, Montmagny said, "One thing is for certain. Nothing good will come of this—they will all be gone within a year," and went below for a nap.

CHAPTER 39

Québec: September 14, 1642—Four months later

As the bells of the Jesuit Chapel tolled the end of mass, the congregation spilled out into a spectacular autumn day, heading for the traditional picnic in the upper town square by Étienne Forton's *L'Auberge Oie Bleue.* Passing by the reconstruction work at the charred parish church of *Notre Dame de la Recouvrance,* Françoise said, "Progress on the rebuilding is certainly slow."

Nicole Boucher replied, "Gaspard says the Father Lalement is very particular about detail. He wants it large enough for the future and solid stone to avoid another fire. They are even going to change the name."

Once they were seated at one of Forton's tables, Xainte Cloutier asked, "What are they going to name the new church?"

"Gaspard told me, *Notre Dame de la Paix*."

As the waiter brought refreshments, Mathurine Guyon added, "I hope something will bring a little peace around here. Did you hear about the couple in Sillery?" Her friends remained silent, so she said, "It was a *habitant* and his new *Métis* wife. They were found dead in their burned-out cabin. I heard they think it was *Iroquois.*"

Françoise replied, "I heard it was from their fireplace."

"No," Mathurine disputed, "Marguerite Martin said it was *Iroquois*. They found arrows outside. She told me her husband said it is all part of these Beaver Wars that are starting."

Françoise began to protest when Remie Giffard added, "I think it is true. My husband said he heard of small raids at *Trois-Rivières* as well as by the Richelieu River—He even thinks they have been sneaking around the new settlement at Mont Royal."

Nicole interrupted, "That's enough gossip about beavers and wars. Did you hear who is getting married?"

The conversation soon turned to safer subjects.

That night Françoise was getting ready for bed when she asked Noël, "Have you heard anything about these *Iroquois* raids?"

Coming around behind her, he embraced her, "A few things, but I think it is all rumor. No one around here has seen anything for certain." Placing his hands on her abdomen, he smiled, adding, "I think you're beginning to show."

She turned to face him with an embrace, "Maybe a little, Mathurine thinks I'm no more than three months." Giving him a kiss, she added, "Let us get to bed. The children have activities tomorrow."

322

The next morning was as bright and spectacular as it could be, even in early autumn in *Québec.* "When you go to the docks, take Robert, Marie-Nicole and Agnes-Anne to the convent school," Françoise instructed her husband as she served breakfast. "I promised Marguerite we would go pick up the chestnuts today. Jean-Pierre will stay with Félicity-Angel."

As Noël sat down, he told her, "Just don't go beyond the pasture."

"We are only going to the big chestnut tree," she reassured him.

Once Noël and the older children had left for the city, she dressed the two youngsters and led them and Tutu over to Jacques-Henri's camp. Leaving young Jean-Pierre with Félicity-Angel, the mother and daughter headed to the giant chestnut tree at the back of their cleared lot, kicking the falling maple leaves as they went. "It is good we are going before the chestnut leaves fall," she told her three-year-old daughter, "It is much easier to pick up the nuts." Once they arrived, she set down her two large buckets and explained to Marguerite how to identify the best ones.

Normally this chore only took a short while, but the day was fine and Françoise had no other jobs so she delighted in her daughter's interest. Picking up each nut to examine it, she would ask, "Is this one good, Mama?" If Françoise said yes, she put it in her bucket; if no, she gave it to Tutu who would bite it before spitting it out while the little girl giggled.

As they began to sing nursery songs to the chirping of the birds, Françoise felt a searing pain in her right thigh. She looked down in disbelief to see an arrow penetrating the leg—an *Iroquois* arrow. Looking up in panic, she saw no one in the forest. She turned to pick up Marguerite but realized the leg would not hold her. As she fell to the ground, she screamed, "Marguerite! Run to Félicity-Angel's!" Her daughter only looked and sobbed. "Go now! Quickly! Take Tutu!" The youngster turned, and calling the dog, began to run for the camp.

From her viewpoint on the ground, Françoise searched the woods to her north but saw nothing. Looking at her bleeding leg, she thought of the Algonquin who nearly bled to death but for the aid of Sister Marie-Forestier at the Algonquin camp. She tried again to stand, but the leg would not hold her. Reexamining the woods in front of her, she decided to attempt crawling back. Her progress was tortuously slow and painful as she made her way slowly south.

TO BE CONTINUED
in
THE BEAVER WARS
Due out next year

324

AFTERWORD

In writing this novel, my intent was to connect the beginning of Canada as a viable community (1634) to the beginning of Book One of my Allards series (1665). It soon became apparent this could not be done in one volume without neglecting many significant events. To read about the continued growth of *Québec*, the evolution of *Montréal*, and the progression of the brutal Beaver Wars as they developed into the French and Indian Wars, we must wait for the sequel, The Beaver Wars, anticipated completion within the coming year.

The interesting solution to the lack of French women in the colony will also be shown in The Beaver Wars as well as the outcome of Françoise's dilemma as she crawls painfully for help.

In the meantime, those unfamiliar with the Allards series can find out more in the archives of my blog on my website at www.wilmontkreis.com.

SELECTED BIBLIOGRAPHY

Charbonneau, Hubert, Bertrand Desjardins, Jacques Légaré. *Le Programme de recherche en démographie historique (PRDH).* Université de Montréal, Montréal (Québec) Canada.

Charbonneau, Hubert, et al. *The First French Canadians.* Cranbury, New Jersey: Associated University Presses, 1993.

Denissen, The Rev Fr Christian. *Genealogy of the French Families of the Detroit River Region.* 2Vols. Detroit, MI: Burton Historical Collection, 1976, 1987.

Dictionary of Canadian Biography Online. Canada: University of Toronto/Université Laval, 2003-2016.

Fischer, David Hackett. *Champlain's Dream.* New York: Simon and Schuster, 2008.

Jetté, René. *Dictionnaire Généalogique des Familles du Québec des origines à 1730.* Montréal (Québec) Canada: Les Presses de l'Université de Montréal, 1983.

Laforest, Thomas, J. *Our French Canadian Ancestors.* Palm Harbor, Florida: The Lisi Press, 1984-1998.

McNelley, Susan. *Hélène's World.* Etta Heritage Press, 2014.

Nortier, Jacques. *L'Emigration Tourouvraine Au Canada.* Municipaité de Tourouvre, Mortagne-au-Perche, France, 1984.

Francis Parkman. *Pioneers of France in the New World.* Boston: Little, Brown, 1885.

Lifelong resident and student of the Detroit River Region, orthopedic surgeon Wilmont R. Kreis has authored nine acclaimed historical novels along with three medical thrillers, The Corridor, The Pain Doc, and The Labyrinth. He and his wife, Susan, a healthcare attorney, live in Port Huron, Michigan.

www.wilmontkreis.com